W9-CDN-002

Just a Dog

In the series
Animals, Culture, and Society,
edited by Arnold Arluke and Clinton R. Sanders

Just a Dog

Understanding Animal Cruelty and Ourselves

ARNOLD ARLUKE

TEMPLE UNIVERSITY PRESS

Philadelphia

Temple University Press
1601 North Broad Street
Philadelphia PA 19122
www.temple.edu/tempress

Copyright © 2006 by Temple University
All rights reserved
Published 2006
Printed in the United States of America

⊛ The paper used in this publication meets the requirements of the American National Standard for Information Sciences—Permanence of Paper for Printed Library Materials, ANSI Z39.48-1992

Library of Congress Cataloging-in-Publication Data

Arluke, Arnold.
   Just a dog : understanding animal cruelty and ourselves / Arnold Arluke.
   p. cm. — (Animals, culture, and society)
   Includes bibliographical references and index.
     ISBN 1-59213-471-8 (cloth : alk. paper) — ISBN 1-59213-472-6 (pbk. : alk. paper)
     1. Animal welfare. 2. Animal rights. 3. Human-animal relationship—Psychological aspects. I. Title. II. Series.

HV4708.A756 2006
179'.3—dc22

                                                                        2005055935

2 4 6 8 9 7 5 3 1

Contents

Acknowledgments

THE GERALDINE R. DODGE FOUNDATION and the Massachusetts Society for the Prevention of Cruelty to Animals (MSPCA) paved the way for my research on animal cruelty. In what has now become a landmark study (Arluke et al. 1999), the foundation and MSPCA enabled me to study the presumed "link" between animal cruelty and subsequent violent crimes toward humans. Findings from this study have been both controversial and important; they have been used in several states to upgrade the seriousness of animal cruelty to the status of a felony crime.

At the end of this project I met with Scott McVay, then director of the Dodge Foundation, to talk about future research on animal cruelty. I could see that cruelty has many different meanings in our society and for each meaning, potentially unique uses for those encountering it. We see ourselves many ways in the face of cruelty. After I explained that researchers had failed to unearth the meanings and consequences of animal abuse and neglect, he encouraged me to write a book taking this fresh approach. I was excited by the scope of the idea but felt more research had to be done before I could start such an ambitious project.

Several organizations allowed me to take these steps. The MSPCA's President's Fund made it possible for me to study how humane agents investigate and prosecute abuse cases. The Edith Goode Trust and the San Francisco Society for the Protection of Animals allowed me to explore the controversy over killing animals in the shelter community and the role that cruelty plays in this debate. The Northeastern University Research and Scholarship Development Fund supported my investigation of animal hoarding as a form of cruelty. Finally, the Kenneth A. Scott Charitable Trust, a KeyBank Trust, enabled me to combine these separate studies into this book.

I thank many for their help. Friends and colleagues, including Spencer Cahill, Nakeisha Cody, Fred Hafferty, Hal Herzog, Alan Klein, Carter Luke, Trish Morris, Gary Patronek, Andrew Rowan, and Clint Sanders, offered guidance along the way. Members of the Hoarding of

Animals Research Consortium and Maria Vaca-Guzman shared their thinking about this form of extreme neglect. Jan Holmquist and the MSPCA provided the cover photo. More than two hundred people whose lives were entangled with animal cruelty allowed me to observe and interview them. At Temple University Press, Janet Francendese backed my original idea for this book and offered good advice as the project evolved, Jennifer French guided the book through the production process, and Gary Kramer created a prepublication copy. Debby Smith provided fine editorial comments. And finally, Lauren Rolfe supported and encouraged me through it all.

Portions of this book are adapted from previous publications: Arnold Arluke, *Brute Force: Animal Police and the Challenge of Cruelty* (West Lafayette, IN: Purdue University Press, 2004), with permission of Purdue University Press; Arnold Arluke, "Animal Abuse as Dirty Play," *Symbolic Interaction* 25 (2002): 405–30, © 2002 by the Society for the Study of Symbolic Interaction, with permission of the University of California Press; and Arnold Arluke, "The No-Kill Controversy: Manifest and Latent Sources of Tension," in D. Salem and A. Rowan, eds., *The State of the Animals*, 67–84 (Washington, DC: The HSUS, 2003), with permission of the Humane Society of the United States.

Introduction

Just a Dog

The judge summarily dismissed the egregious case of animal cruelty against Willa, despite strong evidence that the dog was hideously beaten with baseball bats. People standing near the bench heard the judge glibly mumbling, "It's just a dog . . ." as he moved on to a "more important case," a liquor store "B & E." The humane law enforcement agents who prosecuted Willa's case felt a surge of anger and frustration, seeing their effort go nowhere. The abusers disappeared quickly from the courtroom, still puzzled about why such a "big stink" was made over a dog. At the local humane society, the staff soon got the disappointing news that Willa's abusers walked away scot-free but found much to celebrate that made them feel good about their work—the dog's abusers at least had their day in court, a dedicated and highly skilled veterinary staff saved Willa from death, and an employee adopted her.

—Author's field notes, June 1996

I OBSERVED THE ANIMAL CRUELTY case against Willa in court and overheard disappointed humane agents, who had hoped for a different result, retell the events days later. Two youths brutally beat the dog after accepting the owner's offer of a few dollars to kill her because she urinated in his house. As the beating went on, an off-duty police officer drove by and intervened. Although it seemed as strong as any such case could be, it was dismissed. Like many other cruelty incidents presented before judges, the victim's advocates were let down and the defendants were relieved (Arluke and Luke 1997).

As a sociologist I was more concerned about the process that led up to the dismissal than the outcome itself. To study this process, I asked what the case meant to those present, as it unfolded in the courtroom, and I found that it had many different and conflicting meanings to the humane agents, the defendants, the humane society staff, and the reporters.

For the humane agents, the case represented their best investigative work and had the potential to validate their mission, if a guilty verdict were won. They felt their case was solid—the victim was a dog with severe and telling injuries, there was a reliable witness, and the abusers had no defense. However, the judge's actions made the agents feel dismissed if not belittled, reminding them that many people do not see them as "real" police because they "only" protect animals. To the abusers, it made no sense that people were so upset about their treatment of Willa, since it was *only* a dog and it was *their* animal. What was done to the dog, while undeniably violent, they saw as a form of play— akin to using racial epithets—that is understood to be inappropriate and offensive but far short of constituting serious crime. And for the staff from the local humane organization, Willa was an almost ideal cruelty case that could be used for promotion and fund raising. Although she was not quite appealing enough to get her picture on envelopes soliciting donations, the extraordinary efforts of the humane agents and veterinarians to bring the abusers to justice and save Willa's life, along with her in-house adoption by a popular employee of the humane society, gave staff members many reasons to feel proud about their work and unified in their mission to help animals.

That animal cruelty affects people is an old idea. As early as the seventeenth century, the philosopher John Locke (1693) suggested that harming animals has a destructive effect on those who inflict it. In later centuries, the psychologist Anna Freud (1981) and the anthropologist Margaret Mead (1964) argued that cruelty can be a symptom of character disorder. Children or adolescents who harmed animals were thought to be on a path to future violence because these acts desensitized them or tripped an underlying predisposition to aggression. Once their destructive impulses were released, the floodgates restricting violence opened and their future targets were likely to be human, or so it was argued.

When studies were undertaken to verify what is now known as the "link," results were mixed and sometimes misinterpreted to support this idea. Researchers had a hard time proving, for example, that Macdonald's (1961) "triad"—animal abuse, in combination with fire setting and bedwetting—leads to further violence. Macdonald (1968) himself failed to establish that violent psychiatric patients were significantly more likely than nonviolent psychiatric patients to abuse animals. In subsequent research, the evidence has been less than compelling (see Levin and Fox 1985), raising doubts about the validity of the link. For every study that purports to find a significant association between cruelty to animals and the impulse to violence (e.g., Felthous 1980; Felthous and Yudowitz 1977; Kellert and Felthous 1985), there is another study that finds no link (e.g., Arluke et al. 1999; Climent and Ervin 1972; Felthous and Kellert 1987; Miller and Knutson 1997; Lewis et al. 1983; Sendi and Blomgren 1975). And in studies reporting significant findings in support of the link, methodological problems cast doubt on their results because they rely on self-reports of people who, from the study's outset, were seriously troubled or disturbed, and they treat violence as the sole dependent variable, even though other problems might be subsequently linked to prior abuse. Despite these doubts, researchers continue to replicate old study designs in an unrelenting effort to support this tired model (e.g., Merz-Perez and Heide 2004).

Indeed, if the link were valid, then the reverse should be too: kindness toward animals should predict compassion toward people. However, there are examples of people who are kind to animals but cruel to fellow humans. Some murderers, for example, show compassion to animals. The most famous case is that of Robert Stroud, the Birdman of Alcatraz, who shot a bartender, stabbed an inmate, and assaulted a prison guard while caring for the health of hundreds of canaries (Babyack 1994). And several members of the Nazi general staff, including Adolf Hitler, demonstrated extreme concern for animals in their personal lives as well as through the enactment of animal protection legislation (Arluke and Sanders 1996).

Nevertheless, many people continue to believe the link exists, in part because the idea has strong common-sense appeal and resonates with cultural stereotypes and myths about the origins of violent behavior (Piper 2003). In fiction writing, one of the most effective ways to create a mean, unlikable character is to have the person ruthlessly brutalize an animal because doing so must be a sign that humans are next in line to be harmed. Stephen King confesses that he used this imagery to portray just this sort of person for his book *The Dead Zone*. Speaking about his main character, Greg Stillson, King (2000, 193) writes, "I wanted to nail his dangerous, divided character in the first scene of the book. . . . When he stops at one farm, he is menaced by a snarling dog. Stillson remains friendly and smiling. . . . Then he sprays teargas into the dog's eyes and kicks it to death." In *The Secret Window*, King also establishes a character's evil nature by having him stab an unthreatening, sweet dog to death with a screwdriver. Riding this common-sense appeal and cultural resonance, activists have argued that cruelty should be prevented because it is a nodal event leading to further violence. By the end of the twentieth century, the link became the dominant focus of organizational campaigns against cruelty, such as the First Strike program of the Humane Society of the United States. Even those who do not care about animal welfare might now be concerned about preventing cruelty, given the urgency felt by many to identify adolescent "red flags" that signal a future violent adult.

Others argue that cruelty's destructive impact on people occurs in organizations where society sanctions the harmful treatment of animals. Those who experiment on animals, for example, are thought to endure moral or emotional damage, even though their actions are institutionally approved. Presumed deleterious effects on human character formed the basis of antivivisection campaigns as early as the nineteenth century (Rupke 1987), when calls to end experimentation stressed injustice to animals as well as harm to scientists. The campaigners believed that using animals in painful experiments destroyed human sensitivities by forcing people to distance or coarsen themselves from the assumed suffering of lab animals.

Although most contemporary debate focuses on the moral basis for using or not using animals in experiments, some still claim that using animals in experiments has a negative effect on scientists and technicians. They suffer what is assumed to be lasting moral damage by becoming insensitive to the pathos of the lab animal's situation (Diamond 1981). Yet even those who make this assumption acknowledge that if there is a patent lowering of moral sensitivity, compared with our ordinary attitudes about how animals should be treated, it occurs only in the laboratory (Nelson 1989). The damage, then, is at worst temporary and situational.

Only a few studies, however, have examined the impact of animal experiments on those conducting them, and irreparable moral or emotional harm seems unlikely. Even situational coarsening is debatable, across the board (Arluke 1988). On the contrary, while such work can be stressful at times to those who have direct and sustained contact with certain kinds of lab animals (Arluke 1999), many escape or transcend these negative effects by relying on institutional coping techniques that shield their identities from lasting harm (Arluke 1989, 1991, 1994a). Despite such findings, the belief that experimenting on animals has lasting negative effects on experimentation still lingers and informs many pleas to end biomedical research (Langley 1989; Sharpe 1988).

Three assumptions underlie the belief that harming animals—whether criminal or institutionally sanctioned—has a destructive impact on human character. First, it is assumed that the meaning of harming animals can be independently arrived at and imposed apart from real-world situations where it occurs. Regulatory or legal approaches make this assumption as they belabor the formal definition of cruelty without considering its social context. For example, the 1911 Protection of Animals Act in England defines cruelty as the infliction of "unnecessary" suffering, but this definition ultimately depends on how people in specific situations understand the meaning of unnecessary. Early twentieth-century American state laws continued this ambiguous and context-free approach to defining cruelty (Favre and Tsang 1993), and most maintain the same language today. Massachusetts, for example, enforces a nineteenth-century code that considers "unnecessary" cruelty to include deliberate harm, such as overworking, beating, mutilating, or torturing animals, and neglect by failing to provide "proper" food, drink, shelter, and sanitary environment (Arluke 2004).

Researchers also define cruelty in abstract and socially ungrounded ways, whether focusing on the acts themselves or the motives behind them. Epidemiologists, for example, compile ever longer and more exhaustive lists of cruel acts (e.g., Vermeulen and Odendaal 1993), including burning, stomping, stabbing, and crushing, to name a few. Such list making is uninformed by the way these acts are interpreted by those who cause, fight, grieve, or accuse others of them. Psychologists, or those taking this approach, define cruelty on the basis of intent, or lack thereof, to harm animals (Rowan 1993). While this focus gets closer to the perspective of those doing it, the researcher's thinking is still imposed on the actor's voice; debates over what does or does not constitute abuse or neglect tell us little, if anything, about how it is actually defined on the streets or in police vehicles, animal shelters, people's homes, humane society development meetings, or in the news. Additionally, psychological approaches are limited to the thoughts and actions of individuals, ignoring how mistreatment of animals is defined in social interaction in groups. People arrive at shared agreements about what words and concepts, such as cruelty, mean in given situations. In the end, academic definitions are just as detached from the real-world situations where everyday actors make sense of cruelty as are regulatory and legal ones. What is missing are the voices of the people who encounter cruelty, however and wherever it occurs, as its meaning is decided upon and shaped to address their needs, concerns, and aims.

To capture this meaning, we must not rely on the abstract definitions and lists created by epidemiologists, legal scholars, and psychologists. Instead, we need to hear from those directly involved with cruelty, linking their responses to the larger social and cultural context that shapes whether and how much we appreciate or dismiss the well-being of animals. An interpretive process underlies these perspectives, since cruelty is the subjective experience of animals. The nature and extent of their distress cannot be directly comprehended by humans. One step removed from this experience, people interpret and react to it through various cultural and social filters. *Just a Dog* takes the spotlight off animal victims to consider how these filters shape the meaning of cruelty and, ultimately, shape how we see ourselves.

These understandings reflect, and in turn reproduce, a society that is uncertain and confused about the nature and importance of animals, at times according them high moral status and at other times less (Arluke 1989). Indeed, the entire fabric of human-animal relations is shot through with arbitrariness and anthropocentrism (Serpell 1996; Swabe 1996). Dogs, for example, are commonly beloved as "pretend" family members (Hickrod and Schmitt 1982) but also can be abused and neglected, used for sport, or experimented on as living test tubes (e.g., Jordan 1975). Farm animals, for another, can be shown a great deal of affection, almost as much as the traditional household "pet," only to be "slaughtered" for food (Roth 1994). Even our perception and treatment of "lowly" mice is fraught with ambivalence; in laboratories their status can change from experimental object to pet to pest (Herzog 1988). Indeed, the debate over what to call animals—pets, companions, or nonhuman beings—is a further reminder that this ambivalence runs deep in our culture, leading me to avoid using these terms in the following pages.

In this confused moral context we come to know cruelty in all its contradiction and complexity—no longer just the deceivingly simple definition put forward by psychologists or the apparently straightforward list of abuses codified in state laws. Rather, cruelty is something that people struggle to make sense of everyday in their private and professional lives, making its meaning context-dependent, highly fluid, and to those outside these situations, at times baffling if not offensive.

A second assumption is that animal cruelty has a harmful effect on people, at least reducing their sensitivities, at most setting them on a course of future violence. But the effects of cruelty are not so simple; nor are they only negative. As we see in the following chapters, experiences with cruelty can be used to recast human identities in ways that do not dehumanize us or make us aggressive.

Human identity can be transformed in social interaction, whether with humans (Hewitt 2000; Mead 1934) or animals (Arluke and Sanders 1996). As people struggle to make sense of their experiences with cruelty, they begin to see themselves in a different light. They discover the worthiness or unworthiness of their thoughts, and the respectability or disrespectability of their acts. Thus, encounters with cruelty, like other social encounters, allow us to become aware of, affirm, and declare our humanness. As people undergo these encounters, however, they are not passive and uncreative actors. They do not merely take meanings and roles given to them; instead they redefine and adjust to them (Sandstrom, Martin, and Fine 2003). As authors of meaning, people can define cruelty and exercise some control over how their definition influences their identities in every situation cruelty is encountered. If cruelty's impact varies from situation to situation, then there is no limit to the variety of ways that it can be used to shape identity, whether positively or negatively.

Using cruelty to create a self is an emergent and reflective process that often occurs in subcultures (Prus 1997) and in the course of situated activities (Blumer 1969). Unwanted identities imputed by others can be replaced when members of subcultures assert more favorable ones. For example, people who belong to a disfavored group, perform low-status work, or commit illegal or morally questionable deeds might use an encounter with cruelty to refashion their sense of self and present it to others in a positive light.

A final assumption is that only those who harm animals are transformed by cruelty. As we have seen, two groups of people, those whose harm of animals is culturally sanctioned and those whose harms is not, are thought to undergo identity change as a consequence of their interactions with animals. More commonly pictured are those who deliberately mistreat animals in ways that are criminal. Advocates of the link view this untoward behavior as having a long-term, detrimental effect on the abuser's character and future identity. Less agreement surrounds those who work with animals in institutional settings where the use of animals, even though the law defines such use as proper, is considered cruel by some critics. Whether their treatment of animals is cruel or not, workers in animal laboratories or slaughterhouses, for example, are thought to undergo desensitization as a necessary coping device, if not more major changes to their identities over time.

The power of animal cruelty to transform the human self is much broader than what these examples suggest. Many different groups commit acts of cruelty and many others deal with cruelty in some manner, whether, for example, to prevent it, to punish abusers, to educate the public, or to mourn the victims. All the groups I examine in *Just a Dog* have members who develop their own definitions of cruelty and use these definitions to take on certain identities. I studied five groups, including law enforcement agents who investigate complaints of cruelty, college students who recall their "youthful indiscretions" with animals, hoarders who defend their self-worth from public criticism, shelter workers who battle with their peers over who is more humane, and public relations experts who use cruelty as a marketing tool for fund raising and education. I chose these groups because each exists in an arena where the meaning of cruelty, as well as the nature and importance of animals, are questioned if not contested. Agents, dispatchers, complainants, court officials, and alleged abusers disagree with one another about whether certain acts constitute cruelty; college students realize their former abuse would be frowned upon by many; hoarders withdraw from the community, in part because their way of life—which includes the neglect of animals—would be threatened if people knew about it; shelter workers indirectly accuse other workers of being cruel to animals; and humane society fund raisers and development personnel debate what makes a good or bad cruelty case for public consumption. And in each of these arenas, cruelty has special consequences for how people regard others and think of themselves.

The significance of animal cruelty in modern, western societies is greater than what these three assumptions suggest. Many different groups—however they define or approach cruelty—use it to build or frame their identities in positive ways. Critics will think it unsavory to propose that cruelty can have beneficial effects. Some may be troubled because this proposal focuses on the human side of cruelty rather than on the animal's experience. While it is understandable and proper to focus attention on animals, since they suffer and die, cruelty is also experienced by people—many of whom are not themselves the abusers. Taking the spotlight off the animal victim means that *Just a Dog* is not a polemic against cruelty or an indictment of abusers. Instead it explores the topic without an ideological agenda by giving a voice to those who come face to face with the mistreatment of animals and are forced to deal with it—asking themselves whether what they see is cruelty, whether they or others are cruel, and whether they can approach or use cruelty in ways that make them feel better about themselves.

Others might be troubled because my approach suggests—at a social psychological level—that cruelty can have a positive impact. This suggestion will be considered heretical if misconstrued, even implicitly, to mean that cruelty should be encouraged or at least tolerated. However, by asking how people interpret and use cruelty in beneficial ways, my goal is not to condone it, just as analysts seeking to understand "evil" are not forgiving it (Staub 1989). Despite my intent, readers should be cautioned not to exonerate the perspectives described in *Just a Dog*, since understanding can unintentionally promote forgiving (Baumeister 1997; Miller, Gordon, and Buddie 1999), regardless of an author's caveat.

There are good reasons to study how groups define cruelty and use these definitions to create identities for themselves or others. To start, as in all social science research, it is valuable to explore these questions for the theoretical illumination that can result (Karp 1996). Although we know that identity is achieved through interpersonal human relationships, we are only beginning to understand the ways in which interaction with animals influences the self. In this regard, recent sociological studies are a most welcome addition to the emerging literature on human-animal relationships (e.g., Irvine 2004; Michalko 1999; Sanders 1999). However, the role that interspecies relationships play in the formation of identity needs further study, since sociologists have largely restricted their work to compassionate and caring relationships. We know relatively little about the impact on identity when the connection involves the "dark side" of our contact with animals (Rowan 1992), the side that involves abuse or neglect.

Just a Dog applies the sociological perspective of symbolic interaction to study how cruelty is defined in social interaction and how actors use these definitions to shape identities for themselves and others. This approach argues that meanings, rather than being inherent in objects, events, and situations, are attached to them through human interpretation (e.g., Blumer 1969; Mead 1934). People respond to and make sense out of them in an on-going process of interpretation. Of course, some situations, such as those involving animal cruelty, are more unclear than others, requiring greater interpretive efforts to understand them, in turn inviting conflict over different interpretations.

There also are practical reasons why these questions merit study. Policy makers and the public at large are engaged in an active and ongoing debate about the moral and legal significance of animal abuse and neglect. For example, there is mounting pressure to reclassify cruelty under the law as a felony crime rather than as a misdemeanor, thereby stiffening penalties for violators; and there is growing interest in changing the law's view of mistreated animals as property, thereby recognizing some species as persons, not things, and allowing damages for loss of companionship or emotional distress (Francione 1995). This debate depends on the kind of information people have about cruelty, or what is defined as such, since groups understand its meaning in many different ways. *Just a Dog* describes the nature and extent of this knowledge as people generate and share their conceptions of cruelty with colleagues, peers, and the public or report it in the news.

Examining these questions also can be valuable to those who must deal, in various ways, with those who abuse or neglect animals. Law enforcement agents, veterinarians, psychologists, social workers, public health officials, neighbors, and family members encounter those who harm animals, although they approach them with different goals, whether that is to investigate their potential crime, report them to authorities, rehabilitate them, provide social and medical services, or simply help them cope more effectively with everyday life. Yet they all can benefit from a deeper understanding of how they shield themselves from scorn.

I studied these questions as an ethnographer of human-animal relationships. Using this approach, I immersed myself in my subjects' social worlds, to the extent that it was possible and necessary. At all times, I let these people author their own conceptions of cruelty, no matter how vague, shifting, or contradictory they were, and gave them ample room to explore the particular significance that cruelty had for them. I was able to observe and interview more than 250 people. I listened to and watched humane agents as they investigated complaints in pet stores, farms, and people's homes, college students as they sat across from me in my office and either joked or cried about their former abuse, hoarders as they showed me around their animal and object-cluttered homes, praising their own efforts, shelter workers as they wondered whether their peers were being cruel to animals for either euthanizing them or not, and public relations experts in humane societies as they met in small conference rooms to plan the use of cruelty cases for education and fund raising. And I supplemented these observations and interviews with qualitative studies of newspaper reports about abuse and neglect cases.

My ethnographic goal was to capture their perspectives regarding the treatment of animals—both cruel and humane—not as individuals but as members of groups where they coordinate views and share plans of action (Becker et al. 1961; Mead 1938). Many of the people I studied belonged to groups whose common focus on animals involved working face to face with peers. These included humane agents, shelter workers, and humane society marketers. Not everyone, however, belonged to a group whose members had a sense of "we" when they interacted with animals. Years earlier some of the college students, in the company of friends, had harmed animals, but their current academic subculture had no such component. Hoarders, of all the groups studied, were the most isolated. Although some had friends who aided their efforts to amass animals, there was no wider subculture of hoarders in which they could participate. However, they too can be considered a group that shares—although not necessarily face to face—a similar set of understandings, assumptions, rationales, and expectations with one another as well as a similar set of coping skills to lessen the sting of criticism.

When studying group perspectives, it is not always possible to know whether they are genuine or not (Becker et al. 1961). Do people really believe what they tell us or is it just for public consumption? Sociologically, this uncertainty does not lessen the importance of shared perspectives as devices to give meaning and order to life, to ward off and neutralize public disapproval, and to direct and guide future behavior. Whether sheer ideology or authentic beliefs, whether transparent justifications or genuine feelings, we know from the study of other group perspectives that they are a powerful influence on people's thoughts, feelings, and actions.

Since the power of group perspectives is intuitively obvious to lay people, they often wonder how ethnographers can be comfortable and willing to study, up close, unsavory practices like cruelty. Friends and strangers alike asked how I could do this research. Wasn't I too disturbed by what I saw and heard to do this work, let alone remain impartial? Didn't I become furious listening to people regale me with outrageous reports about harming innocent animals? Shaking heads and rolled eyes were common. Some specifically questioned me because I could pay attention to things that "must be too awful to imagine." Just doing this research condemned me in their eyes, since if I could do it, there must be something wrong with *my* sensibilities. They argued that I must be as callous as my subjects because I could listen to them and try to understand their perspective.

I explained that I was a watcher and witness in the field, roles familiar to ethnographers (Bosk 1985). The roles of watcher and witness provided a convenient shield for my identity, leaving my sensibilities intact and reminding me that I was different from those studied. I was there to capture their perspectives, not to criticize them. And I was there to showcase their perspectives to the public, the humane community, and academe, not to endorse them. Despite attending to these roles, I did not like everything I saw and heard, but the roles enabled me to get through various situations that might otherwise have been more upsetting at the time. Though I was aware of the power of these roles, I sometimes felt it was too easy to hear about or see "bad things." Given what this tolerance might say about me, it echoed the fear that indeed my sensibilities had become blunted. That I needed to intellectualize my lack of response in the situation was itself comforting, telling me that I still cared but needed to put these feelings on hold. For example, I sometimes assumed that subjects exaggerated their cruelty or just made it up to shock me. Most of what I observed also did not upset me at the time, in part because I never actually saw animals being deliberately abused. Of course, I did see animals after they had been victimized, whether through abuse or neglect, and police showed me many photographs of harmed animals, but most of what I saw fell short of the malicious and senseless harm of animals that many people picture when

I tell them about my work. Like my subjects, I was not immune to the potential identity-changing impact of cruelty; it affects those who merely seek to understand it. I noticed this impact in the form of a role "side effect." For example, listening to stories about animals being harmed briefly tainted my behavior. Immediately after interviewing some of the teenage abusers my actions became more aggressive, whether that was driving over the speed limit or being short with friends. I had so thoroughly entered into my subjects' perspective to develop rapport that I exited the encounters a slightly different person, at least temporarily.

Friends and strangers had another question about my studying cruelty-related group perspectives. Rather than asking how I could conduct such research, given its emotional costs to me, they asked why should I do it, given the relative insignificance of cruelty when compared with more pressing human social problems. I heard this concern from fellow sociologists too, although in all fairness, studying human-animal relationships has only recent come into the fold of my discipline. Nevertheless, getting this reaction from academic peers stunned me at first because of sociology's imperatives to examine and understand any encounter between two or more people. However, encounters between people and animals are not yet widely regarded as sufficiently important or interesting, sociologically, to merit the attention of researchers. This attitude should abate as sociologists show through their writing why these relationships are worth a close look (Arluke 2003). *Just a Dog* will, I hope, be part of this vanguard.

The five chapters that follow explore how groups—including but not limited to those who harm animals—shape the meaning of cruelty in social interaction and use this meaning to create identities for themselves and others. Chapter 1 asks these questions about humane law enforcement agents who investigate and prosecute complaints of animal abuse and neglect. I spent one year studying thirty "animal cops" and dispatchers in two large northeastern cities. Most of my fieldwork involved hundreds of hours of escorting agents as they drove to some of the five thousand cruelty complaints made each year. I was there as they spoke with "respondents" or "perps" and walked through their homes or businesses. When not on an investigation, I hung out with them in the department as they mulled over the day's work, wrote reports, or just killed time.

When investigating these complaints, rookie agents think of themselves as a brute force having legitimate authority to represent the interests of abused animals. They see themselves as a power for the helpless, a voice for the mute. With more time on the job, this view changes. For the most part, their experience with cruelty is to see it trivialized. Rather than "fighting the good fight" against egregious cases of harm, agents are overwhelmed with ambiguous, marginal, or bogus complaints that barely qualify, if at all, in their interpretation as legally defined abuse or neglect. In the course of their work, agents also learn that the public does not know who they are, often regarding them as second-rate "wannabe" cops or closet "animal extremists." Having a tainted occupational image with vague responsibilities and a suspect role leaves them with little authority in the public's eye.

Hardly a brute force, agents adapt, at least at first, by assuming a role akin to humane educators as they try to make people into responsible pet owners. However, most agents feel that these informal educational efforts do not work and can, in fact, further impair their already low-status image. Respondents are seen as forgetful, ignorant, resistant, or dismissive when it comes to this instruction and the role of teacher seems to reinforce the misperception that they are not "real" police. Their long-term response to this problem is novel and creative. Agents use their symbolic skills to take advantage of the ambiguity of cruelty and their role as law enforcers. Referred to as the "knack," they create an illusion of having more authority than they do to gain respondents' cooperation. To further buttress the impression of power and authority, agents also suppress their emotions to separate themselves from animal "extremists."

Chapter 2 focuses on late adolescents who harmed animals earlier in their lives, asking how they interpreted these "random acts of violence" and used these interpretations to feel adultlike. To explore this question, I interviewed twenty-five undergraduate students at a major urban eastern university who claimed to have deliberately harmed or killed animals outside culturally sanctioned experiences. They were mostly male, late teen, white, and middle- to upper-middle-class students with majors in a variety of liberal arts and technical subjects. None had ever been arrested for any unlawful behavior. According to surveys of college students, their ability to recount earlier animal abuse was not surprising. Between 20 and 35 percent of students claim to have harmed animals during their childhood or adolescence (Goodney 1997; Miller and Knutson 1997).

Students recounted their animal abuse as a form of "play." At first they described this play as "just" an idle activity because they limited its nature and scope, such as only tormenting an animal psychologically rather than physically. However, as students explored their memories, it was clear that they did not regard their former abuse as ordinary play. They remembered it as having a serious edge that distinguished it from everyday play in general or normal play with animals. Animal abuse was "cool" and thrilling because carrying it out was challenging and harming victims was "fun," given their unpredictable but humanlike responses.

Far from being inexplicable or "senseless," the students explained their prior acts in ways indicating that, at least sometimes, the harm of animals may be a formative and important event in a child's emerging identity. As with other unsavory and objectionable behaviors that occur in adolescence, such as the use of sexual threats or racial invectives, children's defiance can be part of their unfolding adult selves. Students recalled animal abuse as a means to try on and exercise adultlike powers from which they felt excluded, including keeping adultlike secrets, drawing adultlike boundaries, doing adultlike activities, and gathering and confirming adultlike knowledge. These recollections, however, were rife with contradictory views of animals that mimicked society's inconsistent view of them as both objects and pets.

Chapter 3 examines hoarders—those who amass large numbers of animals only to neglect them—and how they are portrayed in the news, what image they provide of themselves, and why stories about them are newsworthy. I reviewed almost five hundred news articles between 2000 and 2003 about hoarding to understand the press's transformation of this behavior into a social problem and to capture the hoarders' perspective. I also interviewed hoarders in their homes so that I could see firsthand their life-style and their animals.

When the media reports hoarding to the public, the abuser's private identity quickly becomes overshadowed as journalists summarize expert opinions about why people harm animals, how often it occurs, and what needs to be done to prevent it. Based on these opinions, reporters write stories about hoarders to make them newsworthy. In so doing, journalistic conventions transform hoarders into three cultural archetypes: they are "bad," "crazy," or "sad" people.

Despite these negative images, hoarders use what the public sees as extreme neglect to craft a more favorable identity. When spoken to about their alleged mistreatment of animals, hoarders present an image that contradicts their overall portrayal by the press. They do this to reassure themselves and others that they are reasonable and good people, claiming to have nothing but the most humane motivations for collecting so many. In fact, they present themselves as saintly for making enormous sacrifices in the interest of helping scores of needy animals. The public's identity also benefits from hoarding, although in a distinctively different way. Readers are shocked and horrified when they read these reports, but they are drawn to them because the stories allow people to consider and work through fundamental questions about their identities.

Chapter 4 looks at how "no-kill" shelter workers—those who consider euthanasia to be an inhumane approach to control animal overpopulation—use the rejection of cruelty as a way to return to their "true calling." I carried out two hundred hours of observation and seventy-five formal interviews in shelters, animal control offices, and sanctuaries in two communities on opposite coasts of the country that have taken different approaches to the use of euthanasia, in one case seeing it as a necessary and humane while in the other as inappropriate and inhumane. I also attended the national meetings of the major humane organizations having conflicting opinions about this matter, examined press accounts and shelter publications relating to euthanasia, and combed Internet news groups that discussed shelter issues.

For most of the twentieth century shelter workers shared a common identity; they accepted euthanasia as the only humane way to deal with the vast number of cats and dogs that could not be placed in homes. In recent years, a rancorous debate has emerged within the humane community about the propriety of "no-kill" strategies that claim it is cruel to kill so many animals just because they are "old and ugly" or somewhat sick. By refusing to euthanize most animals, shelter workers have created a culture that permits them to have certain feelings that are problematic in shelters that routinely euthanize their charges. In a "cruelty-free" environment, no-killers can become attached to shelter animals and devout themselves to "rescuing" them without fearing their death.

Those critical of the no-kill approach feel under attack, now accused of being cruel, and retort by charging that no-killers are themselves cruel. These "open-admission" workers support the use of euthanasia to control overpopulation and contend that it is just as cruel to "warehouse" animals in shelters for months or years or to place them in homes where their proper care is not insured. While no-killers have rallied around their new cruelty-free identity, rediscovering the "true" meaning of being a shelter worker has divided what was once a more unified community, leaving an uneasy tension in its place.

Chapter 5 considers how serious and dramatic cases of cruelty can further solidarity within societies for the prevention of cruelty to animals (SPCAs) and between these organizations and their publics. To explore how these cases are selected and shaped, and why they benefit the humane community's identity, I focused on the public relations and fund-raising staffs of two large eastern SPCAs. I interviewed people at length about their use of certain egregious cases of abuse and neglect to educate the public and raise money for their organizations. I also closely analyzed hundreds of letters sent by community members, hours of television video footage of these big cases, and scores of newspaper articles and letters to the editor that showed the nature and depth of support for the SPCA's efforts, the plight of animal victims, and the ordeal of their owners.

The most horrific cases are discouraging to those who work in SPCAs and their supporters because their numbers never decline, abusers are often not found or brought to justice, and animals suffer and die needlessly. A certain type of cruelty case, however, is thought to be an extremely effective marketing tool because its features rouse the public's interest in abuse and endorsement of humane efforts. Staff members search for and construct these "beautiful" cases by scouring the many instances of cruelty that are reported to the SPCA. Unlike the vast majority of incidents that occur, these special cases have very appealing animals that survive egregious abuse and get adopted into good homes with the help of determined humane agents, caring shelter workers, and skilled veterinarians.

"Beautiful" cases create solidarity. Internally, humane societies are often racked with the same kinds of division and conflict that occur in any large hierarchical organization: departments compete for scarce resources and staff members disagree over organizational policy and practice. Also, staff members are disconnected from one another and disillusioned with the general mission of the society to combat cruelty. Beautiful cases present opportunities for all departments and staff members to put aside these tensions and problems and to work together and feel good about helping animals in need. For the many people outside the societies who support their mission but who have few opportunities to follow and get involved in specific cases, beautiful cases reassure them that these organizations are winning the battle against cruelty. These cases "rally the troops" to celebrate these rare successes and strengthen their identification with the organization.

The book concludes by asking why conflict and contradiction appear throughout *Just a Dog*. To better understand this confusion, I examined three egregious incidents of cruelty that captured widespread media attention—shelter animals beaten to death with baseball bats, a cat set on fire, and a dog crushed to death. These ugly cases expose the general public to the unseemly, sordid, and hopeless sides of cruelty. Animal victims are not always cute and appealing—unattractive pets and unpopular wild animals get tortured or killed. Happy endings almost never occur—abusers are rarely found and their victims usually do not end up healthy and adopted. Most important, abuse is often ghastly. And in addition to egregiously harming animals, people may be victims too.

Inspection of these three cases shows how thinking about animal cruelty is tied to our social context. Collective anxieties and fears filter the way people describe and understand cruelty. Because of this filtering, descriptions of cruelty are not conventionally "objective" or "factual"; they are narratives with many meanings and purposes, not all directly related to the harmed animal's experience. They can also tell a story about the kind of people we are, the kind of society we live in, and the qualities that make us unique as living creatures. Nor are they always simple and consistent stories, because part of our shared identity is composed of modern apprehensions, doubts, and conflicts. These concerns, however inconsistent they are, must be teased out of the mix to help us better understand our confused thinking about the abuse and neglect of animals.

Taken together, these chapters will shake up long-standing agendas and assumptions about what cruelty is, how it affects us, and how it should be thought about and studied. This impact will be greatest in the humane community. Those who formulate its policy have, for the most part, championed the cause of animals at the expense of conducting serious research on questions related to animal welfare and protection. In all fairness to such organizations, they do not claim to be in the business of scholarship. Their goals are more ideological than empirical, as evidenced in humane society publications and conferences that graphically portray numerous "abuses" and make assumptions about what constitutes cruelty and how it affects people. Moreover, discussions about the nature and consequence of cruelty have been left to advocates who have little scientific work to draw on when making recommendations to legislators, courtroom officials, law enforcement workers, teachers, and social workers. And the few studies that are relied on tend to be psychological and clinical. Sociological studies, whether empirical (e.g., Flynn 1999) or theoretical (e.g., Agnew 1998; Beirne 1997), have been slow in coming, but they are necessary to complement, and critique, the work of psychologists in this area.

I also wrote *Just a Dog* with the general public in mind. Future policy debates about animal cruelty must include an interested and informed public. Yet, at present, the public is ill-informed because of the paucity of scholarship on this subject. Much of what is available sensationalizes the alleged mistreatment of animals. Such a polemical approach does little to further our understanding of how people understand cruelty and understand themselves as a consequence. Exploring this question is no less important, even though some regard it as far less "sexy," than detailing purported harm in scientific laboratories, slaughterhouses, or farms. By understanding how people make sense of cruelty and why cultural and social factors encourage its persistence, the public might be better equipped to debate and formulate policies to define and combat it.

Although I take an academic approach to this discussion and debate, rather than an impassioned and ideological one, some readers will still be upset by the book. Cases of cruelty are described in detail and the perspectives of abusers are faithfully reported. This may seem like too much information, but these descriptions are not gratuitous. *Just a Dog* is about the ways that groups construe the meaning of cruelty and its subsequent impact on them, so some forthright discussion, albeit unpleasant or disturbing to consider, is necessary. I excluded many cases, far more unsavory than those that I report, to respect the sensitivities of readers whose distress over specific details would prevent them from thinking about the broader questions posed in the following pages.

1   Agents
Feigning Authority

When you first get here, it's like a cop on a gun run. A cop, when he gets a call for a gun, immediately thinks there's a guy with a gun out there that's going to do harm to somebody. So you're a rookie and you get a job that says, "Dog out with no food, water, or shelter." And you are like [excited voice], "Oh, there's a dog out without food, water, or shelter! It must be dying!" You think the worst. When you have seen as many bullshit calls come through this office as I have, then you say, it could be a neighbor dispute or that dog is out all the time and has a shelter but someone says that "it should be inside with the owner like my dog is." You look at these people, and say, "What, the dog should have a coat on in front of the fireplace? Get the hell out of here."
—Humane agent, five years on the job

PEOPLE DISCOVER who they are by observing the consequences of their actions in the social world. Individuals use this looking-glass self to imagine how they are seen and judged by others, and in this way, they develop self-feelings that tell them who they are (Cooley 1902). Although the looking glass plays a major role in the development of identity in children and adolescents, the process of discovering one's identity continues into adulthood and relies heavily on the reactions people get to their jobs. As Hughes (1958, 42) observes, a person's "work is one of the things by which he is judged, and certainly one of the more significant things by which he judges himself." Indeed, occupation has become the main determinant of status and prestige (Goldschalk 1979). People are granted power or refused it, shown respect or denied it, based on where they work and what they do there. They are not just teachers but college professors at a powerhouse research university. They are not simply stockbrokers but financial counselors at a prestigious Wall Street firm. All of these occupational trimmings reveal things about people to others, who in turn tell them what they think and feel about their work.

Sometimes what is revealed about one's work, and in turn one's self, is negative. Workers suffer low status and tarnished identities for several reasons. According to Hughes (1958), certain jobs involve work that is widely considered to be disgusting, degrading, or undesirable. For example, death work (Pine 1977; Sudnow 1967) and cleaning work (Gold 1964; Perry 1978) offend aesthetic sensibilities, while sex work (Jackman, O'Toole, and Geis 1963; McCaghy and Skipper 1969) and money lending (Hartnett 1981) offend moral sensibilities. Low status is also attached to work that is seen as ambiguous or unimportant, such as that by occupational therapists (Gritzer and Arluke 1985). When the public misunderstands or disrespects what workers do, they will be uncertain about their mission and how to carry it out, especially if they have gone through training that instills high and clear expectations for what they should be doing. They may start to wonder whether their work matters and to question their self-worth.

As workers deduce their identity from the behavior of others toward them, they often try to surmount the tarnished image that goes along with low-status or dirty work. In different ways they control information to buffer their identities from shame and help them feel better about their work. Some attempt to neutralize discrediting reports by justifying the importance of their work, as do prostitutes who claim that their "service" prevents domestic violence (Bryan 1966). Others attack discrediting reports by defining their critics as disrespectable, as do animal experimenters who point to the violent and immoral tactics of animal rights activists (Arluke and Groves 1998). And still others avoid discrediting reports by either hiding aspects of their work that are subject to public scorn or derision, as do shelter workers who avoid talking about euthanasia to outsiders (Arluke 1994b), or by separating themselves from peers, as do bailbondsmen who become social isolates (Davis 1984).

Those who use these strategies view the immoral, unclean, ambiguous, or devalued features of dirty work as constraints that need to be managed and overcome. But such limitations or problems can be seen as resources for workers to use to build more positive identities. In some jobs, for example, unclear or disputed content can allow workers the flexibility to pass in ways that flatter or exaggerate their true authority or expertise. The reverse can be true, however, in those jobs where it is a burden or insult to overextend work roles because doing so diminishes rather than enhances the perception of their worth. For example, regular police expect to go on patrol and enforce the law, but they find that most of their work involves managing many problems unrelated to their legal mandate. Rookies must determine which incidents, outside their mandate, they will police and how they will deal with them. Complaints about "noisy kids hanging out," for example, usually have little legal relevance, but police may resolve the problem by moving juveniles along or telling them to quiet down (Meehan 1992). Doing such extra-legal work, especially when it represents the bulk of what they do, easily raises questions about their identity as law enforcers. However, such confusion can be an opportunity for some workers to stake out their occupational turf and claim wider expertise. In other words, the very fuzziness of core tasks permits people to jockey into a more positive social role because outsiders might not know better.

This is exactly the approach taken by humane law enforcement agents. These agents, or "animal cops," have coped with dirty work since their inception in the mid nineteenth century, when humane organizations in major cities created cruelty agents, entrusted with police authority, to investigate and prosecute cases of animal abuse. Supported by anticruelty legislation that has changed little to this day, the first humane agents focused on preventing the mistreatment of horses, because American society was so heavily dependent on the horse for transportation, industry, and defense. By the end of the twentieth century, many large cities had entire humane law enforcement departments with up to a dozen full-time agents who managed thousands of yearly complaints, usually alleging the abuse of cats and dogs (Alexander 1963).

After sixteen weeks of training at the state police academy, followed by a short course on animal protection, humane agents in Boston and New York are licensed to carry guns and are empowered to make arrests. In New York, they are indistinguishable from regular police, wearing similar uniforms and driving squad cars with shields on the side and sirens on the top, while in Boston their green uniforms, soft caps, and unmarked Bronco wagons blur their police identity. As a testament to the importance of this identity, several agents in Boston want to wear official-looking police hats and drive policelike squad cars, complaining that no one takes them seriously because they look more like park police than real police.

Beyond these superficial trappings, there is a more fundamental difference between regular police and humane agents. Unlike regular police, humane agents enforce only a single legal code, the anticruelty law, which focuses on protecting animals rather than humans. Their investigations and prosecutions are limited to people who are thought to violate this code, and their police authority is restricted to these cases. These cases reflect how seriously society values animals and views their mistreatment. This reflection, in turn, shapes how agents regard themselves.

Agents discover that few complaints of cruelty are serious and clear violations of the law. Many people who report abuse and neglect view them as trivial problems and view agents as either glorified dogcatchers or animal activists. The result is that humane law enforcement becomes dirty work, a notch below the already low status of regular police work (Skolnick 1966; Neiderhoffer 1969). In fact, the occupational status of agents is closer to that of dogcatchers (Palmer 1978) or campus police (Heinsler, Kleinman, and Stenross 1990) than it is to regular police. Dogcatchers collect and dispose of dead, stray, sick, and unwanted domestic animals. They are degraded because they are seen as society's zoological garbage collectors. Campus police jump-start cars, transport students, unlock doors, and perform other mundane tasks. They are demeaned because they are seen as janitors, mechanics, and social workers.

While campus police and dogcatchers cannot overcome the constraints of their jobs to feel that their work matters, humane agents are more successful because they take advantage of what constrains them. Agents use the ambiguity of cruelty law and confusion over their role to craft positive identities for themselves, dramaturgically manipulating symbolic properties of their work in order to be taken more seriously. By passing themselves off as having more authority than their license gives them, agents piggyback on the image of regular police and acquire a courtesy status that would otherwise be more difficult to attain were the public clearer about what agents are supposed to do and what legal codes they are supposed to enforce.

DIRTY WORK

Agents learn that the public has an extremely broad and ill-defined definition of animal cruelty, often including complaints that are not covered by the existing code, which is itself vague. From their perspective, this confusion "stretches" the meaning of cruelty and puts pressure on them to investigate complaints that are beneath their pride and practice. Facing the prospect of carrying out such dirty work, agents try to exert some control over this unselective process by grumbling over the legitimacy of cases. Although this grumbling creates an alternative and more precise definition of cruelty, they still end up investigating many complaints that fall short of what they regard as serious and clear-cut offenses. To agents, the public appears to consider cruelty to be, at best, vague, and at worst, unimportant.

Bullshit Complaints

Constrained by the application of law, agents assess complaints to determine which ones actually constitute animal cruelty. This evaluation shocks rookie agents because they hope to find and fight "real" cruelty but quickly discover that most complaints are "bullshit." They are ambiguous, trivial, or inappropriate. As one discouraged novice said: "When I walked in I wanted to make the arrests. I wanted to do good. You know, I wanted to save animals' lives and jump on everything. You're like 'cruelty—lock the guy up!' But then you find out that the dog has a fly bite on its ear." Agents investigate infinitely more "fly bites" than flagrant cases of cruelty. One SPCA, for example, received 80,000 complaints of abuse between 1975 and 1996 but prosecuted only 268 of them or approximately one-third of 1 percent of all calls (Arluke and Luke 1997). These prosecuted cases come close to what rookies expect to encounter: beating, shooting, stabbing, throwing, burning, strangling, drowning, crushing, poisoning, or hanging animals. Although some egregious cases are not prosecuted because of insufficient evidence or unknown identities of abusers, adding these few cases to the total still leaves agents with the overall impression that clear-cut cruelty is very rare and poorly understood or unappreciated.

Instead, there are endless "bullshit" calls, mostly citizen generated, that make up the bulk of agents' investigations and leave them grumbling about a public that is very confused about the nature and significance of cruelty. One type of bullshit complaint involves borderline situations that are "not straight-out cruelty" but merit attention because animals need help that, for some reason, animal control officers are not providing. Some of these situations are "emergencies" where animals might suffer, in the eyes of dispatchers, but are not victims of cruelty.

Agents might be asked to intervene with injured animals if animal control cannot, as one dispatcher explained: "It's hard because only certain things are cruelty. An animal hit by a car is clearly an emergency, but it's not necessarily cruelty. It's going to be an animal control issue, but if somehow we have an officer in the area and animal control is not around, we'll have an officer go out there and see what they can do." Cases of abandoned animals are also considered borderline. In one case, described by a dispatcher, a woman without family who was institutionalized had three cats at home. "Larry [a humane agent] was going over there every three days and leaving food for her cats because she ended up being in there for a couple of months. Those are the toughest, especially when somebody has no family or friends or anything like that because technically, it's not something we really deal with, but we're not just going to say okay. We're not going to leave the cats in the house, so you try to find something to do." Hearing about stray animals also can trigger a borderline investigation. One dispatcher, for example, was concerned about a cat walking in the middle of a busy highway and asked a sympathetic agent to check on the situation: "You tell Nancy there's a cat in the median and she's probably going to drive up and down the strip a couple of times just to pick up the cat. It's not in her job description to do that. It's not really a law enforcement issue. It's basically a stray cat, but if she's in the area, she will probably stop by to pick it up."

A second kind of bullshit complaint involves situations in which there is a breakdown in interpersonal relations within families or between neighbors. Callers want agents to remedy problems unrelated to animal welfare and will lie or grossly exaggerate, claiming there is cruelty to get police intervention. For example, a landlord who hoped to "clean house" by removing his tenant's animals filed a cruelty complaint. To the agent, this was a bullshit complaint: "The landlord is saying, 'I want the animals out of there. They're shitting and pissing all over the house.' If they're in good condition, then that's not an urgent situation from my standpoint." Other bullshit complaints, according to agents, are lodged to create trouble for people by getting law enforcement involved in neighborhood disputes. As one agent elaborated: "A lot of calls we get are fake. These people, they don't care about the dog, but they get mad at the guy next door and they just want to cause problems." In one case, for example, an agent investigated a complaint of "a dog that was a mess, disgusting looking," only to find a well-groomed dog that was old and overweight. As the agent said: "There's nothing there. [The complainant] called to put the pins to her landlord because he was tossing her out." Civil bullshit complaints also arise when animals are used as pawns in domestic struggles between parents and their children or between spouses. Agents feel there is "no reason" to investigate these cases because animals are not at risk. To illustrate, one agent gave the example of a divorced couple who wanted to hurt each other by making false accusations of cruelty: "People don't always have the best interest of the animal at heart. They have their own agenda when they call. It's a husband trying to get even with his ex-wife by getting the dog taken away. Yeah, the people are separating and the ex-wife's got the animals and the husband's saying that she doesn't take care of the animals and she says, 'Well, he's got a dog over at his girlfriend's place. You should take a look at that one. The dog hasn't been to the vet in two years.' So now you have to go and investigate him and it's just bullshit."

A third type of bullshit complaint involves animal welfare more directly but does not qualify as cruelty under the law. Agents argue that the definition of cruelty used by complainants in these cases exceeds what can be enforced under the law. "It's like everyone has their own definition of what proper care is," one agent acknowledged. "A lot of them are not really cruelty violations, but moral issues with animals—animals are not being handled the way this person feels they should be, but it's not a violation of the law either." A common example is someone hitting as opposed to beating his dog, with only the latter prohibited by law. An agent explained, "You have to understand whether the complainant is just upset because a person hit their animal or in fact actually beat their animal." Another agent offered the example of a complainant who does not like to see dogs in the rain: "I got a complaint— 'two dogs tied out in the pouring rain.' This was on a Friday afternoon. I had just left Ocean City and I had to go back. I got back and I mean there was torrential rains. I knocked on the door and the guy [respondent] comes to the door. I woke him out of bed. He works nights. He comes to the door half undressed. I told him who I was and that somebody complained about his dog. He started— 'You son of a bitch.' I said, 'I understand what you're saying, but we have to respond.' He finally threw a pair of pants on, came outside with no shoes on, walked down to the back in the mud, and both dogs had doghouses. And I was pissed because somebody was just pissed because the dogs were out. The dogs chose to stay out in the rain, but they both had their doghouses. They were both out in the rain looking at me." This type of complainant, while seen as genuine, is "demanding" to agents. "You get a situation where you have to answer the complainant, and they become very demanding as far as 'I want you to do this or that.' I'll say to them, 'Look, I may not agree with the situation, but this is the way the law is.' A lot of people—unless someone is kissing their dog goodnight when they go to bed—they're not happy with the way that animal is being cared for." One agent encountered a demanding complainant who had insisted to a dog owner that he not leave his dog outside at night, or at least keep hay or straw in its doghouse. "I told him about the hay," the complainant reported to the agent, "the dog would be more comfortable with it. . . . But there is no straw there." The agent replied, "Well, I'll be rechecking it, but I can't make him put straw in the doghouse." Most agents are impatient with demanding complainants, sometimes because their exaggerated definitions of cruelty come from the greater value they place on animals than on people. One frustrated agent noted: "Some people will say, 'An animal's life is more valuable than a person's life.' That bothers me." Humane agents are also impatient with complainants' ignorance, which causes them to see suffering or cruelty when they do not exist. An agent gave the following example: "A person could drive by and see a horse with a sloped back and think, 'Oh, my God, that poor thing.' But it's like a person. You've got horses that have sway backs. Either they rode them too early or their spine isn't right, but they are fine. Most of the time when you see sway backs, they are old, their spine just drops. And somebody will call a complaint in and say, 'Oh, the poor thing.'" At other times, agents' impatience is stirred by moral bullshit complaints that stem from mistaken impressions of animal suffering. One complainant, for example, claimed that a dog was a "bag of bones" and was "suffering in terrible condition," only for the agent to find an older animal. "You find out that the owner takes her dog to the vet all the time and the vet says that it's just an old dog. It's not suffering. It looks like hell. Its skin is terrible. It might be missing a lot of its fur or it might have a poor coat. It might be very thin, but there's not much they can do for the dog. It's just getting to be an old dog."

A final type of bullshit complaint are those incorrectly referred to humane law enforcement or left unmanaged by animal control officers, local police, or other authorities. These "garbage" or "nuisance" complaints have nothing to do with cruelty but result when other organizations, at the town or state level, shirk or inadequately perform their duties. For example, odor problems with big farms might get "pushed off" on agents when the town's sanitation department should be the first agency to be called and take action. In one case, agents repeatedly investigated a pet store that violated numerous regulations involving proper sanitation and hygiene because the department of agriculture failed to monitor and prosecute these civil violations. In another case, an agent had to pick up and transport the decomposed body of a Beagle, a dirty job that in his opinion should have been done by the local animal control officer: "It really bothered me. I just don't like seeing something so decomposed. I just couldn't look at it. It's kind of evidence, I guess. I had to carry it about a quarter of a mile. I had it double bagged, but it was dripping on me. I wouldn't have felt right leaving it there, plus the woman was standing behind me saying, 'I can't believe that the animal control officer wouldn't take this.' He left it there. I didn't want to do it either." Humane agents often get calls from people who "get no satisfaction" from their animal control officer. "'The dog barks all the time,' [they say,] and we'll say, 'Sorry, there's nothing we can do about that. We do cruelty.' We get a good percentage of that, and that's frustrating because it's not our job and you get out there and we are driving a long way to come up there when it's probably going to be a waste of time."

Although theses cases are considered bullshit, if animals can be helped, most agents approach them cases as professionals and conduct investigations when necessary. Nevertheless, they disparage the complaints and grumble about having to check them out. What frustrates them is not only that many of these ambiguous or trivial cases waste their time but that they jeopardize their precarious and limited authority by reinforcing the public's confused perception of them as either low-status workers or political activists.

Dogcatchers and Extremists

Just as cruelty is ambiguous, so too is the role of agents to enforce the code. Newcomers quickly learn that many people accord little status to their work, viewing what they do as dirty—and not very important—work and confusing them with either animal control officers or animal extremists. These flawed images challenge the authority of humane agents to investigate complaints, carry out the law, and prosecute cases. If agents can disconnect themselves from these images, they can regard themselves more positively and perhaps be taken more seriously.

The most common image problem is for agents to be mistaken for "dogcatchers" or animal control officers. "You know," one agent explained, "I've got a mouthful of food and people come up to me and say, 'Oh, the dogcatcher's here. Sorry to bother you, but there's this barking dog in my neighborhood.'" This confusion feels like an insult to agents, as one complained: "My good friends, like from college and stuff, they still don't understand what I do. They introduce me like, 'This is my friend the cat cop.' People are like, 'What do you do, rescue cats out of trees?'" These encounters frustrate and anger agents. Many, for example, point to pretrial hearings or trial experiences gone sour because court officials question their status as police officers. One agent described such an experience: "I got pissed off. The defense attorney came up to the judge and said, 'The dog officer came up to his door and saw the dog.' I felt like saying, 'Gee, did somebody else come because I'm a police officer?' It bothers me to some extent. I don't like being called a dog officer. We work hard and we have to go to the police academy, so we should get some recognition."

Humane agents are also mistaken for environmental police, fish and game wardens, park rangers, and other officials whose work has nothing to do with animals. For example, while standing in downtown Boston, one agent was approached by out-of-town tourists who opened a map of historic sites in the area and asked him for advice about what to visit, thinking that he was a park ranger, whose uniform, except for the brimmed hat, was very similar to those worn by agents. And on rare occasions, they are seen as security or delivery personnel. As one agent admitted, "I had someone think I was from UPS once. I like what I do and I feel comfortable with what I do until I hear some comment that shouldn't affect me, but it does."

At other times, people know that humane law enforcement agents are police of a sort but realize that they are not "regular" police and therefore do not take them seriously. This dismissive attitude is especially irksome to agents when it comes from regular police, who agents see as colleagues. In this vein, one was troubled by the reaction he got from regular police when they were asked to investigate a case of a teenager beating his dog: "Quarrytown pissed me off really bad. Mind you, six or seven of them were good friends of mine at the [police] academy. I tell the lieutenant what's going on. I said, 'Look, I was wondering, while you guys are patrolling, if you could just take a peek over there and see if you see the dog maybe, and get me some information on the kid.' 'Hey pal, what are we, the fuckin' puppy police? Let me tell you something, we have outstanding warrants for home invasion and stuff like that that we can't execute. You want me to go harass some kid for beating on his dog? We've got better things to do.'" Regular police showed their disregard by ridiculing agents. Ridicule from regular police is hard to write off as just innocent teasing or to forgive because of ignorance. Every agent confronts this attitude as a rite of passage into humane law enforcement work. One talked about the dismissive feeling he got on the first days on the job: "You can get that feeling right away when you walk into a police station and they say, 'Here's the dog officer.'" Another recounted his bad experience with police: "District Five, that's the one I hate the most. When I go there, I always hear cracks and comments. So I went to meet this officer. And I'm standing at the general public counter because I'm not allowed behind it, and this guy looks up, 'Yeah?' 'I'm here to meet Sally Smith.' So he gets on the intercom to call her, and goes, 'Woof, woof, your doggie guy is here.' I was like, 'Hey, thanks buddy. Call me when you're in a jam.'" Similarly, two agents in a marked car resembling the city's police department were embarrassed and angry after regular police officers pulled up next to them at a street light, loudly barked over their car's loudspeaker, and broke into raucous laughter. Regular police also conveyed their disregard by referring most cruelty cases directly to animal control, even though they knew that humane law enforcement wanted to manage such cases. Agents felt that regular police, who saw them as lowly dogcatchers, did not consider them to be fellow professionals engaged in important work with valued victims and serious or even dangerous criminals. And when the occasional case of extreme cruelty to a dog was handled by regular police, they dismissed all other animal cases as insignificant.

If not dismissed as lowly dogcatchers, humane agents are criticized for being zealots or animal rights activists. As with the dogcatcher image, regular police often level this charge, according to agents, who hear it very negatively. In some towns, one agent reported, the police "just think we are idiots—we're way off base—we're animal rights type people—not in the real world." Another agent recalled the following incident: "I ran into a police officer and he saw a bunch of our people at court. And he said, 'Gee, I didn't even know you guys were cops until I saw you at court. I thought you were back-of-the-woods, tree-hugging do-gooders.'" Environmental police also consider agents to be extremists who "make a big deal" over animal cruelty, especially those working in rural areas. For example, two agents found a film crew mistreating crows and pigeons that were being used in a movie and reported what they saw to the local environmental police office only to be "laughed at because there's basically an open season on crows." "You can go out and shoot them any time you want, so why are you making a big deal about these crows?" they were told. "And we contacted federal people because they're migratory birds, but they didn't give a damn. We took a lot of harassment." Another agent explained, "Environmental police feel like the SPCA is trying to outlaw everything that's their job. Like we banned traps and the next thing you know we're going to stop hunting. Next thing you know we are going to stop fishing. That's their outlook."

Agents who are accused of having the wrong priorities, for going to extremes to protect animals, fear being labeled as animal activists. One agent said of his father: "He doesn't get protecting animals. See, protecting people is a noble job. They need protection. They're civilization. Animals, well, they're things for people to own or possess or use. He doesn't think that an entire police department should be dedicated to helping animals—that we go a little overboard for protection. He doesn't look at it as though helping animals is important."

Devaluing the importance of fighting animal abuse undercuts what little legitimate authority agents have to investigate what are often vague, borderline, or bullshit cruelty complaints. Even with good cases, their efforts are encumbered because people are often confused about who they are or write them off as second-class law enforcers. Moreover, they are protecting animals from cruelty—a notion whose inherent ambiguity makes it easy to challenge the propriety of many complaints. To effectively counter the perception of their work as trivial and vague, agents may present themselves as having more authority than they do, though usually after first taking a softer, more educational approach to respondents.

MANAGING IMPRESSIONS

Initially, agents tend to downplay their authority when investigating cases. They take this approach because many respondents are unnerved or even angry when they find a uniformed police officer is "checking" on their animals because "complaints" alleging their mistreatment have been made. De-emphasizing the law enforcement role can calm these riled respondents. Agents also downplay their limited authority because so many of their cases are ambiguous, not clearly constituting a legal definition of cruelty, or they are too minor or excusable to call for a law enforcement approach. One agent estimated that only 10 percent of his job constituted law enforcement work, saying "most of what we do isn't really law enforcement. Well it is, but most of the things that we see, we couldn't arrest someone or drive them into court. Most of what we see is just ignorance and just plain not knowing."

By abandoning, at least temporarily, most trappings of law enforcement and adopting an instructional stance thought to be more practical and effective, agents become humane coaches and teachers more than police. One experienced agent spoke about the need to give up the rookie's "toughness," noting, "At the academy they drum into you that you've got to be this tough officer. So you come out and you're tough, but through the years you learn that you really can't get your job done if you continue down that path. I educate people on what they should have done or what to do in the future." Many agents rethink their occupational identification because so much of their work puts them in the position of humane teachers rather than law enforcers. One admitted, "I don't look at myself anymore as a law enforcement officer. I think of myself as an educator. . . . Law enforcement is very minor."

Part of agents' educational approach is to teach respondents to be more responsible animal owners. "You always try to better the situation if you're there, although you find in most instances that it goes in one ear and out the other," one agent pointed out. This approach can involve teaching respondents to be more sensitive or thoughtful about their animal's needs, especially in "borderline" cases where "some things are not quite right, but not really bad enough to seek a complaint." When respondents are not seen as "cruel" or criminal, agents give advice to push them gently to be more caring or sensitive owners of animals. This "humane standpoint" seeks to improve an animal's quality of life beyond that stipulated by law. An agent gave the following example: "Say it's summer time, we get a complaint—'dog tied out, no water.' The law says dogs are to be provided with proper food, drink, shelter, or protection from the weather, so they don't necessarily have to have water in front of them twenty-four hours a day. From a humane standpoint, it would be beneficial to the animal, especially if they're outside for long periods of time, to have access to water, especially if no one is home. You'll explain to the person, 'Gee, it would be better if you leave the animal out there for long periods of time to have water out there for the animal.' Say you get a comment: 'Oh, the animal spills it if I put it out there, so I don't leave water out there.' So then you try and give them a solution as far as how they could secure it, so they're not going to spill it." The decision about how far to exceed the legal definition of cruelty is left to individual agents, who base their thinking on what they believe is best for animals and what they can reasonably expect of respondents. Some agents suggest changes that are clearly beyond the cruelty code but that are part of their own admittedly blurry definition of suffering. In this regard, one agent talked about where she drew the line when owners were doing the minimum they had to by law: "I've sort of tried to tell them things that they could do to make it better. For instance, with psychological needs of dogs, everyone's standard is going to be a bit different. I don't go to a place and expect them to— I mean, my dog has been fed and is on the couch, spoiled rotten. I don't expect everyone to do that, but I also don't expect them to keep them chained twenty-four hours a day and never spend time with them. You kind of try and tell them. But they could choose to or choose not to, and I can't do anything about it, so you just close it."

Most agents, however, do not believe their teaching will result in lasting change. They see respondents as adults with long-term, ingrained beliefs that resist change. One reported, for example: "We try to get them [respondents] involved, but generally people's attitudes are made up. You're not going to change this guy's attitude on Maple Street about how he's going to care for his dog. He's a grown-up. He's not going to change. You can go and get frustrated trying to get him to play with his dog and take it in and socialize with it, but if he's not going to do it, and it's not a violation of the law not to do it, well what are you going to do?" Agents also consider some respondents not only ignorant or devious but also too disadvantaged to care for animals properly.

When agents see that respondents neglect their children or themselves, it is hard for them to imagine that these people will be concerned about their animals. As one observed: "It's difficult to explain to people that they should be caring for their animals in a certain way when they don't care for themselves as good or any better than they do their animals. Or they don't care for their kids any better than what they do for their animals. And yet you're trying to tell them, 'You need to do this and you need to do that and you need to have all these stupid things for your animal,' but yet they don't have it for themselves or their kids. So if someone is living in squalor, you can't expect them to give the dog steak. If you look at their house and their house is basically a shack that's falling down and their animals basically have a shack that's falling down, well, you know, everything's relative there." And finally, many respondents ignore advice when they believe their firsthand knowledge of and experience with a particular animal trumps the agent's. This attitude, combined with the perception of agents as having little if any authority, often inspires rudeness and disrespect. Agents have doors slammed in their faces, business cards ripped up in front of them, and obscenities yelled at them. Recalling such a moment, an agent said, "So I knock on the door and I say 'Hi, I'm with the SPCA and we got a call on your dog.' And they go, 'What's your fucking problem pal? It's my fucking dog. I'll do what I fucking want.'"

The humane educator approach, which fails to make most respondents into more responsible owners, is dangerous for agents to use because it feeds into the image of low-status work they so resist. Unless they show some authority, they see themselves as perilously close to being not much more than animal control officers. To transcend this problem, agents use their symbolic skills to capitalize on the fact that most people do not know the substance or extent of their license to enforce the cruelty code or the content of the law itself. The very constraint posed by the vagueness of their work allows agents to present themselves as having more authority than they do.

Bluffing Power

To encourage more humane behavior, agents create an illusion of having more authority than they do. Some of this illusion, referred to as "the knack," depends on respondents' making mistaken assumptions. For example, the mere appearance of a law enforcement officer, according to one agent, can make respondents comply: "I have a certain amount of power. I have my presence. I have a gun belt, wear a gun, wear a holster, wear an OC [oleoresin capsicum, also known as pepper spray], I carry extra ammunition, I carry handcuffs, the radio, the baton. All of those things present a certain picture and a certain message for people." He continued: "You want to go there and be able to say to them, 'I'm telling you, this is what you've got to do.' And hopefully, just from your presence, they're going to listen to you."

Agents show their presumed authority by the way they speak to respondents. Some admit that they carefully word their statements to respondents to increase the likelihood of gaining access to property and viewing animals. How they word their statements makes it possible to "go in giving people the attitude 'I have the right to look at these animals.'" Regarding a case where he spoke with a respondent on the telephone and wanted to visit the latter's property and examine his dog, one agent noted: "I said to him, 'I'm going to go down and check on the dog.' He didn't say I couldn't go down and check on the dog. Until he tells me I can't go in his backyard and check on the dog, he's given me permission to go back and check on the dog. Just like I'll say to people, 'Why don't we take a look at the dog?' or 'I'm going to take a look at the dog and I'll come back and talk to you.' Sometimes I'll ask them if we can look at the dog. Sometimes I'll tell them we can look at the dog. Or I'll say to them, 'Can we look at the dog?' I'm saying to them, 'I'm going to look at the dog.' People are under the misconception— if people knew what you can do and what you couldn't do, we wouldn't get our job accomplished. You bullshit your way into a lot of situations. I knock on someone's door and say, 'I had a complaint. You've got some cats in poor condition. Where are the cats? I'd like to see them.' They invite you in and you look at the cats. All they have to tell you is, 'Screw you, get off my property. I don't have to talk to you.' And there's nothing you can do." Aware that strict interpretation of the law could discourage responsible animal ownership, agents speak vaguely when giving advice to respondents to create the impression that advice is legally required when it is not: "People are not legally obligated to accept your advice, but you can plant the seed. Like, by law, you don't have to have water out for a dog all day long, but nobody ever questions you when you just tell them that. I say, 'Gee, it's a hot day, put some water out for the dog.' But you can't say to them, 'Look lady, the law says you don't have to have water out,' because if you do you're kind of defeating your whole purpose of being there."

Agents realize that their advice will sometimes be ignored no matter what or how they speak to respondents. And if prosecution seems out of the question, agents can do little. As one noted, "If it's not a violation, I really have no right to go back. Some people, you'll approach them. The animal will be in a situation that's not the best for them, but it's not the worst. You can try to improve it. Talk to them. But if they're like, 'Get the hell off my property you little —' or 'Don't ever come back here,' there's nothing you can do if they're not breaking the law." Another agent described a case where a dog did not have water: "Bottom line is, if they say, 'Screw you, I'm not going to leave water out there for the dog,' and the dog's condition doesn't reflect the fact that it's not being provided with adequate water, then at that point, yeah, you can educate them. But as far as prosecuting them, there is no prosecution as far as that's concerned."

In such cases, agents know successful prosecution is out of the question, but they do not tell respondents, hoping that this uncertainty creates a veiled threat that will push people in a humane direction. Agents do take some action, however, so that they do not turn their backs on cases where the welfare of animals could be improved. They continue their coaching by returning to "recheck" respondents, providing clear advice with each visit and warning of future checks if respondents fail to act. An agent gave the following example of his response to an obstreperous respondent: "The complaint was this dog is full of fleas. It's got a tumor on it. It runs loose all the time. I said to the woman, 'I'm here concerning your dog.' 'The dog's not around anymore.' 'When was the last time you saw the dog?' 'A day or two ago.' 'Okay, fine. Does the dog have a tumor on the side of its back?' 'Yes, it does.' I say, 'Last time you saw the dog, was it full of fleas?' 'I didn't really notice.' I said, 'We got a complaint that the dog was full of fleas and had an ear infection.' She says, 'I really didn't notice.' I say, 'As soon as the dog comes back, I want you to make sure you notice. If the dog has those problems, you've got to get it to a vet or else you've got to take it to an animal shelter and get rid of the dog.' She said, 'I can't afford a vet.' 'When you decide what you're going to do, here's my card. But if I don't hear back from you, I'm going to be coming back.'" By relying on the unchallenged assumption that they have a right to make these revisits and hold respondents to a higher standard of animal care, agents create a sense that respondents are humanely deficient, even if the law does not say they are.

If the situation calls for it, agents escalate the knack by threatening to seize the respondents' animals. In one case, an agent investigating a complaint of a dog without shelter spoke to people in three different units of the multi-family building. After long questioning, they all denied knowing who was the owner. But, the agent pointed out, "When you threaten to take an animal, the calls come real quick." Agents have mixed feelings, however, about seizing animals and would rather not, although they do not share these misgivings with respondents.

Threatening to take an animal can backfire. One agent pointed to a rookie whose efforts to seize animals jeopardized her future interactions with an animal hoarder. "Anna went out to one of these cat collectors and she was real tough, and she ended up getting them signed over. The lady still has about sixteen cats. She ended up hiring a vet to come in and take care of the cats. And now, I can guarantee that Anna is not going to get back into that house. I go the other way. I bend over backwards for these animal collectors." Taking respondents' animals can cause significant emotional distress for respondents and their families. One agent said that the situation of "needy" families might call for the surrender of animals but that doing this might seriously disturb children: "You have cases where it's a family that's having a hard time and can't afford the feed or the dog or cat needs medical attention. It's real hard when you go in and you got some children there, and they're not even taking care of the kid properly. They're living in a dump or whatever and you have this dog and because they can't really afford to take care of it, do you take it away from them and upset the children like that?" Adults, as well, are not spared pain. An agent was surprised in one case because he assumed that the respondent was a "cruel person" until he started crying after relinquishing his dog: "I had a case where a Rottweiler's leg was broken and it eventually fell off the dog. It was up by the elbow, and it was just the bone sticking out. It upset me very much. I was real hard on the party and said, 'You'd better sign this over to me, and if you don't I'm going to lock you up right now.' And so they agreed. The ambulance came out and the guy turned around when we put the dog in the ambulance and he was crying. He had a love for the dog. The dog loved him. You get a sense whether the respondents are caring for the animal or whether they don't give a damn. Like this guy with the Rottie sounds like he cared for the dog but just didn't have money. I turned around and read it all wrong. When I got there, in my mind he was just a cruel person. And it made me think when I saw his emotions." Agents, too, can be upset when seizing animals because they feel partly responsible for their deaths. One spoke about this dilemma: "When you take animals away you end up turning them over to the shelter, but they end up being euthanized because when you take them away, these animals need special care, medical attention, and you just don't have the money to do it. So you're kind of signing a death warrant for the animal."

Depending on the animal's situation and the respondent's attitude, an agent can use the knack to push harder for humane changes by resorting to the "next step"—threatening the respondent with court, even if prosecution is unlikely. An agent described this graduated approach to working with a respondent who, after reason and education have failed, continued to leave her dog outside in the sun without shelter: "At that point you go to the next step where you say to them, 'Hey look, this is the second time I've been here. I keep getting complaints. You say you only leave the dog out a certain period of time. I'm finding out that you are leaving the animals out. Look, I've spoken to an individual and she says that yesterday it was ninety degrees and your dog was out from ten to two. The only thing I can tell you is that one of your neighbors wants to get involved and will give me a statement that keeps track of the amount of days the dog is out. If she wants to keep track of the amount of time that the dog is out and the weather conditions, and I feel it's adequate to pursue a court case, you're going to find that you're receiving a notice from the court.' Then at that point, you've gone just that one step further."

Trying to preserve their image as "good guys," agents threaten but do not pursue court action. As one noted, "Whenever I am working on something I say, 'Look, if you don't straighten this out, there is a possibility I may have to sign a complaint against you.' Try to tell them, 'I don't want to sign a complaint because it is paperwork for me, and once I sign a complaint, we have to go through with it. So do yourself a favor and correct it.' So you try to get them to think you are the good guy, you are trying to help them." No matter how hard they try to preserve their good-guy image and avoid court, agents still encounter respondents who remind them that they are "assholes." In one case, an agent recommended that the respondent have his Lhasa Apso euthanized because it was in "real pitiful shape." But then, the agent reported, "He starts to cry. He says, 'I realize that, but I haven't had the heart to do it.' So you sit there and you try to reason with them and explain to them that this is what he should do. I went back two weeks later. The guy still hasn't made any decisions as far as having this dog euthanized and it is starting to look much worse. And the guy's like, 'I'm at the point now, I really can't face the decision.' I say to him, 'I hate to put it to you this way, but you're just not being fair to the dog, and right now the way you're keeping the dog, you're in violation of the law. I would really hate to have to take you to court, but if you don't do something fairly quickly, like within the next week or so, I'm going to end up having to pursue a court case against you.' So he takes the dog two days later to get it euthanized. Then he turns around and basically his attitude is, 'You're an asshole for making me put my dog to sleep. Thanks for making me kill my dog.'"

Agents take this next step because they believe that most respondents help their animals only to avoid legal repercussions. Complying with agents becomes a way to avoid the time and expense of going to court. As one noted, talking about horse owners and farmers: "I think mostly with them, if you tell them what the law is and they know the law, then they have to make a decision that 'I'm either going to do it or I'm going to have to go to court and explain why I didn't do it.' And most of them don't want to take the time to come to court, so they just do it."

Humane agents are most likely to threaten court action with "jerks." Some respondents with "bad attitudes" lie or conceal information in serious cruelty cases. One agent confronted a respondent who denied killing his dog, despite strong evidence to the contrary: "I told him, 'If we find out different, if the animal was inhumanely killed, there is a good chance you could be prosecuted.'" Other jerks are respondents who create difficult encounters and are extremely frustrating for agents to manage. In fact, one devised a special coding system on his day sheets to indicate particularly difficult respondents by noting "AH," for asshole, next to a person's name. In one such case, an agent explained why one pet store owner was a jerk who needed threatening: "Supposedly there's an injured kitten there that's for sale. If the injured kitten hasn't been treated and they don't take it right away to a veterinarian, then I will take out complaints against this guy [the store owner] in criminal court for cruelty because he's such a jerk. Since the day he opened his store— we went to the place once and we saw him hiding under the counter." And yet other jerks blatantly neglect animals, "bullshitting" agents directly to their faces. One agent on a no-shelter complaint found a dog without water in extreme heat separated from her eight puppies, which were crammed into a small, stifling hot shed: "I said, 'No good. Why are they separated from the mother? They still need their mother.' And the kid said, 'My father said she's a bad mother because she won't nurse.' And all of a sudden all of the puppies headed toward the mother and starts nursing these puppies. And I'm like, 'Obviously the mother wants to nurse.' So he said, 'Well, my father wants this and my father wants that.' And I handed him my card and said, 'If your father doesn't want to go to court have him call me.' Because I mean, this kid was really giving me an attitude. And he didn't even care that the dog didn't have any water and it was ninety something degrees out that day. I made him bring all the dogs inside downstairs into the basement. It was cool down there and they could all be together. He didn't want them in the house."

Even with jerks, agents believe that threats of court action must be used cautiously and selectively. Some respondents shut down when court is mentioned and do not hear what agents say and are unreceptive to them in the future. As one agent warned, "If you use 'SPCA' and you threaten them that if they don't do something, you're going to take them to court, you're probably not going to get through to the person and you're just going to create problems. Next time, they won't let you in." Agents feel, however, that there is a limit to how many times they can warn a respondent before they lose all credibility. In some cases, agents believe that court action must be pursued: "How many times are you going to speak to them? After a while they know you're just bullshitting them, that you're not going to do anything, and it loses its effect after a while. You can only speak to someone so many times." If agents reach this point, they need to follow through. According to one officer, "You never want to tell them that you are going to take them to court unless you are going to take them because if you say that, and you don't take them, your credibility is gone." For example, an agent described how he handled a respondent who did not telephone him after he left his business card: "If I know that the allegations are such that I might want to pursue it further, I might in some cases put on the card, 'Failure to contact me may result in court action without further notice.' Most of the time, if you put that on the card, the next day the people are on the friggin' horn. I don't put 'will result.' I never do that unless I know that there's a possibility that I might be pursing some type of further action. You never draw lines in the sand unless you're willing to step over the line, the reason being you lose your credibility. If I was to put on something, 'Failure to contact me will result in court action' and two or three weeks down the pike or a month down the pike the people don't get a notice to appear in court and then six months from then I get another complaint on this individual, and you go out there and you have to catch them there, and the first thing out of their mouth is gonna be, 'I thought you were going to take me to court three months ago.'" Agents also avoid going to court if winning a conviction seems remote. In this circumstance, they will be reluctant to pressure respondents, as the following example illustrates: "Sure, I could have said, 'That's a violation of the law relating to the dogs in the sun and blah, blah, blah.' She could have really went off. If I back myself in a corner like that, she could tell me to go stuff it. Then if I really felt that strong about the violation of law, I'd have to go to court, and I'd probably be laughed out of court."

Nevertheless, once an agent's' bluff is called and he or she is unable to work with a respondent, court action is often taken. Frustrated agents who feel they have been "strung along" can take out a complaint against a respondent. The result is that "most the time, they will scurry and get things done." For example, over the summer one respondent repeatedly ignored an agent's advice and failed to build an appropriate shelter for his farm animals. The agent finally stopped "working" with the respondent and gave him an ultimatum: "'John, you have until next week. If it's not up by next week, I'm signing the complaint.' I go back the next week. No shelter. So I went down and I signed the complaint. Two days later he calls me, 'The shelter is all done.' I said, 'It's too late.' I signed the complaint." After this encounter, the agent warned the respondent that any future mistreatment of animals would result in immediate legal action. As he said, "Hopefully now he is going to know that if I go there and see a problem, I'm not even going to fool around with him. I'm not even going to call him up. I'm just going to go down to court and sign a complaint."

The danger in taking court action is that the agent can be hurt more than the respondent if the illusion of authority is exposed. Complaints are often refused, and those that ultimately lead to trial are usually dismissed or given no hearing. Respondents walk away unscathed, without even a stern warning that what they did was wrong, while agents leave court wondering whether what they do has value and meaning. Without a different kind of impression management to further buttress the agent's image of power and authority, the knack would certainly fail.

Suppressing Emotion

In many ways, agents' decisions about handling complaints, investigating cases, and prosecuting abusers are influenced by the specter of the extremist label. "I don't want to be seen as a crusader," one agent said, "because I don't want to be labeled as a radical. I don't want any part of that. I just want to be categorized as a professional in my work." Behaving unprofessionally, agents believe, risks denigration by the public and likely failure on the job. Indeed, their ability to successfully bluff power is thought to depend on their coupling it with actions that will be seen as professional.

Agents use their understanding of what it means to be professional to organize how they think about themselves and act on the job, as well as to manage the more unprofessional aspects of humane law enforcement. They are not alone in this regard; others describe themselves as professionals and use this folk symbol in strategic ways (Becker 1970), especially to justify their structurally subordinate positions by putting a positive spin on demeaning aspects of their jobs. Paralegals are one example (Lively 2001). However, agents use their front (Goffman 1959) differently than do paralegals, for whom professionalism calls for their ability to be nonpersons and remain invisible during interactions, reaffirming their subordination and lack of power relative to attorneys. In contrast, humane agents' use professionalism to gain authority in encounters with outsiders who might otherwise question their mandate.

Agents think of professionalism as an ability to maintain emotional distance from cases. Maintaining such distance is not a problem for those who view their work as "just a job" and not a mission. "I mean, my life doesn't revolve around animals. It's my job," one agent admitted. "I don't think I ever went home and cried. I mean, it's never affected my life in a negative way. I can honestly say I've never gone home and felt bad because that poor dog's out in the rain." Others admit to being disturbed but attempt to avoid such sentiment, as the following agent suggested: "I do my best to not get wound up about any of this. You can't take it personal. If there's a problem, you deal with it."

To avoid getting "wound up" in their cases, agents try to suspend personal beliefs and emotions about how best to treat animals. They claim that it is wrong to expect respondents to behave toward their animals as they would themselves. "Let's get this straight, I love animals. I have a dog. I'd run through fire for him. But am I one of these people who is going to break into somebody's property for a dog with no shelter that is healthy just because my heart tells me to? If I arrested everybody because of my heart, half of Queens would be locked up." Another agent elaborated the problem: "You can't take every dog home and cuddle it. You can't expect every respondent to take their dogs to bed like you do or to have them all wrapped up in a rosy blanket. People aren't going to do it. And if you go out there thinking you're going to get that done, some people will say, 'Get the F out of here. It's my dog. I'll leave him out there if I want to leave him out there. And I'll feed him when I want.' Like you go out there and somebody is feeding their dog table scraps, somebody will say, 'Well, you can't feed him that.' And it's like, where in the law does it say you can't feed him that? Come on. You can't go in there with your emotions flowing." Being bothered, then, by respondents whose mistreatment of animals is not illegal is thought to feed into an image of agents as "overly sensitive" or "too emotional."

Some opinions are more extreme, according to many agents, and come close to espousing an "animal rights agenda" that criticizes the traditional use of animals for food, experimentation, or entertainment. One agent acknowledged that most people doing humane work are on the "extreme side" when it comes to animals, but they should not condemn people for having different views: "My dogs, we treat them as part of the family, although I never played with them like they were babies. I never talked to my animals like they are babies. I don't put hats on them. It's just how you feel about animals. Just because someone's going to raise an animal for foodstuffs and kill it doesn't mean that they don't take good care of their animals and feel for them. It's just how it is." Having strong enough views to be labeled an activist by respondents is thought to "block" agents' effectiveness. For example, one department member criticized a colleague for her uncontrolled thoughts and feelings: "Helen is a vegetarian. I don't think there are any problems with that, but I think if she was out in the field and told people that she was a vegetarian or she's working for an animal rights group, that could block her. If she told a farmer that she had a complaint on him, in his mind, she's just an animal rights person and that's going to create a problem."

Agents who espouse such "extreme opinions" can further jeopardize their investigations because they become too eager to find "abuse." One agent, for example, considered his colleagues to be "unrealistic" about what they expected a pet shop owner to do because they let their "personal opinions slant the way they do their job." In his words: "They lose some of their objectivity and get very picayune about different things. You've got to realize that there are a lot of times that things just don't go the way you want them to go. Maybe the place didn't get cleaned as good as it should have because they were short help and it didn't get done in a timely a fashion. I take all of that into consideration when I'm doing a pet shop inspection."

Agents are concerned that peers eager to find abuse may also become too "aggressive" with respondents, and that such behavior is very unprofessional. One explained this concern: "I've always loved animals and I've always wanted to help them, but I know that you can't overstep your boundaries and become a fanatic. Give the animal its proper needs. And yes, if you can get a little more by working with the person, but don't make it— 'You should do this.' Say, 'Well, it would be nice if you had this or you had that or if you could do this or that.'" This alleged "aggressiveness," according to agents, means that their colleagues lack "good judgment" about when to intervene in cases, reacting too quickly to perceived "suffering" in animals. Another agent pointed out that it is sometimes necessary to walk away from suffering, allowing it to worsen until prosecution is justified: "You've got to realize when you're at a point when there's no more you can do until things either get worse or something can happen and you can prosecute the individual. You can't take it home. You can't be going to the house every day bugging them because that doesn't work. It's just a waste of time and everyone else's time. That's when you've really got to have good judgment and when it gets bad enough, do something about it. And a lot of people can't accept that. 'I gotta do something now because the animal's suffering.' It might be, but what are you going to do?"

Rather than allowing their "personal opinions" to stretch complaints so they can be seen as cruelty, agents believe that doing effective animal police work requires them to narrowly interpret and strictly apply the cruelty code. One agent talked about how he focuses only on respondents' legal infractions, despite personal feelings: "I don't think you can take the job too personally. Yeah, it bothers me, but I try not to take everything personally— go after people that way. You have to kind of keep an open mind and say, 'Okay, this is the complaint I got and does it violate the law—yes or no?'" Indeed, some agents sympathize with those having a broader conception of cruelty than that supported by law, but they nevertheless put these feelings aside and stick to the law, as one explained: "Complainants say, 'The animal should be treated this way.' My personal beliefs may agree with them, but the law allows the animals to be treated differently. For instance, someone leaves their dog out twenty-four hours a day tied to a doghouse. I don't do that to my dogs. That goes against what I believe, but the law allows them to have their dogs out as long as they are caring for them properly. Whether I agree with something or not doesn't even come into play. What comes into play is whether it's a violation of the law."

Agents also claim that being professional means "playing the game" with other professionals. Playing the game means not getting too "personally involved" with work, to ensure that regular police, court officials, and others take the department seriously as "objective" and "professional." As one agent said of his animal-inclined colleagues, "If they go into court and are vocal about some of their views, I think it affects their credibility. If we are perceived as an animal rights group, I don't think we can function as we do today." "To be a successful officer," another agent noted, "you have to not get too fanatical. You can't allow your personal beliefs or feelings to affect your job because you lose your objectivity and either drive yourself nuts so you can't do the job or you become totally ineffective. There are a lot of things that I believe personally but I try, whenever possible, and sometimes it's difficult, to not let personal feelings or attitudes get involved."

They argue that missionary zeal and emotionality lead "people to look at us like a bunch of nuts," one agent explained. "The way I look at this department," he continued, "people won't take you seriously if they think you are too extreme. I don't like people looking at me as though I'm an extreme animal rights person." Even worse, personal involvement in cases risks "radicalizing" humane law enforcement. As another agent said, "Some people have problems differentiating organizations like ours that have 'animal protection' type people and organizations that have 'animal rights' type people or people who tend to be more radical." If the SPCA is perceived as an "animal rights" group, agents believe that people will see them as "very fanatical, very unrealistic," and the organization will be "stigmatized." To make this point, one agent noted that he has a good relationship with local police because he is not seen as a "wacko who pushes that animals have these rights and all that. I'm reasonable and we can work together." Those colleagues who do not "play the game" with regular police officers will compromise their effectiveness, agents claimed. For example: "You have to be realistic. Some officers really have a hard time playing the game. If I'm dealing with the police and they say, 'Aw, it's just a stupid dog complaint,' if you start pissing and moaning 'Oh, yeah, but this dog wasn't cared for properly and this and that,' you lose your credibility. So you say, 'I know what you're talking about, but over the scope of things—' or you make a joke out of it. Some of our people have a problem dealing with that, but you have to do that because if you don't, you come across too fanatical. If you come across as though you're off in left field some place, people look at you and before long you don't get any cooperation and you don't get any help. Nothing."

In the end, agents take advantage of the ambiguity of the cruelty code and their role to enforce it. By suppressing sentiment and bluffing power, they convince themselves, and perhaps others too, that "their" legal definition of cruelty is worth upholding. They also convince themselves, and again, perhaps others, that enforcing the cruelty code is professional police work rather than mere dirty work.

Resistance

Not all agents agree with these interactional strategies for defining cruelty and enforcing the code. In the opinion of many of their peers, those who resist the department's conception of what it means to be professional are compromising their effectiveness with respondents and officials. For workers whose job already is not taken seriously by some because they "only" work with animals, emotionalism only intensifies the problem. In more sociological terms, it would seem that they also impair their ability to transcend a conception of themselves as dirty workers. Yet they too use the ambiguity of cruelty and their role to enforce the law to transcend dirty work. To them, work matters precisely because of their unprofessionalism. They have redefined their core task as a mission that requires an unusual degree of personal investment in the job.

Fewer in number, but definitely present within the department's culture, are agents who have a different identity and relationship to cruelty than those concerned about presenting a strong professional front to respondents and officials. These agents see humane law enforcement as an extension of their lifelong passion for animals and desire to improve their lot, leading them to approach work in ways that reinforce the department's negative image of animal rights activism. One such agent spoke of his own zeal to have other people care for animals as he would himself, even when the anti-cruelty code is not broken: "If you own a pet, you do everything for it. I don't care if you don't eat for a week, but not everybody feels that way and that's not the law. But I can show up at someone's door and make someone listen to me on how they should treat their animals. That's where my heart and soul is. I couldn't see myself doing anything else and really be happy because my life is so centered around animals." Another agent was disturbed when a respondent violated no law but completely ignored his Shepherd, which was chained in the backyard to serve as a twenty-four hour watchdog. She commented, "I feel bad because they [dogs] just want company and to be loved and played with. A dog like that is probably one of the saddest things I see in my work. It's not a way to keep a dog. Why have one? The dog is going to spend its entire existence on that chain running back and forth. That's the sweetest dog, it wouldn't bite you in a million years— That's what bothers me, that I can't make them look at their dog the way I look at my dog and my cat that are side by side on my bed when I leave in the morning and have a bowl of water. Every time I give them a bowl of water, it just blows my mind that there are dogs that are begging for water. And that's why I'll probably never get satisfaction from this job."

By their own admission, these agents blur boundaries between work, professionalism, private life, and ideological conviction. For example, one in his free time raises funds and writes a newsletter for an animal shelter and "fosters" stray cats until homes can be found for them.

He spoke proudly also about how his concern for animals influences his dating habits: "After the first couple of dates I would be like, 'Here's a multiple choice question. We have tickets to *Phantom of the Opera*. We've waited months to see this and paid hundreds of dollars, but we are running late. We are flying down there and see an animal thrashing in the street that was just hit by a car. Do we: (*a*) keep driving; (*b*) keep driving till we get to a telephone where we call someone that hopefully will respond and pick it up; or (*c*) pick it up, forget about the show, and bring it to an animal hospital?' Anything less than *c*, I don't see her again. Well, the answer came from a situation. It was a ballet. There was a cat jumping around in the street. I stopped and said, 'Sorry, we are going to an animal hospital.' She broke up with me. She said that I was too— animals came first in my life and that she couldn't handle someone like that. I said, 'Thank you. I'm glad I found out now because, yes, animals come first.'" And another agent found it difficult to separate feelings for her own animals from those she had toward the respondent's animals. Investigated animals "all become mine," she said. "They're all mine. Even if I haven't seen it, it's still mine. I don't care if the owner is sitting there, that's my dog, you know. It's always been like that. Every animal that I talk to is automatically mine."

Unable to separate work from personal belief, these agents admit that investigating cruelty complaints "bothers" or "gets to" them, a reality that their colleagues decry. One agent compared her work to that of a traffic officer: "I have a strange passion for animals. I'm not a normal person when it comes to them. It makes it a lot harder when things bother you as opposed to writing a speeding ticket for somebody. There's nothing emotional about that." These agents admit that even the most minor cases trouble them. As one said, "I say that when I look at a dog tied to a doghouse and it doesn't bother me, that's when I should quit, because that's something that will always bother me." Some of these agents talked about how the job still "gets" to them even after years on the job, unlike their more "hardened" colleagues. An agent commented: "The first few years of this job, you really have to play a lot of head games with yourself and get over it. Sometimes I think I'm dealing with this job a little bit better, then I'm like, I've been doing it for ten years! Eventually I hope to deal better with it." Unable to turn off their feelings, these agents admit that they "take their work home" and worry about their cases—again a point of contention with the majority of their peers—as in the following case that "just really stuck" in one agent's mind: "It was a real friendly, white, fluffy medium-sized dog with a muzzle embedded in his mouth. The muzzle cut and scraped him since it was too tight and it never came off. I can tell them to leave the muzzle off until its face heals, but there's nothing illegal about putting it on. How do I know they didn't just say, 'Yeah, whatever,' and when I left put the muzzle back on the dog and the dog is still sitting there?"

They become angry at respondents for their treatment of animals and it affects how they manage cases—making frequent rechecks, insisting on specific changes, and showing their displeasure. As one agent said, "I've seen stuff that's really bad and you just go, 'You've got to be shitting me. Look at this dog. You are a piece of shit!'" Another added: "I feel horrible for the animals and I get very, very angry. It's directed toward the people because it's not the animal's fault. I get mad at people. I don't mean mad like I'm going to go out and punch them. But I mean mad, like what can I do to these people to get this dog out of there or to get them to improve the situation." Especially with rookies, anger can create edgy, even hostile encounters with respondents. One agent talked about how she handles cases: "I'm preachy and I'm critical of people. I mean, I'm working on toning that down. Like, the dog will have no shelter and I'll go, 'The dog needs to have shelter.' And I'll get one of those blank stares, 'It does?' And that kind of gets you going a little bit. 'Well, would you like that?' 'But it's a dog.' I may sound condescending to people, but I'm brand new, cut me a little bit of slack."

These agents feel that their peers do not handle cases aggressively enough. One agent said: "I think Alan is laid back. Sometimes he'll spend too much time giving the people the benefit of the doubt and not really get tough on them quick enough. That doesn't work for me. I get really emotionally involved." In a similar vein, another agent says: "Like Danny, I think he's an excellent police officer. But he has no emotion. I think he goes out there and if he doesn't see a blatant violation, I don't think he's going to say anything." These agents believe that the less aggressive approach of peers can jeopardize the well-being of animals. In the following instance, an agent is critical of a peer's inaction: "We got a complaint on a guy who was out of his mind on crack. He owned a dog that he wasn't taking care of. He was feeding it raw chicken to make it vicious and he was beating the dog. I was out sick, and I said,

'Look Jack, go deal with it.' And he comes back and goes, 'He's got a plastic container under the house that the dog can crawl in for shelter and it really wasn't much, but he was really strung out on crack.' That meant to me to get that dog out, regardless. Well, the dog was very thin, and he talked to him. He went there with 'no shelter and thin.' Well, 'Yeah, I feed it raw chicken.' Well there's no law against that, if it keeps him healthy, which eventually it won't, but— so when I came back, he told me that, and I just shook my head. I went over there and put the guy through the ringer and the guy gave me the dog. Its primary diet was raw chicken and orange juice. So that right there indicates a health problem, okay. The dog had never seen a veterinarian, it was way under weight, and the shelter was not adequate. But Jack didn't find the same violations that we would."

This advocacy reminds agents that their separation from animal control and animal rights activism is more symbolic than real. By having this connection, they jeopardize their image as police officers and endanger their ability to tell themselves, if not others, that they are a brute force for animals. Securing a safe identity removed from the "unprofessionalism" and "fanaticism" of these groups is impossible, leaving agents confused about who they are and what they should and can be as police officers. They are left with two identities that result in different approaches to cruelty: viewing cruelty work as a job akin to regular policing, and viewing it as a personal mission.

Although the police orientation is dominant, both identities are tolerated if they do not become too excessive in the eyes of agents. Alternative styles of humane law enforcement are carried to extremes when agents become overly absorbed with the police or the mission side of their work. Police-oriented agents occasionally take the "it's only a job" attitude to extremes when they become desensitized to the needs of animals and unwilling to push respondents to become more humane. They express this attitude when they do not take the animals' perspective in complaints, fail to intervene in cases, or become pessimistic about accomplishing anything with respondents. Mission-oriented agents periodically carry their charge too far and show signs of oversensitization or work addiction (Schaef and Fassel 1988). They may feel overly responsible for "rescuing" animals, believe they are irreplaceable on the job, or have an exaggerated "we versus they" perspective with clients and the general public. When carried to extremes, these two opposing approaches cause friction between agents, who can become frustrated with and patronizing toward each other. The result is to stifle identification with animals and not press the envelope of the anti-cruelty statute, on one hand, or to soften the police perspective and increase their identification with animals, on the other.

For the most part, though, conflict is rare between these two kinds of agents. In its place lingers uneasiness and confusion in the department about the propriety of each identity that is expressed in debates over the humane correctness of matters that are sensitive and important issues to agents, such as vegetarianism, rodeos, and hunting. Agents' thoughts and feelings about these issues convey moral statements about their character. The following agent, for example, explained why she feels that she is not humanely correct because her views on these issues are different from those of the SPCA and some of her colleagues: "I have my views. Trapping—I don't like that. But I like rodeos. I don't like calf roping. I think that's a big danger to the animal there. But I like the sport of rodeo and I think the people take pretty good care of the animals. But when I'm working, if someone asks me on the street what do I think, I'm representing the SPCA, so I have to give them the SPCA point of view—'rodeos are bad.' But personally, I would probably go to a rodeo if I had time. And John [a fellow agent] knows it and he's like, 'Oh, you—' And I'm not a vegetarian, although I tried. I ate Fritos for about a month and that was about it. And I'm seeing this guy. He hunts and traps. And people are like, 'How could you go out with someone like that?'" Other agents do not see her as an "animal rights" person and claim to have a different reaction to events such as rodeos. As one said, "I can't say that Marilyn doesn't care about animals because she must, but she certainly isn't on the same level of protectionism as myself or even Tim. I would consider us closer to animal rights than anything else. Marilyn loves the rodeo. If I go to the rodeo, the only thing I want is to put handcuffs on everyone in sight and help those animals from the legalized torture they are enduring." Another agent also falls short of the department's standard for humane treatment because he does not oppose ox pulls or pet stores and does not condemn those who own these stores or participate in these activities. He explained: "I don't think that because a guy pulls an ox, uses oxen, that they're bad people because they do that. We have some officers that think that. If a guy owns a pet store and the guy is pulling horses or oxen, he's a jerk or he's a bad person. And I don't categorize people that way. That's their party. If they choose to do it, and they do it in a responsible manner, I don't think they're a bad person."

In the end, the debate over what constitutes humane treatment is more than an internecine squabble over who likes rodeos and why it is good to be a vegetarian. Seeing it this way trivializes the tension and portrays it as just a local issue. On one hand, it should not surprise us that agents place themselves and their colleagues into one of these camps and have an opinion about their correctness. Individuals whose work is defined by some abstract principle or standard of behavior often compete to achieve their goals. This competition is aggravated when the primary mission of the group is vague, as it certainly is for humane law enforcement agents seeking to prevent and prosecute cruelty.

On the other hand, the tension is more profound, reproducing larger societal issues about the meaning of animals and the importance of cruelty that have serious implications for the identity of humane law enforcement agents. How they come to regard themselves will mirror how we all think about animal cruelty. Our thinking about cruelty is confused because American society is divided over how humans should relate to animals, seeing them either as utilitarian objects to be used or as valued companions. Those who regard animals as objects tend to take the mistreatment of animals less seriously; those who regard animals as valued companions take it more seriously. Humane agents capture this dualism; the former identity encourages them to be "objective" in their management of cases so they do not become emotionally involved, while the latter identity allows for more passion and connection to animals and their plight. That agents should be unsure about whether they are truly a force for mistreated animals or more of a parody of one is the dilemma we should expect. Further confusing the picture is the fact there also is division about the nature and significance of animals and their mistreatment even among those who regard them as valued companions. Here, too, we see this conflict played out in agents' two identities.

Although such uneasiness reproduces wider societal confusion about the proper treatment of animals, people actively create their identities rather than merely inhabit those available. This self-creativity is most apparent when people use cruelty as an opportunity not just to clarify a status as agents do but to develop entirely new ones, as we see next.

2 Adolescents

Appropriating Adulthood

There was a little farm. They had a cow and pigs and stuff. We thought this was crazy. Five or six of us went back there at night and we kept luring the cow to the electrified fence to shock himself, and he'd shock himself and then walk back. We kept on doing it and doing it because it was funny to us. It was entertainment for the people who were there. Something different. A rush.

—Business major, male, twenty years old

To those who treasure animals and want to protect them, intentional cruelty and extreme neglect are inexplicable crimes that demand some explanation. Unfathomable events, such as these, are just too disturbing to be flippantly dismissed. They cannot happen without a bad reason. While almost everyone wants to know why abusers harm animals, including humane law enforcement agents and the human victims of animal abuse, the abusers' explanations are understandably simple and disconnected from their own reality. Agents, for instance, write off most cruelty to "ignorance." If they just knew better, they would not harm animals. More extreme cases are written off to "sickness." "Look what they do to children? They cut up little babies and stuff them into garbage cans. You have to put it into perspective—it's a sick mind. A sick individual. I don't think you can rehabilitate these people. I feel that it starts out with animals and goes on to humans."

Humane agents do not understand the abusers' perspective, one that makes their acts intelligible, reasonable, and even enjoyable to them, in part because capturing this perspective humanizes the enemy and comes dangerously close to justifying or excusing bad behavior. As we see in this chapter, agents are not alone in this regard. Many people, including mental health professionals, whose attempts to understand animal abusers lapse into tired formulaic explanations, join them. Even more disappointing, they cannot answer why cruelty is so common— even a rite of passage for some adolescents. By trying to fathom the abuser's "mind," psychologists and psychiatrists have missed something larger and perhaps more important than the abuser's personality—they have missed the abuser's social context.

Until recently, understanding violence toward animals was the sole province of psychologists and animal welfare advocates (e.g., Ascione and Arkow 1999). Their approach sees animal abuse as an impulsive act that reflects psychopathological problems within the offender. In one typical psychiatric study (Tapia 1971), the author suggests that children who are cruel to animals suffer from hyperactivity, short attention span, irritability, temper, destructiveness, and brain damage leading to poor impulse control. Like bedwetting and fire setting, animal cruelty is one more sign of "impulsive character development" (Felthous 1980, 109). As such, the act of abuse has no social context and is likened to angry or irritable aggression that provides an emotional and perhaps rewarding release to aggressors.

From a psychological perspective, animal abuse provides sought-after emotion and reward. One approach holds that animal abuse displaces frustration by making the aggressor feel better. The displacement approach to abuse sees it as serving no purpose other than hurting animals and venting anger. In fact, until recently, mental health experts supported the therapeutic value of mundane animal abuse as a "healthy" form of displacement. Psychologists argued that dogs, in particular, were "satisfactory victims" for children in need of power. "The child who is commanded all day long may be commander over his dog. The child who is full of resentment over what he believes is his bad treatment by adults may kick at his dog. Though this use of a dog, if carried to extremes, is not exactly commendable, there is some therapeutic effect for children when indulged in within reason" (Bossard and Boll 1966, 128).

A second, and increasingly common, psychological approach to abuse posits an "angry child" with "destructive energy" that needs to be released. Unlike the displacement model that sees abuse as a safety valve to reduce internal pressure and further aggression, the graduation model argues that attacks on animals are early stages of a progression of aggressive responses that mature into later violence toward humans. Humane organizations, in particular, are quick to raise the specter of future Jeffrey Dahmers when asked to weigh in on the developmental significance of animal cruelty during childhood (e.g., Moulton, Kaufman, and Filip 1991). Most cases of abuse, they claim, should be considered for their potential to forecast future violence. Pressure to pathologize abuse has led to its incorporation into the *Diagnostic and Statistical Manual* (APA 1994) as a warning sign of conduct disorder.

Yet, as discussed earlier, when researchers have studied the graduation model, their results have been mixed (Felthous and Kellert 1987). More recent sociological research on the relationship of animal abuse to subsequent violence highlights the fact that many cases appear to be terminal, not linked to later violence or other forms of antisocial behavior (Arluke et al. 1999). These results suggest that not all cases of abuse have the same significance, calling for researchers to examine the meaning and use of abuse when it does not escalate to serious aggression. Of course, parents or other authorities should dismiss no case of animal abuse. However, lumping together all instances of harming animals as impulsive and pathological does not allow for the possibility that abuse can be instrumental and normative, in the sense that abusers may gain things from their acts that are essential to and supported by the larger society.

To allow for this possibility, we need to listen closely to young adults who have abused animals to discover their perspective. The traditional psychological approach to cruelty does not give enough credit to children for their actions. The view that children are active social agents who shape the structures and processes around them (e.g., Morrow 1998) and whose social relationships are worthy of study in their own right (e.g., James and Prout 1990) raises an interesting question about the part that animal abuse plays in children's lives.

Exploring this question demands that we establish how young adults define the social meaning of their abuse to understand why it does or does not occur. To capture their thinking and emotions, we must not assume that these youths are "psychopaths," "cold-blooded killers," or "sadists" who act impulsively without reason. Instead we must recognize that they have a complex subculture of their own worthy of serious study (Fine and Sandstrom 1988). This approach makes cruelty intelligible by constructing it as ordered and rational, unpacking the reasoning, logic, and decision making that inform the actions of abusers, as researchers have done with thieves, murderers, and other criminals (e.g., Katz 1988). If some abusers describe their actions as fun and thrilling, then we need to discover what this experience means, feels, sounds, tastes, or looks like to them. In short, the development of a general theory of animal abuse must go beyond narrow psychiatric models to include interactional theories of behavior that can approach "cruelty" as a complicated phenomenon having different meanings and consequences for different types of animal abusers (Agnew 1998), as has been done with other kinds of human experiences with animals (Arluke and Sanders 1996).

From this perspective, more is going on than abusing animals simply to discharge pent-up frustration or to release anger. Although we may not be able to answer why children pull off the wings of flies, we can examine how this experience lives on in the memories of adolescents and young adults who went through it when younger. This approach can tell us how adolescents understand their prior actions toward animals and what role, if any, this prior abuse plays as adolescents move into adulthood. Sociological research on children's play suggests that some expressions of animal abuse may qualify as play. Children's play is never idle in the sense that it can teach them things. If it existed, idle play would teach children nothing. On the contrary, children learn through "ordinary play" and what they learn is diverse, with some of it relating to the development of their moral selves (Mead 1934) and their future ability to assume adult roles (Borman and Lippincott 1982).

Sometimes, however, such play can be offensive to those given the task of guiding children's development. For example, it is common for preadolescent boys to engage in a class of activities that includes aggressive pranks, sexual talk, and racist remarks. Fine (1986) argues that these forms of activities, or "dirty play," are connected to the child's social development, much as is ordinary play. Although adults usually view dirty play as childish or immature, children do not. On the contrary, by engaging in what is described as "deep play" (Geertz 1972), children are interpreting where they stand in the social scheme of things and mastering what is ordinarily denied them by more powerful others (Piaget 1962). They are attempting to live up to adult standards of behavior and address claim-making issues from which they had been excluded. As a claim-making behavior, each instance of dirty play makes a implicit statement about the rights of preadolescents to engage in a set of activities and to have a set of opinions in the face of adult counter pressures.

There is good reason to extend Fine's (1986, 1988) model of how children shape their identities. Certainly, the process of identity shaping in childhood, and the need to experiment with claim-making behavior, is not resolved in preadolescence or limited to boys. Boys and girls continue to struggle with their transition out of adolescence by living up to adult standards of behavior. If anything, older adolescents are likely to be more preoccupied and perhaps feel more urgency about becoming adults than are their younger peers. Play will continue to be a vital mechanism in efforts to explore and claim these new identities, although the specific types of play involved may be quite different from the aggressive pranks, sexual talk, and racist remarks noted by Fine among younger children. Compared with these activities, other types of play will entail more serious deviance where the risks to adolescents are larger and the outcomes more valued than those obtained from aggressive pranks and the like.

To what extent is Fine's (1986, 1988) analysis applicable to more deviant forms of dirty play? In particular, does it help us to understand the experience of animal abuse by children and adolescents? This chapter explores three questions, in this regard. First, will young adults consider more deviant variants of dirty play as fun, despite their unsavory character and potential to stigmatize? If so, then animal abuse should be recalled as a special kind of play with an exciting edge, unlike everyday forms of play that are merely "fun." Second, does the added risk of dirty play, when it involves more serious forms of deviance, offer greater rewards to adolescents in terms of what they learn and the kinds of adults they become? If so, then animal abuse as dirty play should entail far-reaching appropriations of adult culture. And third, do deviant variants of dirty play have some positive outcome as children enter into adulthood in terms of their presentation of self, no longer claiming that it is "just good fun," instead experiencing guilt and shame over it? If so, then animal abuse should pay off as children enter young adulthood, now admonishing themselves for their prior acts.

PLAYING SERIOUSLY

People undergo an endless stream of social experiences over a lifetime, but most of these experiences are trivial. Trivial social experiences have little impact beyond the time in which they transpire and are forgotten almost as soon as they are concluded. Other social experiences, however, are consequential and unforgettable. They have a lasting impact on people's lives and are remembered long after the experience took place (Athens 1989).

Animal abuse had this significance for students. It is interesting, in this regard, that some students claimed to have long forgotten their former cruelty but recalled it in great detail when asked, while many others seemed never to have forgotten their experience and remembered it vividly. The recollections of the students who spoke about their former abuse with great subtlety and immediacy have some parallels to the recollections of adults who recount childhood traumas to themselves or passages to new statuses in minute physical and emotional detail, such as how those present were dressed and how they felt at the time.

The significance of experiencing abuse was not evident at the beginning of many interviews. Several features of abuse lead students to compare it to idle play. First, it was seen as "just one of the things that we were up to, to fight boredom." As a form of everyday play, students remembered their abuse as an "entertaining" distraction, given limited appealing options. For example, in one case, a student described her drowning and burning of kittens as an activity to combat her boredom: "It was fun at the time, but I can't answer why. I just thought it was. I don't know how else to explain it. We didn't have anything to do besides having work and stuff. You were finished with your yard chores. You were finished with everything and the adults wouldn't let you be glued to the TV. It was like we didn't have anything to do and we're bored, so it's like, 'Okay, let's go torture some cats.'"

Second, students likened their abuse to specific examples of play. Some compared their abuse to playing Nintendo games or burning toy soldiers, others to sports. "It was more to occupy the time," one student reported. "Usually I skateboard. 'You wanna go out and do something today?' just meant we're going skateboarding. This day was just hot. It was like 'We're not going to skateboard, it's too hot. Let's fill the time up with something.' Shooting animals just appealed to us for the day." Another said: "On certain days, we'd play basketball, but on other days, we'd feel like shooting birds. I'd either ask friends to come over and shoot birds or come over to play basketball."

Students also claimed that the psychology behind their abuse resembled that of everyday play. One reason they gave was that they did not remember losing control of their emotions and becoming explosively violent. Had they lost control of their emotions when harming animals, students claimed that it would have been harder to define their acts as mere play. Unchecked, intense emotions would have suggested something more serious than play; so would have intent to harm animals. Another reason is that, students claimed their cruelty was idle play because there had been no intent to torture or kill animals. As one student said, "We didn't go, 'Let's go kill some birds and hang them on the wall.' It was just to hit them. And as soon as we started to hit the targets, they would have a problem with their wings. That hit home 'cause all they do is fly. So I would feel guilty after." Another student felt that his abuse was play because it was not premeditated: "I wasn't like all out burning the cat's head off. It was still play. We were doing it for fun. It wasn't like I had this devious plan—like I'm going to my cousin's house to torture the cat."

Finally, students remembered their abuse as idle play because they claimed to have kept it within certain bounds. Some thought they limited their abuse to psychological torment, inflicting no physical harm. In one case, the student described teasing a cat but not causing it serious physical harm. As he recounted, "I thought it was funny what we did to the cat. It was mean, but it was not harmful I guess, at least not physically harmful. We'd tape its two front legs together, and it was funny to watch. It was like a kangaroo." To prevent pain, the student applied a special tape that did not pull hair when removed. When physical harm was involved, students claimed to have limited their abuse as well, stopping themselves from causing excessive suffering. One student remembered: "I definitely made sure that I didn't hurt it. I made sure that we were just having fun, and maybe it would get hurt a little but nothing serious or that I could get into trouble for. I'd get scared if I actually broke its leg and it was hobbling around. I'd feel bad. I definitely had limits." For other students, the possibility of death checked their actions. One student said he "only wanted to toy" with the parakeets that he harmed: "We didn't try to kill them. I didn't squeeze it hard or smash it or anything like that." Students also considered their abuse to be play because they claimed to have limited the duration of their animal tormenting. As one student recounted: "We wouldn't always just sit home and do this [abuse] for hour on hour. We'd do it for a little while, and then we'd go out and actually do something."

As students explored their memories in the context of the interview's quickening rapport, however, it became clear that they did not regard their abuse as ordinary play. They remembered their animal abuse as having a serious edge that distinguished it from everyday play in general or normal play with animals (Mechling 1989). "Like with hide and go seek," one student explained, "it's fun. But it's hide and go seek. Like what can you do really? This stuff [cruelty] was more serious."

The emotions associated with abuse were different from and more intense than those associated with regular play. Students remembered their cruelty as a "thrilling" childhood activity that provided them with strong positive or negative emotions, unlike memories of everyday play. Being cruel to animals gave one student what he described as a feeling similar to the "rush" he felt before playing in a "big game." "You definitely feel something different," he explained. "Just before you do it, you feel that difference. Right before you play a big game or something, you get this feeling, kind of a rush. That's what it's like. It's like a rush." Another student spoke about a similar rush, comparing abuse to wrestling with his friends. "See, we might just be like playing around wresting, but then we get a little serious and we started getting angry at each other and you started wrestling—like trying to hurt each other. That's when you get that feeling of a super rush, when you hit him and he hits you and you realize that it's not like a game anymore."

Some students were drawn to the challenge of carrying out abuse. For example, living targets were more difficult to hit than were inanimate objects. As a student explained, "It was fun to shoot, to begin with, even at stationary targets. I'd take a milk jug and throw it out in the lawn and we'd shoot it around. But it was more fun to shoot at moving things, especially if you couldn't predict where it was going. Like, if you throw something and you shoot at it, you know it's going up, it's going down. Where these [squirrels], they're going here, they're going there, you know what I mean?" Another student recalled, "When my friend got his gun it was like 'cool.' And we were shooting cans, and then it was like let's see if we can shoot a moving target. So that had a lot to do with it. It was a challenge. It was a lot more difficult than throwing up a can in the air and shooting it. This was something, not that they can reason, but they knew to run."

The coolness of abuse stemmed from its "exciting" consequences—living targets responded unpredictably when harmed. One student, for example, described the "fun" of tormenting a hamster: "A lot of people would think it's mean, but I had fun seeing what happened. I put a blow dryer up to a hamster and saw what happened to him. All his food and stuff went all over his face." Another student recalled that he did not "think about hurting" a rabbit when he and his friend shot it with a BB gun. Instead, the two of them focused on seeing the rabbit "flip," and that response made it interesting and cool to them. As one student claimed, "We used to shoot road signs and trees and stuff, but that wasn't really exciting. That wasn't as good as hitting a bird. It was about hearing them cry out."

Students remembered their play as cool because their abusive interactions with animals had a pseudo-human quality; animals responded to abuse in ways that were similar to the reactions of humans with whom students played. One student, for example, compared her animal abuse to playing tag: "I would torture this neighborhood dog. I used to get the vacuum and tease him and he'd be howling forever. He hated it. He was so scared, so I used to go after him with it. I liked his reaction. It was like playing tag. You run after a person to tag him, then you run away because they are going to get you back. That was the thing with the dog." Another student said that he had "pushed" animals to get a certain reaction, much as he did with people: "They got so fed up, they reacted. I used to do that with my cousins too. Try to see the point where somebody just loses it and they're going to punch you. I guess I tested them to see where they would break and they can't take it anymore."

These recollections of abuse as serious and cool resonate with Thorne's (1993) description of cross-gender borderwork among children. Although such play is episodic, like animal abuse, its dramatic, ritualistic, and highly emotional qualities make it particularly memorable. It is not just "play" or "fun" because more is going on at an unarticulated and volatile level as ambiguous meanings and culturally expected identities are explored and experienced. Play, according to Thorne, is a fragile definition despite efforts by participants to maintain boundaries between play and not-play; more serious meanings lurk close to the surface as children use cross-gender play to try on, enact, and perpetuate cultural constructions of masculinity and femininity. Similarly, the thrill of animal abuse as play is due to the opportunity it affords adolescents to contemplate, sample, and appropriate adult identities.

Appropriating Adult Culture

Memories of strong emotional reactions, such as those described above, are a major reason why animal abuse is remembered as different and more serious than everyday play. However, as a type of serious play, animal abuse is much more than a recollection of strong emotion. Students remembered their troublesome acts against animals as cool and thrilling because these are part of the process of interpretive reproduction (Corsaro 1992) whereby children usurp adult information to address their own confusions, fears, and uncertainties, including those relating to their transition out of adolescence into adulthood. What makes the memory endure as a thrilling experience, then, is that it is part of a larger process whereby adult identity emerges in adolescents as they appropriate adult culture.

Engaging in such behavior, adolescents form, belong to, and maintain their own peer culture that tries not only to make sense of the adult world but to resist and challenge adult standards and authority by asserting autonomy and control over their own lives or those of other living creatures. For the students examined in this chapter, this resistance provided an opportunity, even if briefly, to try on and exercise four kinds of adultlike powers that were sought after by their younger, curious selves. They took charge of their transition into adulthood by keeping adult-like secrets, drawing adult-like boundaries, doing adult-like activities, and gathering and confirming adult-like knowledge.

Keeping Adult-like Secrets

Adults in organizational settings commonly resort to a variety of secondary adjustments to lessen the institution's power over their behaviors and identities (Goffman 1961). Children, too, in the face of organizational restrictions will evade adult rules through jointly created and concealed secondary adjustments that enable them to gain some control over their lives in these settings (Corsaro 1997). The problem of gaining control over one's life is more pronounced in the context of formal organizations, whether nursery schools or mental asylums, than it is in everyday life, yet the issue is no less important in the latter setting, especially in childhood and adolescence when adult standards of behavior are first being discovered, made sense of, and perhaps experienced as unduly constraining or even oppressive.

In both everyday life and formal organizations, these control-enhancing secondary adjustments are concealed from authority figures. Control afforded through concealment, when it occurs in childhood and adolescence, can be part of a transition into adulthood. A child's sense of control derives as much from carrying off this concealment as it does from the rule-breaking activities themselves. The awareness that one has the power to remain silent, which comes from the experience of keeping and sharing secrets (Bok 1982), is linked to the understanding that one can exert control over events and that one is not at the mercy of adults. From the child's perspective, part of the allure and power of adulthood comes from the control of information. Parents and other authority figures are perceived as privileged by having access to private and perhaps controversial knowledge of others. Conversely, children may feel that they have no secrets from adults, at least regarding morally controversial matters. Secret keeping is therefore empowering because the ownership of privileged information, from the child's perspective, is a marker of adulthood.

Students I interviewed felt they were piercing adult morality when they took pains to hide their animal cruelty from the scrutiny and presumed criticism of adults. If "found out" they believed that adults would berate them because they had violated moral standards regarding the proper treatment of animals. The belief that parents, animal owners, or other adult authority figures would berate them for their acts, if discovered, made students feel as though they were "getting away" with something wrong. The secret of wrongdoing gave special meaning to abuse. It was a serious offense, from the students' perspective, because in their imaginations it could elicit a strong reaction from adults and was by definition in a different category from other, tamer play that did not test adult moral standards or risk punishment if caught doing it. There was a nasty or antisocial side to abuse that was unlike ordinary play. As a student recounted, "It's just basically playing around, but in a malicious sort of way." A few compared their abuse to "petty" crime. One student compared the "fun" of luring a cow to an electrified fence to other "hell raising" and "common, petty vandalism, like throwing eggs at cars, stealing signs, smashing mailboxes, and snooping around the neighbor's houses."

So they took pains to hide their abuse from adult authorities. One student, for instance, recalled his abuse of cats as something he did "behind closed doors" to prevent discovery by his parents. He elaborated, "We weren't gonna get in trouble for this because nobody was gonna know about it. I didn't want parents to know." Another student talked about concealing his actions from camp counselors: "We would hunt chipmunks with rocks— I remember skinning one. I cut the tail off and it kind of slipped right off. That amazed me. It just slipped off like that. I was definitely aware that I shouldn't be doing this. We didn't want to get caught by the counselors." Another student talked about hiding his animal abuse from teachers, as he and his friends "would poison fish that were in the classrooms with bleach and cleaning products. So nobody would say anything, we would only kill a couple of them [otherwise] they'd know right away."

Many claimed that this hiding contributed to the "rush" of tormenting or killing animals, a description that has been used with other adolescent risk-taking behaviors (Lightfoot 1997). Abusing animals, according to students, was not the end they sought. Their primary goal was to risk getting caught. As one student said, his abuse was "exciting" because adults could "discover" his actions: "I was afraid that I would get caught by someone. I got more like a rush from just the fact that any minute somebody could turn around a corner. It was more like fear that made the whole situation exciting. Part of the thrill [of abuse] was the idea that we might get caught by the people in the house. We used to think of all these plans to get back because we would do stuff to try and get ourselves on the edge of getting caught and see if we could get away with it." Another student compared the "fun" of abusing animals to the fun of "sneaking out" with friends at night: "It was a little bit off color. That definitely did play a part in it. It was sort of like when we used to sneak out of the house in seventh grade and go see our friends at night. Once my parents knew I was going out, it wasn't really as fun. A lot of the fun is the risk. If my parents found out they would have killed me. I would have gotten in a lot of trouble. That's what made it fun because you're not supposed to do it. It's knowing that if you get caught doing this, then you're in trouble. It's like a risk. At that age it was a big one— getting yelled at by your parents."

While they claimed to have enjoyed the risk of getting caught, students took steps to avoid it, such as abusing animals in ways that would not be discovered easily by others. In one case, the student decided against burning a cat because that would be hard to conceal from adults.

As he said, "I knew I could get into trouble. I knew if I burned a cat, the family was gonna— you just can't ignore that. I thought it was all right to smack it around because nobody would know. I didn't want anybody to know. Even then I didn't want parents to know. We didn't want to get into trouble." Also, to avoid detection, students said they did not abuse animals in certain places or at certain times. As one student commented, "We did it away from the house. We were always careful where we did it and when we did it. If my parents came out and saw it, I am sure they would have been like, 'What the hell are you doing?'"

Measures such as these allowed students to create and experience their furtive abuse in a relatively safe way with the support and aid of peers. Sequestered acts and private information bestowed upon students a sense of power, as does privileged knowledge or even gossip among adults (Levin and Arluke 1986). Breaking adult rules and keeping this information from adult authorities empowered them simply because they could do what they did and "get away" with it. In the end, abuse made it possible for them to have and share a secret that simultaneously signified both their independence from and their co-opting of adult culture.

Drawing Adult-like Boundaries

Children learn that boundary issues are significant to adults. They see that if adults regard certain people as "not us," they become suitable subjects for scorn or attack. When speaking about their former cruelty, students appeared to mirror the significance of such boundary drawing, except "not us" became animals rather than people. In one case, the student talked about how, from his child's perspective, harming cats was different from harming people: "The cat wasn't— I didn't consider a cat a person. It's not like I'd go beat up people. I felt bad when I beat up people. I always felt bad. But with the cat, it wasn't really important to me." To another student, classifying animals as "not us" was more complex than merely distinguishing humans from all nonhuman animals: "Killing an insect wasn't as bad as killing a bird, which wasn't as bad as killing a squirrel, which wasn't as bad as . . ."

At one extreme, some students said that only insects were remote enough to qualify for abuse. All other living creatures were off limits. In this regard, a student spoke about how she was comfortable abusing flies, ants, and other bugs, but not frogs. "We just took the legs right off of flies. We thought it was fun. We took one wing off to see if they could still fly. And centipedes, I used to cut those with a knife, stick, anything. When I would touch them, they would roll up in a ball, so I used to play with them. And ladybugs, they were in the shower. So I put soap on them to see if they would die. And with my friend, we would light up on fire whole ant trails or we tried to burn them with a magnifying glass. I think that was cruelty. I was torturing something, but it was okay to me then because they were insects. I thought they had no purpose in life. It was kind of cool to just kill them. But when my friend took a frog and hit it to play frog ball, that was when I was like, 'No, that's wrong.' When I actually saw their eyes, I kind of felt sorry for them. I was like, 'No, leave the frog alone.'"

At the other extreme, students drew boundaries that included many "higher" species as "not us," making them eligible targets for abuse. Domestic animals were most often spared the designation of target. A typical comment flatly ruled out all cats and dogs: "Like I would never— like I have dogs, I have a cat, and a bird. I would never think of touching them, but for some reason with frogs it didn't seem like a big deal. It just didn't. Back then I didn't think it was mean, like I looked at them differently. It just didn't seem like on the same level as a cat or dog or something for some reason." Another student felt that birds or squirrels were "not us" compared to pets, which were part of the family: "Dogs and cats are like the closest things to humans compared to like a bird or a squirrel. I remember shooting birds and squirrels for fun and that didn't bother me at all because they are not like part of the family— like, 'Oh he's my little pet.' Some families treat animals like kids."

There was no consensus, however, about which domestic animals were off limits to abuse. Some students saw only certain cats and dogs as "not us," claiming never to hurt their own animals but abusing those owned by other people. As one student explained: "You know, I never really abused any of my cats, to tell you the truth. It was always like I'd be over my friend's house or my cousin's house and they always had cats. So when I was a kid, I used to tie them in a bag and spin them around, or tie them in a bag and smack one side, then smack the other side, so they wouldn't know where to get out." Other students claimed not to have abused cats and dogs if they or others owned them, but those without proper domestic status were targeted for abuse. As one student noted, "Strays I would throw. But if it was someone's— like if

I knew it belonged to somebody, I wouldn't do that. But if it was a stray, like a stray cat, I would have thrown it. I didn't like boot them, but I kicked them."

If owned and treated as pets, animals other than cats and dogs might also be spared mistreatment because of their special status. Students recalled being confused about the propriety of harming these "lower" animals because in their eyes they were not full-fledged pets and therefore could be victimized. Recognizing that animals such as rabbits were owned as pets gave students pause but did not necessarily stop them from inflicting harm. "Maybe if rabbits were more of a household pet," one student said, "I would have thought twice about it [harming the rabbit]. They're not that popular a pet and it's not really as much of a domestic animal. It was a wild rabbit. I never really had a kinship with any kind of rabbit."

In quite a different manner, students appropriated the adultlike ability to draw boundaries. Through their collaboration in abuse, students explored adult's facility in drawing boundaries between human in and out groups. Learning to establish boundaries and their moral significance entails both excluding others as "not us" and including others in one's inner circle as "us." Those who are allowed or encouraged to harm "not us" usually are seen as most "like us." To the students, abuse of animals was a ritual of inclusion, an event for including those deemed closest. When students recalled their former abuse as fun because it was done as a group activity with their playmates, it was clear as they spoke that this companionship was more important to them than the abuse of animals. In fact, many seemed nostalgic about their prior harm of animals because it was an opportunity to spend time with friends in the face of what were perceived as less attractive options "to do something." As one student said, "The hunting of chipmunks in a group would be kind of like a clanny, bonding kind of thing. Or when we trapped a big lizard in my friend's backyard. We all took turns shooting it, and it took a long time to die." Like a child's "mooning," "egging," or other pranks, students often "got away with something" as part of a group activity, with their best friends as collaborators. One typical report, for example, recounted how a student took turns with friends as they tortured insects: "I was between five and seven, and I was hanging out with a couple of friends in the front yard. One of us got the bright idea to start messing around with bugs, and we captured some flies and some grasshoppers. I don't know exactly how the mechanics worked, but we took turns pulling the wings off the flies, burning the grasshoppers—someone got a lighter from their parents who smoked. I remember that part of the reason I did it was because everyone else was, and I wanted to fit in with the group." Of the twenty-five students studied, only two reported harming animals by themselves.

In the vast majority of cases, students claimed that friends initiated or strongly encouraged the abuse. For example, when one student was asked why he shot a rabbit, he said: "I think a lot of it had to do with the fact that I was with John. It was actually his idea to begin with. I don't think it would have occurred to me, 'Hey, let's shoot a round at the rabbit.' If I was alone with a gun, I'd probably watch TV and not even touch the gun." Another student recalled firing a BB gun at a cat because he was "dared" to do so by a friend: "There was this neighborhood cat, it was always hissing and scratching people. So one of the guys took out a BB gun one day and dared each of us to fire at it. And we all did. That was something that was done in secret—we never told our parents about it." And yet another student talked about being "egged on" to abuse animals: "Your friends, they see you do it [abuse] once, and they egg you on for the second time."

Friends rewarded students whose play violated adult civil behavior. According to students, their primary concern was not to make animals suffer but to gain renown, even if momentarily, for being daring—and the status and identity attribution that followed. One student recalled that he and his friends vied for whose animal abuse "could be cool—who could come up with the funniest thing [type of cruelty], you know?" To another student, the goal of abuse was to be seen by peers as a wise guy." As he said, "It was just mischief to see who could be the wise guy and not get caught." And if not competitive, students and their friends were strongly supportive of each other's "successful" abuse. One student recalled shooting birds: "It wasn't really competition because we'd all be happy for each other if you hit them." And yet another spoke about how being cruel to animals gave status to members of his group: "Like the cat thing [thrown off roof], I think the motive— if I came up with the idea, that would place me in the creative part of our group. A lot of us in the group wanted to be the popular people in school, but we just weren't. By doing this [cruelty], it defined our roles in the smaller group and it at least made us feel comfortable with what we were doing."

As a ritual of inclusion and exclusion, whether between humans and animals or between humans, animal abuse allowed students to designate what constituted "us" and "not us" and to find meaning in boundary demarcation in ways that corresponded to classifications made in adult culture. As adolescents they were continuing the kinds of preadolescent clique dynamics observed by Adler and Adler (1998) that teach them to reproduce society's feelings of differentiation between in-groups and out-groups. Certainly, the mistreatment of animals is not the only device children and adolescents use to build and maintain peer-group boundaries, but it certainly should be recognized as an important and perhaps common one. Like other techniques of out-group subjugation that children see as "just fun to do," such as picking on lower-status individuals, badly treating animals that are perceived as outsiders helps maintain a group's exclusivity and contribute to its cohesion.

Doing Adultlike Activities

Animal abuse can be inspired by children's interest in being like adults, particularly when what they do is forbidden. As was true with acts of abuse for other reasons, these instances were less about causing harm to animals than they were about making claims. Harming animals was a means for these children to become interlopers of adult statuses.

For example, some students saw animal abuse as a way to experience and rehearse an adult form of hunting, based on what they saw and heard from parents, relatives, acquaintances, and popular culture. Some did acknowledge that as children they realized there was a difference between their cruelty and genuine hunting, the latter called "*hunting hunting*" by one student. Another remembered: "My friend's father was a big hunter, so we were like, 'We should try it.' But it wasn't like we went out with blinds and camouflage." And yet another recalled distinguishing his uncle's hunting from his own, saying, "I sort of hunted, but what my uncle did was much neater. I almost glorified it because he was at the top— he had guides, he had videos, he had trophies."

They also distinguished their "hunting" from the perceived adult version of it in a different way. Many remembered feeling uneasy when their activities came too close to the real thing. Some students, for example, claimed that they were troubled if their hunts led to the death of animals because, ironically, they did not want to "harm" them. In one case, the student and his friend succeeded in shooting a possum but suspected that it was not dead. If they left the animal alive, it would presumably suffer, and that would constitute "harm" in their opinion. So they made sure it was dead for the animal's sake rather than for the conquest of hunting.

Nevertheless, students saw their hunting as fun and thrilling because it resembled the adult version. One feature that made it adultlike was that they used weapons to torture or kill animals. When asked to account for their prior behavior, some students claimed that they had no interest in hurting animals but were preoccupied with firing various weapons that adults often discouraged or prohibited. One student talked about the allure of using "weapons" that made it seem as though he was on a hunt: "[We wanted] whatever explosive or firearm we could get our hands on [as long as] it could kill. We also loved burning things with magnifying glasses. These [exploding, shooting, burning] were better than just throwing them [animals] in the air. The weapons like the explosives were very interesting and I loved them. I knew it was sketchy and not right, but it was fun. It was like hunting, looking for them and then finding and getting them. That's exciting."

A second feature of their hunting that made it adultlike was that it involved "planning." One student said of his approach to shooting birds, "It involved a sort of hunt, planning it out, even though it was cheesy. We got the cereal. We put it out there to see if birds came. We'd change the food—bread, croutons, whatever they were. There was a planning to it, a method—loading the gun, hiding, keeping your sight on the target, survival techniques, as childish as it may sound, it's true." Similarly, another student spoke of the excitement of stalking and successfully hitting animals during hunts with friends: "We used to go back in the woods, and you'd search around back there, you'd just walk around trying to find an animal to shoot. And it was a thrill, it was a rush, it made your heart pound. If you hit it, then you'd feel like you accomplished something."

"Hunting" also made students feel as though they were developing certain adult "skills." One student, for example, talked about honing his marksmanship abilities on squirrels: "I'd hit one with my BB gun; they would react vigorously, but they wouldn't die. And then this one squirrel, I shot about five times and it kept on popping up, but it would never die. It was fun to shoot the BB gun at them. It helped me learn to shoot straight and skills like that." Another student talked about how he acquired a blowgun as part of his adolescent interest in "ninja stuff" and used it to hunt a duck. However, he claimed his interest was not to kill this animal but to practice his shooting skills.

Certainly "hunting" was not the only way that students remembered their abuse as a rehearsal of adult behaviors, although it was the most common way. Students saw their animal abuse as constraining the behavior of animals that were seen as overstepping their "limits," whether that involved barking "too loudly," biting "too hard," or defecating on the family rug. Some likened their animal abuse to parents who discipline bad behavior in children. If students saw animals behaving in ways that seemed to violate adult codes of conduct, their abuse could be seen as similar to the exercise of control by parents. For example, when students spoke about abusing "misbehaving animals," their actions can easily be interpreted as attempts to exert the type of control over someone or something to which the child is regularly subject at the hands of adults, whether that might be constant reprimands or spankings. In these instances, animal victims became surrogate humans who violated norms, and their harm mocked how students envisioned adults responding to deviance. Thus, one student spoke about how she "spanked" a dog because it misbehaved: "I would visit these neighbors, and they had a poodle named Spot. And the poodle was the nicest dog—sweet, very sweet. Once a day, I would take the dog for a walk. This one time I was mean to the dog. I was tugging on the leash and I hit it. You know, I spanked it for no reason. I would purposely make the dog do something wrong, like make it walk when it wasn't supposed to. This continued for about ten minutes. I probably hit him half a dozen times. I was belting it. I was spanking it, like you would whack the dog for wetting the floor." As Corsaro (1997) observes, such acts reflect children's focus on adult's power over them, especially in physical ways. Their response to this powerless through animal abuse, as a form of dirty play, differs in important ways from psychological displacement models of the same act. By seeing abuse as simple displacement, the significance of the act is limited to seeing it as a coping technique to improve a child's mood state. As dirty play, however, the child's casting of abuse as similar to the expression of power and control by adults permits us to understand it instrumentally, rather than impulsively, as part of a larger social process of appropriating adult culture.

Others saw their animal abuse as a test of membership in the adult world of work. In these cases, animal abuse was seen as a way to nurture skills that adults were thought to possess in various occupations. One student remembered beheading cats to test his future ability to work for the secret service: "I'm not sure this is exactly the right word, but like [it had] something to do with personal development. Like I've always had the fantasy of one day being in the secret service or something like that, and I know there's a lot of questionable things you need to do in terms of— maybe you need to assassinate a human being or you're ordered to— I was wondering if I was capable of that kind of disconnection."

In short, whether it was hunting, disciplining, working, or engaging in other adult-like activities, animal abuse facilitated students' youthful exploration of a variety of adult social roles. Thus, abuse was not the end but a means by which students could cross age-status boundaries to rehearse their imagined future participation in adult society. Although students appeared anxious to assume adult statuses, they felt illequipped to do so because too little trustworthy knowledge was available about the workings of the social and physical worlds around them. Abuse was a way to get this sought after knowledge.

Gathering and Confirming Adult-like Knowledge

Students remembered their former cruelty as a device to verify information from adults or to create it when unavailable. According to students, this information was suspect because being told something by adults did not guarantee its accuracy. From the abuser's perspective, then, cruelty was a tool to gather firsthand knowledge that could be trusted. At the least, by taking this approach, students challenged the assumption that children automatically accept the "factual" veracity of the adult world.

Students commonly spoke of their "curiosity" to "see for themselves" what others had told them to be true. In one case, the student said that he and his friends gave Alka-seltzer to a pigeon that subsequently died to conduct a test because "I heard that it would kill them and I wanted to see for myself whether it would." Another student explained why he stoned and hurt a skunk, saying "I was curious to see what would happen if I hit it. Would it spray a mist or a stream of water or what? I guess I didn't know what was going to happen and I just needed to see what would happen." And yet another student described her disbelief in what adults told her about the ability of cats to survive falls from great heights. Because she doubted this was true but was curious about the validity of the idea, she decided to test its accuracy by dropping a cat off the second story of her home.

Sometimes students recalled their curiosity as a method to obtain information that adults withheld from them. For example, one student said that he was frustrated as a child because he could not acquire information about death, forcing him to explore this topic by abusing animals: "I always had an interest in death and stuff. When you're young, you don't know a lot about questions about life and death and stuff like that. You know, they don't teach you about death in school or anything and you can't do it to [kill] another person. You're curious, you know, and I didn't want to go out and kill somebody and cut them up. I was curious about death, curious about harm. I was curious about what you can do to something living. At the time, I had my own theories. What I did to animals was a way to learn this."

Many students remembered their curiosity as having had some general intellectual purpose. They recalled their former acts as driven by "wonder" about how their cruelty would affect animals. As one student said of her abuse of centipedes: "I would cut it up and try to see if it would live. The whole thing was curiosity. I wondered what would happen. Cutting them, I wanted to see what they were like inside." Another student spoke similarly of her treatment of cockroaches: "We would put a toothpick through a cockroach, and it would keep crawling. It just kept walking, so we were like, 'Wow.' We picked it up. It was fascinating trying to see if it would croak." And yet another student said of his burning of insects: "It was curiosity— trying to, I don't know what it was curiosity about, but mostly it was, 'What would happen if we did this?' I didn't have any hypothesis, any thinking, beyond 'What's going to happen if we did this?'"

Some of this curiosity was to confirm specific cultural knowledge or beliefs, especially the saying that cats have nine lives. For example, one student explained: "We lived in a two-story house, and we used to always want to know if a cat really had nine lives. So we would kick them down the stairs and make them fall. Instead of landing on their legs, they would roll over and keep running. We were just curious besides being mean." Indeed, several students mentioned curiosity about a cat's ability to survive substantial falls, including one who remembered that he was "surprised" and "amazed" after he dropped a cat off a balcony: "We were drinking beer, just having a good time. My parents were out of town. We were like, 'Yeah, I heard cats always land on their feet.' So, we had like a balcony upstairs. We were like let's see if we drop the cat off here, if he'll land on his feet. We didn't think it would be that bad, it was only about ten feet. We just dropped it off there and surprisingly, amazingly, it did have nine lives." This student went on to compare it to "the public hangings that they used to have. I guess this was something like, 'Hey, let's go watch. This is interesting.' It was like, we did it, that's neat."

Other students remembered their cruelty as a form of "experimentation" on animals that was both fun and a source of knowledge, however rudimentary or redundant, though a few students viewed their experimenting more as a "crazy thing" rather than as a form of knowledge creation or verification. In one such case, the student described his experimentation on frogs: "We'd try to catch stuff in the woods. If it was something like a squirrel, we'd just try to kill it. But if it was something like a frog, we'd try to catch it and experiment with it a little. We used to play Frisbee with them. Throw them and catch them. We would do crazy things like that, not for any purpose, not to learn anything, just to like harm it. We would just throw it back and forth, and we didn't know if it was still alive or not because we would just keep tossing it. Yellow stuff would come out of it and stuff like that." Similarly, another student talked about feeling "pumped up" when he "experimented" on fish by stabbing them: "Instead of putting them in the bucket, I would throw them on the rocks, watch them flop around, take a knife and just drop it from a certain height. They would like wince. When it pierced them you could see the blood and they would flap around a lot more. And then you would stop for a little bit and then you'd drop it again and they'd start flipping. It's like experimenting. It's like, 'Wow, that's cool.' That gets you pumped up and you just keep going."

Yet many students talked genuinely about their prior interest in "experimenting" on animals, usurping this concept from the adult world where talk of experimentation gave credibility to the use of animals in ways normally disallowed. To students, the fun of this form of experimentation came from using ingenious methods to harm animals, with the methods themselves holding the students' interest because they seemed novel, illegal, or creative to them and because their use would allow students to observe certain responses in animals that they could predict but wanted to cause and witness themselves. In such cases, developing and using methods of "experimentation" were in themselves more appealing to students than causing animals to suffer. For example, one student described how it was "cool" for him to invent unusual ways to "experiment" on and kill frogs after catching them with fishing poles: "My friend John would spin the frog around and around the pole, so it would get some good momentum. I would take a paddle and the next time the frog came around, I'd just sort of wind up and give him a good smack. And then you usually lose about half the frog. And we'd do that until the frog was all gone. It was like, 'Let's see what it can take.' Like an experiment. Sometimes, the larger ones would take a couple hits before it was all gone." Another student talked about how it was "fun" to build and use a "stun gun" to "experiment" on his cat, for which he claimed fondness.

Comments such as these paint a picture of adolescents who crossed intellectual barriers through their harm of animals. Knowledge whose accuracy was doubted or knowledge that was unavailable could be gained, from the perspective of children, through firsthand exploration with animals. Once again, abuse appeared not to be an end in itself but a means, albeit an unfortunate choice of method, by which students questioned the adult world's truthfulness and undertook an adultlike "experimental" approach to satisfy more than just their simple "curiosity."

THE PAYOFF

Fine (1986) maintains that as children grow older and their needs for presentation of self change, they no longer regard their former dirty play as fun. Instead, they see it as morally offensive, and they feel guilty. This "payoff" of dirty play was evident among many students in this study, who as young adults seemed, on the whole, quite different from the "wilders" of popular culture who seek fun to relieve their boredom and suffer no remorse even if people and property are harmed along the way (Derber 1996). While students reported a period in their lives where their reckless abandon entailed harming animals, this may have been more of a cultural "time out" than a lasting sign of incivility or anti-social personality. Indeed, some groups, such as the Amish, anticipate and acknowledge these adolescent behaviors by permitting children between the ages of eighteen and twenty-one to leave home and experience what are regarded as unacceptable or immoral behaviors, only to return to the community morally intact despite their episodic waywardness during this "rumspringa" or "running around" period (Kraybill 2001).

Consistent with Fine's argument, many but not all students presented themselves as morally troubled by their former abuse, although they did so in different ways. Some claimed to have experienced guilt at the time of their abuse, specifically naming this emotion in their talk. As one student said of his stoning to death a snake, "I felt like I tortured it and basically that I felt guilty. I started in on myself, like, how could I torture something? It made me question myself, like why would I do that? It wasn't like I was in love with the snake. It's not like I was going to cry over it being dead. But it just made me question myself, like what kind of person did this make me?" In the wake of his self-doubt, this student admonished himself for the abuse.

Other students claimed to feel guilty because they did not recall having this emotion years earlier when they harmed animals. The fact that they had been comfortable carried the implication that they were and are not decent people, and this implication haunted them. From their current perspective toward animals, not having had regret or guilt was hard for them to explain or to face. One student, for example, killed a friend's hamster and was "freaked out" later because she was not upset at the time over killing the animal. She spoke of her continuing distress over not having had the appropriate feelings: "I started picking up my friend's hamster and throwing it back in the cage. I was picking it up and throwing it in. I especially remember squeezing the hamster hard but not squeezing it as strong as I could. I wasn't doing it intentionally to hurt it. Then I put it back in the cage and there was like a little bit of blood on the side of the cage. And then I went downstairs and I didn't think anything of it. I didn't even feel guilty about it. I wasn't upset that the hamster was dead. I forgot about it for a while, but that kind of freaked me out later on. I am upset that I hadn't been upset about it. I can't believe I didn't feel bad about it. That makes me feel bad now, because that's not how I am. I mean, I'm a compassionate person."

A few students conveyed their guilt more graphically by describing themselves as "killers" or "murderers" who lacked empathy for their victims. In this regard, one student spoke about how he could no longer shoot a possum as he did when he was fourteen because he now could identify with the needs of animals: "I just went out to kill something. But in my head, it is like what if it was going out to get food for babies and by me killing it, those babies died because there was no one to provide for them. If I went and killed a human being and people cared about it, I'd be a murderer. I feel like a murderer for killing an animal just because I had a gun in my hands and I felt like it."

Further support for the idea that dirty play, such as animal abuse, can pay off positively came from the shame underlying students' nervous laughter. For some, at one level such laughter may have been due to their feelings of uneasiness and nervousness because they could not make sense of prior acts. As one student said, "I laugh when I don't understand something." It also is possible that they laughed at the disconcerting image of themselves that emerged in the course of the interviews because of the sheer incongruity between their prior and current selves, at least in regard to their ability to harm animals. One student laughed as she noted about herself: "If I look at it right now, I just laugh because I'm like 'why did I use to do it?' I don't understand why I used to do it. I just look at how I was then and how I am now. I wouldn't do it now to a cat."

Perhaps the laughter exhibited by students in this study is more akin to that witnessed during Milgram's (1974) experiment on obedience to authority, when several students laughed as they inflicted what they thought were life-threatening punishments on the experiment's confederates. Social scientists have speculated that this laughter may have served more as tension release than as a reflection of flippant disregard for suffering. Others have noted the value of black humor as a coping device for people to manage emotionally difficult, situations, such as performing surgery, by making what can be a very serious situation into something that seems smaller or more normal (Koller 1988). Students' laughter then, may be more of a reflection of their discomfort describing their former behavior than their disregard for animals.

These interpretations of laughter belie deeper emotions among students. The fact that some students laughed while also denying that their former acts were humorous spoke to this deeper understanding; it was a different kind of laughter than that normally associated with the trivial or unimportant in that it was ironic or parenthetical. For example, as one student laughed, she pointed out that her former actions were not humorous: "I was so mean to them [cats]. It's not funny right now, but looking back, how we used to treat them, it's like 'Wow, I used to do that!'" While Goffman (1967) claims that laughter can define a situation as unserious, the very fact that students attempted such a redefinition suggests that they recognized its potential seriousness. Students may have used this laughter as a dramaturgical signal to the interviewer that he or she no longer approved of such acts and was no longer capable of committing them, whether or not these assertions were true. The emotion they had trouble naming was a sense of disgrace in the presence of the interviewer. In this sense, their laughter may have been a marker or outer indicator of shame (Scheff 1990), further evidence for the sociological "payoff" of dirty play.

Some interviews, however, did not support Fine's (1986) suggestion that as children mature their presentation of self will no longer define prior dirty play as fun. It is true that the students were late adolescents who might continue to mature into adulthood and develop sufficient guilt about their abuse to present a repentant self to others. Nevertheless, some still spoke about their former abuse as fun and showed little evidence of presenting themselves as ashamed or guilt-ridden for having harmed animals, even though they remembered thinking at the time that what they did was not quite right. A student illustrated this when he said, "I kind of realized that it was bad, like maybe I shouldn't have done it, but then I'd think about how much fun it was."

Many of these students thought animal abuse was a "normal" part of growing up and a reflection of childhood "innocence," forgiving themselves and others for such acts. In this regard, some relied on a vocabulary of motives that dismissed their abuse as a "rite of passage." This approach asserted that their prior behaviors were normal for children, and they no longer were children, having long stopped such play. From their perspective, animal cruelty was something that children do because they are children, or as one student said of his earlier act of throwing a cat through a basketball hoop: "We were young. We were kids. It was a stage for me." Similarly, another student said: "It was just what most kids will go through. If you don't torture a cat, you are going to torture some type of animal. It doesn't matter how big or small."

And yet another student described his abusing frogs some years earlier as just one of those things that "young guys do." "When I was six or seven," he said, "me and this kid, Henry, we would kill frogs. We would run them over with our bikes. We would totally abuse them, like fry them with a magnifying glass and like put fireworks in their mouths and everything. We'd just pick them up and destroy them. I never really loved doing it. I mean it was fun. We had nothing else to do. A lot of guys, when they're young do things. . . . It stopped like in the fifth or sixth grade because I grew up. When you are young, you don't really think of the social consequences to killing frogs. You know, you don't think about the karma of it."

There is good reason to think that this split in self-presentation, between those students who admonished themselves and those who still felt entitled to see their abuse as fun, is not due just to differences in students' maturation, as Fine (1986) might explain. Students' appropriation of the adult world had parallels in broader institutional and cultural themes about animals in American society that are equally confused about the proper treatment of animals. As a form of deep play (Chick and Donlon 1992; Fine 1988, 1992), animal abuse allowed students to discover these themes and connect them to their everyday behavior. By drawing on these themes, students could reflect on their abuse—planning it, carrying it out, and concealing it—and tell conflicting stories about harming animals that supported alternative presentations of self. They could talk, on one hand, about how disturbed they were about their former abuse and on the other hand, how entertaining they still considered it to be. They could tie their abuse, along with their reputed compassion and kindness toward animals, to a larger society that is confused about how we regard the moral status of nonhuman animals.

Our ability to switch from treating animals as objects than can be abused one moment to treating them as members of the family that are adored the next has been widely documented in many American institutions and customs. Biomedical scientists, for example, typically tout their love and admiration for animals, especially their own pets, while carrying out experiments on animals of the same species (Arluke 1988). And school programs in biology dissection have a hidden curriculum that teaches young people how to construct and effortlessly shift between categories that objectify animals in certain situations while personalizing them in others (e.g., Arluke and Hafferty 1996; Solot and Arluke 1997).

When they remembered their abuse as fun, students might selectively tune out media attention given to extraordinary acts of altruism by humans to save endangered animals and instead hone in on slapstick portrayals of animal suffering common in mainstream popular culture (Melson 2001). Such humorous slants on cruelty are built into a social order that makes light of animals being harmed or even killed (Gerbner 1995). For example, the media industry is guilty of using cruelty to get laughs. Movie viewers snicker as Jack Nicholson, in *As Good as It Gets*, decides to dispose of his neighbor's yapping dog by throwing it down a garbage shoot. And in *There's Something About Mary* the audience roars as a dog is thrown through the air. Radio, too, is not immune to joking about animal cruelty. The former Boston talk show *Two Chicks Dishin'* devoted two programs to listeners who called in "tales of childhood animal torture." The hosts engineered the show to have a light and humorous tone and admonished callers who did not find the discussion funny. And certainly books do not spare making a good joke out of cruelty, using humor to cloak our ambivalence toward animals. Cats, for one, are viewed with ambivalence. The September 21, 1981, issue of *Time* reports that a book entitled *101 Uses for a Dead Cat* sold 600,000 copies in just a few months and that there were 575,000 copies in print of *The Second Official I Hate Cats Book*, which followed the earlier *I Hate Cats Book*. Twenty years later saw the release of *I Still Hate Cats* and the *I Hate Cats Calendar*. There are even Web sites that feature ingenious devices to torture animals, all in the name of "good fun," such as "bonsai cat" sites that show how to force kittens into bottles.

Similarly, when students recalled their abuse as "something normal," they also could selectively ignore media stories about unusual human kindness to animals and focus on instances in popular culture where extreme mistreatment of animals goes unpunished. Such abuse is often used as a literary device to construct character. For example, in the play *Rent*, although a landlord throws a dog out of a window to punish renters who fail to pay him, he suffers no incrimination or penalty for doing so. Also, in the movie *Straw Dogs*, Dustin Hoffman is not distressed that his girlfriend's cat has been hanged to death by a group of handymen who killed the animal to show the couple that they are unsafe and that no part of their home is off limits. The men unnerve

Hoffman more than their act of cruelty, which he does not protest, despite appeals from his girlfriend to confront the men about their abuse. Some instances of unpunished brutality are used for their shock value but still convey the message that hurting animals is no crime. In one story about the now staid and mainstream rocker Ozzy Osbourne, we are reminded that years ago the legendary bat-biting singer committed a "sick act of animal cruelty" by "slaughtering" with a shotgun the family's seventeen cats (*National Inquirer* 2002). Similarly, *Hell on Earth*, an industrial rock band from Tampa, Florida, received national attention when the group allowed a chronically ill and depressed person to commit suicide on stage during one of its concerts. Readers were reminded, as an afterthought, that the band had a history of doing unusual things during concerts, including grinding up rats in blenders.

That students could experience animal abuse as deep play illustrates how children appropriate information from adult culture and creatively use it to address their own concerns. Virtually all of their appropriation of adult culture had parallels in our wider society. For example, when students borrowed the adult facility of drawing boundaries between human groups, their talk of harming victims because they were "simply" animals, "only" strays, or "just" other people's pets" closely paralleled our cultural typifications of animals that legitimate their inconsistent and dismissive treatment. Permeating adult thinking and action toward animals in many western societies is a sociozoological scale that specifies our conceptions of the moral relationships between humans and nonhuman animals (Arluke and Sanders 1996). The less some animal is regarded as "like us," the more we will tolerate, ignore, or even condone its mistreatment. Certainly, the deep play of animal abuse was not limited to the ability of students to couch their acts in the sociozoological scale. For example, when students borrowed and used information about common adult rituals and occupations, their talk about the fun of "hunting" or "experimenting" closely paralleled how adults in the United States treat animals in harmful ways that are sanctioned by customs and legitimized through institutions.

In the end, then, what students derived from dirty play with animals was far more profound and complicated than the control and empowerment realized through their appropriation of certain features of adult culture, although that alone is no small accomplishment. Since dirty play is a reflection of, rather than separate from, the values of society

(Fine 1991), its identity-conferring properties, in the case of animal abuse, will mirror our conflicted attitudes about animals. When students reflected on and grappled with what their animal abuse said about them, the stories that they told themselves about themselves were no more or no less contradictory than those writ large across our society's ambiguous and shifting canvas of human-animal relationships. Much like Clifford's (1992, 100) rethinking of culture, the adult world that students creatively borrow from, refashion, and apply to their own mundane activities is a "multiply authored invention, a historical formation, an enactment, a political construct, a shifting paradox, an ongoing translation, an emblem, a trademark, a consensual negotiation of contrastive identity, and more." Students' identities are formed from the multiple and contradictory layers of society, making it possible for them to present themselves as young adults now deeply disturbed by their prior acts or still entertained by them.

3   Hoarders

Shoring Up Self

Cat "Hoarders" Are Usually Victims of Mysterious Obsession. Nearly 90 cats
had taken over Terry's home in the Bronx. . . . The thought of giving up any
of her cats . . . hurt. "I got so close to the baby cats that I couldn't give any of
them away . . . I figured no one else could take care of them like I could." . . .
When officers last week entered a Petaluma home filled with about 200 cats,
they found floorboards soaked and warped by urine and feral animals bur-
rowed inside walls. Some of the cats were malnourished or sick. A few had
already died. Barletta told *The Chronicle* last week that she was trying to find
homes for her cats. . . . Their numbers simply spiraled out of control. "I know
this sounds bizarre," she said. "But I'm a rational person."
                              —*San Francisco Chronicle*, May 27, 2001

WHEN ADOLESCENTS EXPLAIN their prior cruelty, many are distressed by memories they cannot readily excuse. Although they recall
their unsavory behavior as a way to "try on" adult identities, this
account does not entirely numb whatever guilt or uneasiness they still
feel. Others are indifferent, viewing their memories as unimportant
matters that neither help nor hurt their self-image, but they too com-
partmentalize their former abuse by linking it to a transition out of
childhood. They have moved on; memories of abuse are just that. Their
sense of self is not based on relationships with animals—whether
positive or negative.

Mistreating animals, however, can play a more vital role for the self
when people base their entire identity on such harm. It is not a memory of a random event, a lapse in judgment, or "going crazy" but the
essence of who they are as people. They use cruelty—or how they redefine it—to build their sense of self, define their purpose in life, and most
important, console themselves that what others see as loathsome if not
criminal, mentally ill, or pathetic is no such thing. They tell themselves
and others that they are decent and kind.

Severe neglect plays a vital role for the self of animal hoarders. Their
identities hinge on amassing dozens or even hundreds of cats, dogs, and

other assorted creatures, purportedly out of concern and love for them (Lockwood 1994), only to withhold the rudiments of humane care and the necessities of life. Law enforcement agents, animal control officers, housing officials, shelter workers, and veterinarians often find these animals in pitiful condition, chronically underfed or even starved, living in inadequate, overcrowded housing, and sometimes harboring painful diseases, behavioral problems, or physical impairments (Campbell and Robinson 2001). They also find hoarders and those living with them to be socially isolated and to suffer ill health. Sanitary conditions frequently deteriorate to the point where dwellings become unfit for human habitation.

On their surface, incidents of hoarding make for good news stories because they are so extraordinary, baffling, and sad—scores of sick and starved animals being kept in filthy, cluttered homes often by people who claim to "love" them. "Experts" who must deal with them all weigh in on what they think causes people to grossly neglect their animals, homes, families, and selves. The result is that hoarders' identities become a matter for public speculation. Various experts alternatively portray them as mentally ill, criminal, or simply pitiful.

Speculation about the nature of hoarding can easily shame hoarders when it is both public and negative. One hoarder claims that such thinking implicitly asks her: "How can you do it? How can you live like this? How can you live with animals, it's filthy, it's dirty, if nothing else, don't you care about other people? Don't you this? Don't you that? I never hear the end of it." In response, hoarders justify or excuse their behavior, in the press and in person. Hoarders' justifications and excuses seem as outlandish as their behavior toward animals and property, starkly contrasting the grim "reality" of these situations. Yet, that they have them is unsurprising. Others who feel maligned resort to similar "accounts" or "neutralizing techniques" to normalize the behavior in question (Hewitt 2000). Hoarders, too, craft personal narratives that reveal how they wish to be regarded by journalists or sociologists who interview them as well as neighbors, friends, family, and strangers. When hoarders are accused of wrongdoing, these accounts lubricate awkward social interaction and protect the hoarder's threatened identity.

That hoarders explain and defend their behavior is not unusual; it is how they do so that merits attention. Their identity work does more than neutralize and deflect unwelcome or derogatory views, it paints a flattering self-portrait that is firmly anchored in widely accepted and rewarded roles borrowed liberally from our general culture. Unlike the adolescents described in the preceding chapter who were either remorseful or indifferent about their cruelty, hoarders are passionate and proud about the many animals they acquire and claim to "care" for in self-proclaimed roles such as parent or shelter worker. Hoarders emphasize that, even if sacrifices are necessary, they can be counted on in tough situations to constantly keep in mind and help needy creatures. In other words, to console themselves, they present an image of themselves as saints.

IDENTITY AS A PUBLIC ISSUE

Private troubles are converted into public issues by the media, which selectively gathers up the building blocks of individual experiences, invests them with broader meaning by drawing on the opinions of experts, and makes them available for public consumption. Individual cases become symptomatic of a larger problem, as specialists or authorities offer their explanations of the problem's causes. And when crimes, homelessness, or unemployment are reported in the news, certain types of social control agents—police, social workers, housing authorities, physicians and others—become identified with the proper management of people thought to pose serious social problems (Best 1995; Mills 1959; Sacco 1995). Each agency questions the personal identities proffered by those being managed and provides them with alter identities compatible with the agency's own perspective. Depending on the institution, people can be defined as "bad," "mad," or "sad" (Schneider and Conrad 1992), when the criminal justice, the medical care, and public health systems manage them.

In the news, hoarders are not associated with any of these institutions, since no one agency claims to best manage them. Readers are left with a bricolage of reports about these people from various experts that are interpreted and summarized in the news. As they try to limit or stop the harm of animals, people, and property, these reports show that organizations have conflicting conceptions about hoarders' identities and the meaning of their neglect. They are painted as criminal, mentally ill, or pathetic.

In this mix of opinions, journalists who write about hoarders become significant players because they cull and report the views of various authorities. How we come to regard hoarders and assess their relationships with animals depends on the willingness and ability of journalists to capture not only the perspectives of organizations dealing with hoarding but the perspectives of hoarders themselves. Although the news is a platform of communication, hoarder's voice is permitted expression only within narrowly confined limits. The constraint to present "balanced" stories with many sides and viewpoints, and to defer to the opinions of "experts," leaves scant room for this voice.

The Person

The hoarder-as-criminal identity stems from the press's crime-story convention. These stories typically begin with complaints about hoarders from neighbors who report "strong," "obnoxious" odors or "stench," and occasionally nuisance problems such as "barking loudly." Neglect is seldom the initial complaint because animals are usually concealed inside hoarders' homes. Hoarders are usually described as "uncomfortable around people" or as "quiet and somewhat reclusive," boarding up windows, rarely appearing outside, and not answering doorbells. This isolation makes it difficult if not impossible for neighbors to know much about them or their animals. Law enforcement authorities are eventually called to the scene, typically discovering many suffering or dead animals that are taken away from angry or grieved owners who potentially face charges of cruelty and possible conviction and sentencing.

Presenting hoarding as a crime story means that articles often emphasize, in dramatic terms, the perspective of those who intervene to help animals harmed or put in danger by hoarders. Use of terms such as "rescued," "seized," or "raid," rather than the more neutral "confiscated" or "claimed," underscore the law enforcement approach to managing hoarders and the aggressive steps needed on behalf of animal victims who apparently need to be "taken away" with some urgency. This perspective also paints each case as the "worst" or "most horrifying" incident, describing animal neglect in superlative terms. One article cites a humane official who said, "'You can't imagine people accumulating that sort of filth and garbage.' . . . Frazier said that it was the most foul scene he had encountered in his six years on the job.'" Another official maintained that a different case involved the "largest number of neglected animals ever seen."

Since the law enforcement viewpoint dominates these articles, hoarders do not routinely comment on these actions and when they do, they, predictably, protest unlawful and unnecessary seizure of their "children." Some hoarders are characterized as resistant to authority. One is described as "so belligerent the police were called to help," at which point the hoarder wrestled with police, who sprayed him with pepper spray and finally arrested him. Others have histories of being uncooperative or hostile. It is common for articles to describe repeated attempts, sometimes spanning years, to take animals away from hoarders who resist these efforts by authorities. In one case, an article features the headline, "Notorious Cat Hoarder Jailed" and details the exploits of a "wily and elusive foe." Another article notes that "as is true of most animal hoarders, Becker had a track record," listing her history of being deceptive and difficult with authorities as she chronically acquired animals.

Although the crime-story format sensitizes readers to view hoarders as criminals—they violate the law and get "busted" by agents who seize their "property" (i.e., animals) and possibly take them to court—articles show them being handled leniently. Reports of cruelty charges actually being filed are uncommon. When charges are filed, they tend to be for other problems like child endangerment or assault and battery of an investigating police officer. Guilty verdicts or no contest pleas are rare. Most often, if any sentence is passed, hoarders are ordered to give up animals, not get any more either temporarily or permanently, or stop breeding them. Occasionally, they are modestly fined or made to reimburse shelters for the cost of food and veterinary care. Jail time is almost never imposed, despite frequent mention of maximum sentences, such as "Helen Miller [a hoarder] could face up to 17 years in prison." In rare reports of hoarders receiving jail time, the sentence was usually for crimes having nothing to do with animals. For example, one hoarder, charged with "extreme" neglect of twenty-eight animals, was immediately jailed because of child neglect and charges of "felony child endangerment." In other cases, hoarders were sentenced to jail for contempt of court, fraud, and violation of probation.

There are many ways to explain this apparent leniency, although hoarders think it is stern to impose any limit on their animal ownership.

Certainly, hoarding—despite the numbers of animals involved and the extent of their suffering—will be overshadowed in court by the many serous crimes against humans that officials see, and hoarding is classified under the law as neglect rather than abuse, calling forth more sympathetic than punitive responses. However, a second image of hoarders in the news—that of the eccentric perhaps even mentally-ill animal owner—is most likely why their criminalization seems inappropriate.

Psychological interpretations are common in reports about hoarding. They rely on a medical model that views this behavior as an individualistic, idiosyncratic symptom of a disordered personality. Hoarding is assumed to be a psychopathologic problem and hoarders are assumed to be "sick," irrational, or at least seriously "misguided." Conjectured causes for hoarding fall short of overtly psychotic behavior (Worth and Beck 1981) but include addiction, attachment disorder, obsessive-compulsive disorder, and zoophilia (HARC 2000).

Many articles provide a quick diagnosis of animal hoarder "syndrome" by citing any authority figure present with an opinion about their motivation or behavior, including housing inspectors, firefighters, police, animal control officers, and humane officials, as well as unnamed "researchers" or "authorities." Typically, these comments lack much psychological depth, sophistication, or consistency. "Symptoms" of this "disorder" vary from article to article and are often vague and clinically questionable, such as the suggestion that a hoarder has "too much love" for animals. One article, for example, is heavily sprinkled with a journalist's and a humane official's talk about "obsession" and "addiction," at one point comparing hoarders to "tobacco addicts or shopping addicts." The effect of such popular psychologizing is to create a folk diagnosis of hoarding, in the absence of any official category for animal hoarding as a mental health problem or clinical diagnosis by trained mental health professionals.

Despite occasional references to being "crazy," "far out of reality," or "not all there," these folk diagnoses do not claim that hoarders suffer from serious mental disorders. It is far more common for articles to paint a picture of them as eccentric or "wacky," arguing that the difference between "sensible" pet owners and hoarders is that the latter "don't stop at a few dogs or even a dozen." One article, for example, portrays a hoarder of dogs, birds, foxes, guinea pigs, iguanas, and a baboon as bizarre but well meaning, calling her "a nice woman who needs a little help." The major thrust of another article is that the hoarder is an eccentric, cantankerous fake—a real "character." The article suggests that she falsified her college attendance, used a phony English accent, lied about her age, used many aliases in court, wore fake animal clothing, and earned a living as a psychic. Moreover, the article lightheartedly questions the seriousness of her neglect, asking, "Her alleged crime?" and answering, "Owning Bugsy, Vampira and their kittens." In the same light spirit, the article notes that this hoarder had been "playing cat and mouse with animal control officers for 13 years." Similarly, a reporter asked a humane official, "What drives people to take in more animals than they can handle and how [can] people spot hoarders in their neighborhoods?" to which the official replied, they have an "illness" but "they're average, normal people."

Press reports of judges' actions further the image that hoarders are not seriously disturbed. Judges rarely suggest or require counseling. Indeed, even when they allude to possible mental health problems in hoarders, they may not order or recommend therapy. In one such case, the judge simply commented, "I think it's clear you are fixated on animals. In your obsession, you really are misguided." This reticence to recommend psychological help is surprising for three reasons. First, a number of hoarders' behaviors seemed symptomatic of serious psychological disorder based on how badly they neglected their animals, homes, and themselves. Second, sometimes hoarders' own attorneys cited their clients' histories with mental illness, suggesting chronic and serious problems. And third, sometimes investigators specifically asked judges to approach hoarders as irrational or disturbed individuals.

Instead of serious mental disorder, hoarders are more often thought to have a "blind spot" that prevents them from seeing the ill effects of their basically good intentions. Many articles characterize the impulse to "save" animals as a matter of having "too much love" or "compassion." Hoarders were animal "lovers" and headlines such as "Compassion Unleashed" or "Animal Passions" emphasize this point. The text of many articles elaborate this theme. One, for example, notes, "This woman loved animals so much she could not turn them away." Another cites the hoarder's lawyer, who claimed, "This is not an animal abuse case. It's an animal loving case that went too far." Other articles claim that hoarders love their animals too much to give them up, even though they cannot care for them.

Sometimes hoarders' presumed strong love for animals is not specifically stated but implied as though a mysterious force drove them to amass animals. One hoarder explained that he had eighty-eight dogs because "it was impossible to give them away." In another case involving sixty-eight dogs and cats discovered in squalid conditions, the officers conducting the investigation said that the hoarder appeared to be unable to turn away a stray because of her feelings for animals. And in a case involving two hundred cats, a humane society representative said that the hoarder "can't seem to get rid of" the animals.

A few hoarders showed some awareness of the problem, acknowledging that their love for animals had "gotten a little out of hand." One hoarder, charged with animal neglect for failing to sufficiently feed and water forty-eight horses, ponies, and donkeys, and thirty-two dogs, wept in court, explaining that "her intentions were to save animals, but she had acquired more animals than she could handle." "Between sobs," the article reports, the hoarder "said she was sorry she had not cared for the animals properly. 'I would go hungry myself before my animals would go without.'" Similarly, a hoarder in another case said: "I have loved animals all my life and would never set out to make them suffer. But because of my stupidity and arrogance in thinking I could cope, I made these gentle creatures suffer. It is something I will never forgive myself for." And yet another hoarder admitted, "I just got a little overwhelmed. I'm just a good person whose heart was bigger than my abilities."

Given that they had so much "love" for their animals, hoarders retreated from human contact because of the enormous responsibility of caring for their charges. This retreat furthered an image of eccentricity more than mental illness. Hoarders' animals were their "only family and friends," "babies," or "children." The title of one article reads, "Dog Owner Is Told to Curtail His Collie Clan" and elsewhere refers to the hoarder's "pack." Another article points out that because the hoarder has so many animals, she does not take trips or use television or radio. A number of articles, somewhat pathetically, note that hoarders feel as though their entire purpose in life was taken away from them if their animals were seized and destroyed. "What else do I have anymore?" one hoarder said.

This blind spot casts hoarding as a minor psychological problem rather than as a serious pathology. Saying that hoarders suffer from "too much love" assumes strong positive feelings toward animals that might include nurturing and other socially sanctioned behaviors. That these feelings for animals simply went astray problematizes this behavior as an inability to control impulses that are almost admirable, and certainly not criminal. As one hoarder said, "These people act as if you have a psychological problem if you want to help animals. I did nothing illegal, yet they treat me like a common criminal." In the end, hoarders are classified by the press as a highly eccentric subset of "animal lovers" whose quirkiness falls short of full-blown mental illness.

For the most part, then, the news does not report hoarding to be a serious mental disorder. Judges almost never order psychiatric counseling for hoarders and theories of causation supplied by various authorities and experts equate their actions with everyday impulse-control problems like smoking or gambling. Indeed, these theories often provide sympathetic portrayals of hoarders as people who simply "loved animals too much," images supported by hoarders and their friends and lawyers who, when permitted, defend their actions as well meaning although excessive.

If not portrayed as seriously ill, hoarders are characterized as pathetic and sad people who live in nightmarish "squalor" that is hard for most people to comprehend. As the news describes the drama of the "worst" cases, it often concentrates on hoarders' life-styles and living conditions in ways that might elicit pity or even disgust in readers. Such a strong reaction is likely because hoarders are reported to violate taboos against excessive filth and disorder. As such, their public identity becomes more animal than human.

Articles about hoarders often paint a picture of domestic squalor. Typical headlines read, "Man Cited in Keeping 60 Labradors in Filth," "Cats Seized from Squalid Home," and "Menasha Woman Gets Jail Term for Keeping Pets in Filthy Home." The article headlined "Dog Lover Gets More Time to Clean" describes the case of a woman with 140 dogs (not reported as neglected) whose house was declared a "public nuisance" by health department officials because its floors needed scraping and scrubbing to get rid of the feces and roaches. Some of the articles noted that, in addition to being extremely unkempt and unsanitary, the hoarders' homes were abandoned, falling apart, or burned because of their owner's neglect. In one case, the hoarder had a candle on her television set that dripped on an adjacent plant that in turn ignited the television, causing it to explode, blow out the front window, and start a more general house fire.

Descriptions of stench-filled, dilapidated, run-down homes create an image of hoarders as pathetic, troubled people whose life-styles clearly separate them from prevailing community standards. Detailed descriptions are common of feces, urine, and spoiled food found throughout hoarders' homes, defying conventional cultural norms that restrict domestic animals' movement, excretion, and eating to limited and specified areas. Not merely unaesthetic and chaotic, hoarders' homes were uncivilized. Homes and yards also were littered with animal carcasses, further contributing to the image of uncivilized chaos. A few reports describe scenes of carnage and death, with animal corpses scattered throughout the hoarders' homes in varying degrees of decomposition, sometimes partially eaten by other animals. One article describes a house "covered with feces, several inches thick in places" with "dead, dying, and half eaten cats" throughout. When humane workers arrived at one home with over two hundred dogs, they found "dead dogs hanging from windows. There were pieces of bodies of dogs. Some dogs were dead in their cages. . . . Some adult dogs were feeding on puppies." Several articles report that animal cadavers were discovered in refrigerators. One, for example, reports that investigators discovered twenty-nine dead cats and a decomposed six-inch alligator in the hoarder's freezer. One bag of frozen cats was marked "S. Sauce." There was some question about whether five bags and a large pot of spaghetti sauce also in the freezer might have been made from cat meat.

The result of the urine, feces, decomposed food, and cadavers was utter chaos and "overpowering stench," as though hoarders and their animals had sunk to a level of existence that was far below civilized standards. Articles suggest that this squalor was so bad that neither humans nor animals should live in such uncivilized conditions. Rather than simply describing this squalor, media accounts usually quote humane officials, house inspectors, or firefighters who recount in graphic terms the extreme clutter and stench they encountered, how it affected them, and the steps they took to overcome it.

Officials typically report that hoarders' homes and lives are "out of control," noting that animals "overrun" homes or have "total run" of them. Two headlines make this point: "Home Found Overrun with Birds [215 birds "in cages stacked from floor to ceiling in every room"]:

Resident . . . Found Dead" and "More Than 100 Dogs Take Over Home." The text of the accompanying articles elaborates this out-of-control image. In one case, the hoarder lived in the attic because she had turned over the rest of her house to animals. Another article says, "It was like a jungle in there. They had plenty of food, but the cats were living almost one on top of the other on one floor of the house. It was appalling." In another case, an animal official claims that the house is literally "running with cats. . . . [They] were observed perched on top of appliances, living inside furniture and cabinets and ranging through the several rooms." In yet another case, cats were found living in the crevices of the walls. The animals appeared to be in control, free to do whatever they wished. Once the animals are in control, hoarders' homes lose their human nature in press reports, where they are instead described as "zoos," "menageries," or in one case a "feces clogged urban Noah's Ark" full of "strange creatures" including small birds, a wolf, foxes, hedgehogs, snakes, raccoons, guinea pigs, iguanas, fourteen dogs, and a baboon. Investigators also thought they saw an orangutan.

With animals "in control," hoarders' everyday habits appear less human. Their eating patterns, for example, could resemble those of animals. One article notes, "She eats dog food and grain along with her animals." Another article reports that the hoarder's son "has to eat in the loftier of the bunk beds to keep Spot, vaguely Dalmatian and the unquestioned leader of the pack, from picking his plate clean." Sleeping, too, became animal-like for some hoarders. Other articles describe this behavior in a hoarder who "sometimes slept" with her two hundred rabbits in "two cramped and filthy sheds," a hoarder who lived in a six-foot square rabbit hutch with her dozen cats and dogs, and a hoarder who said that she "used to sleep on the bottom bunk, . . . but I kept waking up with too many dogs on my chest. They were cutting off my air supply."

Once hoarders lost control of their animals, their squalor and subhuman status suggested their acts were more pitiful than criminal, more sad than seriously mentally ill. Indeed, it was common for the press to quote people who felt "sorry" for hoarders. For example, in one case of dozens of sick cats living in squalor, a "code compliance officer" said "he felt sorry for the 57-year-old owner of the home. . . . He said the man was probably just trying to care for stray cats and they multiplied to the point that they were no longer manageable."

Overall, then, the press presents a confused picture of hoarders, who are variously portrayed as criminal, mentally ill, or loathsome. But this inconsistency is not the press's fault. It reflects society's confusion about how to view these people. Much of what people read in the news is a distillation of how social problems are made sense of by organizations that enforce laws, rescue survivors, and otherwise intervene in these situations (Fishman 1995). Because hoarding is a relatively new and complex social problem, organizations that deal with hoarders are themselves unsure how to think about or best manage them. Although experts are reluctant to deal with hoarders, they still get involved and express opinions about what kind of person commits such chronic and severe animal neglect. In turn, journalists do their best to present these ideas, however conflicted and tentative they are, to readers of the news. The one consistency is that all the characterizations are negative, from the hoarders' perspective.

The Problem

The press has a bigger hand in shaping a different aspect of these cases. In addition to classifying the kind of person hoarders are, news coverage influences how the problem is portrayed and who should be blamed for it. Many articles appear to de-emphasize the severity of animal neglect, while some deflect blame away from hoarders.

Several articles mention animal neglect but give little detail. While there were reports of animals suffering from respiratory diseases, eye infections, heartworm, diarrhea, conjunctivitis, flu, ear mites, fleas, and malnutrition, only a few articles elaborate or emphasize these conditions. Instead, emphasis is placed on the disgusting or horrifying state of hoarders' homes and life-styles, overshadowing reports of animal suffering. There were even more superlatives used to describe squalor and uncivilized behavior than there were to describe animal suffering. And photographs of neglect were uncommon. Rare exceptions show a young horse with debris on its forelock and mane, a badly matted cocker spaniel, and a horse whose hooves were untrimmed and beginning to curl upward.

Other articles are mixed or ambiguous in their reports of animal neglect. Some note neglect in certain animals but not in others. According to the animal control officer involved in one case, nine cats were in "tough shape." "You could tell those animals were pretty sick," he said, "just by looking at them" because they had "severe ringworm" and "various respiratory ailments." Yet, 6 dogs and over 20 cats left in the home had "no serious ailments." In another case, a humane official said that the hoarder's dogs were "mistreated and badly cared for," but only 20 out of 249 seized dogs were "put down . . . because they were in extremely poor health." In other articles it is unclear how many animals were involved, how many were neglected, or what their condition was when the case broke. For instance, one reported "dead from neglect and starvation," which in its brevity could make it hard for some readers to imagine the nature and extent of suffering experienced by these animals. Another article merely says that the animals "were not cared for properly and were living in dirty cages."

And some articles make no mention of animals' poor health or suffering, describing them as healthy and active, or at least not suffering serious health problems. One such piece notes that the hoarder's ten horses and nearly one hundred ducks, turkeys, and chickens "aren't in good condition. . . . [But] most are suffering from the types of ailments you would expect from animals living without proper nutrition or medical care. None of these ailments are life-threatening." Photographs of hoarders' animals in their homes often feature animals that appear healthy and active and, less commonly, in "normal" interaction with hoarders. One article, for example, uses four photographs, all of healthy or active animals and a sign outside the hoarder's "sanctuary" reading, "Beyond These Gates Lies a Safe Haven for All of God's Creatures."

When victims get center stage in these reports, they are more likely to be human than animal. For example, child neglect by hoarders trumped animal neglect in both headlines and text. In one such article, the headline reads, "8 Children Taken from Squalid Home" and text describes a couple charged with child endangerment for letting their eight children live amid animal carcasses, excrement, and spoiled food. Toward the end of the short article, there is brief mention that the local humane society "was expected to cite the couple" because a horse and cow were found dead from neglect and starvation on their property. To some extent, these articles position animal hoarding as the cause of child endangerment or "environmental child neglect" rather than a problem in its own right. For example, one article entitled "Girl's Escape from Filthy House in Detroit Leads to Kids' Rescue: Animals and Garbage

Filled Home" details the chaotic and unsanitary mess in this home, including "clouds of fleas," animals standing in feces and urine, caged animals, broken toys, human feces, and "crumpled religious pamphlets and posters." Most of the article chronicled the "pitiful" plight of the children, who were severely neglected by their parents. A single sentence notes the condition of the animals—an undetermined number of cats, hamsters, and a guinea pig were "so diseased that they were put to sleep."

That neglected animals and their harm receive short shrift is consistent with studies showing that the news in general focuses much more on criminals than on victims (Graber 1980; Sherizen 1978). Here, the "disaster" of squalor is given much more attention and detail than animal neglect, which appears to be a less important issue or even an afterthought. Because these articles focus on the hoarder's living conditions, readers may be less horrified about animal neglect than they are about squalor. To the extent that the press can rouse public interest for new issues and problems, articles de-emphasizing animal neglect may not elicit enough horror in readers to lead them to regard hoarding as a serious problem or prompt them to take action to prevent or better manage it. There also is the possibility that the de-emphasis of animal neglect might lead some readers to question the legitimacy of shelter workers who seize and euthanize these animals.

Indeed, to some readers, the real "criminals" in these cases are humane law enforcement agents and shelter workers who are seen as insensitive and cruel to victimize hoarders by seizing their animals. Rather than eliciting public indignation toward hoarders for putting animals in this position, readers can be inflamed by the actions of agents and workers who can appear in newspaper reports to be in a rush to dispose of these animals. At least a third of the articles report that humane workers killed hoarders' animals because they were considered unadoptable in their current condition. Animals were "euthanized," "destroyed," or "put to sleep." At other times, this outcome is suggested as a possibility. For example, a few articles report that "making room" in shelters for hoarders' animals meant that humane workers "might" have to euthanize healthy shelter animals. Other articles are blunter and could easily make humane officials appear to bear total responsibility for killing these animals, even though hoarders created the problem in the first place. One headline, for example, notes "55 Cats

Given Death Penalty: Owner to Pay Up to $5000 to Try to Save 10 Other Felines."

Other elements of news reporting make it easy to blame these workers and think of them as cruel. While some articles describe the ill health of animals that apparently justified their killing, not all provide such detail and some only briefly mention animals' veterinary condition. To the uninformed reader, it may not be clear why these conditions warrant killing animals rather than having veterinary personnel treat them. For example, in one case, an animal control officer confiscated 143 dogs, "many of which were in such bad shape they had to be put to sleep right away . . . [and] many of the dogs had severe mange." It was unclear, however, exactly how many dogs were killed, whether mange was their only problem, and why mange was such a difficult problem to treat. In another case, a hoarder's 205 dogs were seized, 25 of whom were "in such bad condition that they were euthanized"; the only ill health noted, however, was that the dogs' problems ranged from "lack of food and shelter to oozing sores," conditions that would appear to be treatable. Nor is there discussion about the behavioral problems of these animals that would make their adoption unlikely, and that might make the public more sympathetic to the plight of officers and shelter workers who must deal with these animals.

And finally, articles never report humane staff members' feelings or reservations about euthanizing these animals. Without such reports, these workers might appear to be heartless or uncaring, despite the fact that they experience considerable distress over euthanasia (Arluke 1994b). In one news story, a humane official acknowledged and bemoaned this unfavorable press image, noting: "When you go to court, you're the one who looks like the bastard." While humane officials, in a few articles, acknowledge the sadness of hoarders when their animals are confiscated, most articles do not report the feelings of animal control officers about the plight of hoarders' animals—feelings that might soften the media image of these officials. In one of the few articles to describe such feelings, the animal control officer said, regarding two hundred sick rabbits confined to small, unsanitary sheds: "It made me very, very sick. Because I'm an animal lover, it made me very, very sad because they couldn't get out. They were imprisoned in there." Less emphatic was one humane official who said that the hoarder's situation was "upsetting to anyone who cares at all about animals."

Media coverage can elicit public criticism of humane societies and their employees. In one case picked up by the media, a woman with eighty cats and two dogs moved to a motel with her animals because she claimed her water pipes had burst. Since the motel permitted only one pet per rented room, the hoarder surreptitiously smuggled her animals into the room. The motel staff had no idea that the animals were there because the woman declined maid service and the animals were not inside the rooms long enough to create an odor. A motel spokesperson claimed that had the hoarder been there a full week they would have smelled the animals. Tipped off that there might be a problem, officers entered the motel room, where they found "wall to wall cats." Although one newspaper article quoted an officer as saying the cats "were quiet and friendly. Most of them didn't seem sickly," they were seized by law enforcement officers from the local humane society and taken to shelters for evaluation. One person on the scene who was not a law enforcement officer said, "It will have to be determined which cats are healthy enough to keep alive. That's their call. I would hope that the decision would be made fairly quickly so that the cats won't have to suffer." However, all were found to be extremely sick (rotted-out eyes, leukemia, respiratory illnesses, ringworm, and other parasites) with very bad prognoses, and they were unsocialized. Despite humane society press statements noting that it was always their goal to save animals and make them available for adoption, all were "destroyed" because they had an extremely low possibility of adoption even if a lot of money and time were spent on making them healthy, and they would use much-needed cage space. Media coverage alerted concerned animal people, who read the story and became outraged that the humane society would kill all of these cats. Headlines in local newspapers included, "Animals Found in Motel Destroyed."

Press coverage of this bad case created a number of problems. In one letter to the editor, an irate citizen decried the destruction of the cats, writing "It is unfortunate that the humane society, with its vast resources, felt it expedient to put these animals to death rather than treating those that might have been curable." Other people threatened to stop making donations to the society, and these threats continued for months after this news broke. Feeling the need to respond to this public outcry and criticism of the seizing of these cats and their subsequent destruction, supporters of the agents and the society wrote a number of letters to the editor and op-ed articles to defend their actions. These letters and articles reiterated the society's position that their destruction of the cats was not a cruel, heartless act but rather an act of mercy. "Our mission," a member of the society wrote, "is to help reduce animal suffering, and the cats were euthanized purely out of humaneness to them." In another response, the author tried to create some sympathy for the officers by making it clear that the hoarder victimized the animals: "It is not unusual for law enforcement officers . . . to wear protective gear to mask the stench caused by the accumulated mix of feces and urine of dozens, even hundreds of cats or dogs crammed into houses. Pathetic pictures of rescue raids show them crammed into spaces no larger than a phone booth or in stacked filthy cages often deprived of light and human companionship. Hoarders obtain their victims, for victims they are, by any means, often taking household pets that are 'let out' in the belief that they are being rescued."

Such defenses, however, may do little to allay the concern of some people that hoarders are being unfairly pressured to relinquish their animals. Indeed, in the wake of charges suggesting the culpability of agents and shelter workers, along with news that questions the extent to which animal suffering occurs in these cases, if at all, readers are likely to be confused about animal hoarding—how wrong it is and how hoarders should be seen. Further confusing readers are defenses by hoarders themselves.

SAINTLY ACCOUNTS

In the public arena, there is little room for the hoarder's voice because it is overshadowed by the opinions of various authorities whose presumed expertise trumps the occasional defense of hoarding. Nevertheless, hoarders are not passive actors who watch on the sidelines as the press constructs a confused and unflattering identity for them; instead, they confront it head on as they strive to refashion pity into praise, horror into honor. Hoarders resist professional knowledge, despite its widespread legitimacy, by reasserting who they think they are and why they believe that others "have it wrong." These presentations of self are not constructed in a social vacuum but are shaped by what hoarders learn through interaction with others. At least in a general way, they discover how society defines animal neglect and regards those accused of it. They also learn culturally derived vocabularies of motive that diminish responsibility or deny wrongdoing (Mills 1940). These excuses or justifications enable them to frame their behavior in a positive light or cast aspersions on law enforcement officials and others, just as do members of any group whose identities are questioned or stigmatized (Lyman and Scott 1970).

Given the derisiveness of "expert" views of hoarders, we would expect them to use these vocabularies of motive to counter with a more amenable self-image—one that they can live with and use in their interactions with others. They transform what others see as neglect into something positive by portraying themselves as saviors of unwanted and helpless animals for whom they make huge but worthy sacrifices so that these needy animals can have better lives. In their talk they imply that their behavior is saintly. Although hoarders merely insinuate their saintliness, it underlies and informs how they characterize their feelings about and actions toward animals.

Hoarders portray themselves as saviors who are on a rescue mission to save animals from death or euthanasia. They believe that only they come through for animals in need, seeing themselves as the last outpost for many animals that would have nowhere else to go and no one else to care for them. Most see it as a "duty" and feel "guilty" if they turn their backs. One viewed her acquisition of scores of dogs and cats as a "wake-up call" from a higher power to help animals: "Well, God, this is the way you made me. You made me to love animals and I'm proud of it. It's not something that I need to make excuses for. I don't hurt people, you know." Hoarders see homeless animals as "abused" and say, in the words of one, they "cannot live knowing that they are being abused and not taken care of." Hoarders worry, indeed a few say they are "terrified," that something tragic will happen to animals—cars will hit them or "butchers" will sell them to medical labs—if they fail to act.

For example, a man found living with sixty dogs and two cats claimed that nine dogs were his, while the remainder belonged to people who asked him to care for them. "It was a goodwill gesture. I want those animals to live. I'd rather be put to sleep myself," he said. Another hoarder of thirty-one cats said he did not take the felines to the animal shelter because he wanted to prevent their euthanasia. "I love animals and I don't feel any animal should be put to death," he said, citing religious reasons. And the owner of sixty-four pit bulls and a Rottweiler claimed: "That was my family. I took care of dogs people were trying to kill." For hoarders, then, death is an unthinkable option; any other possibility, not matter how horrific, is better for the animals.

Hoarders feel highly responsible for the welfare of animals in general by maintaining vague and shifting boundaries between their animals and others. Almost any animal they encounter can easily be seen as "their own" and one they feel an obligation to help. Their sense of responsibility also comes from having a very broad and ambiguous definition of what constitutes a "needy" animal, and therefore one that should be helped. This perspective guarantees many situations that call for their intervention. There are always strays to be found and helped or unwanted animals from friends or strangers to be taken in. Shelters, too, offer unlimited numbers of animal "projects," as one hoarder calls them, to provide homes for the unadoptable. Some hoarders even feel responsible for the welfare of wildlife in need of shelter or care. As one observes about the endless number of animals waiting for her care: "It could go on forever. If one came to my door, I'd take it in." The result is that hoarders have endless opportunities to feel selfless, and they take advantage of many.

Hoarders provide dramatic accounts of rescuing and caring for animals. Their talk becomes very animated when they describe how much effort, emotion, patience, time, and money went into saving tragically injured, sick, or troubled animals that survive dire conditions. One hoarder recounted staying up all night to nurse stray kittens and another detailed how she followed one of her feral cats into its underground burrow and took food to it for over a month until it decided to come out. These excursions to save the cat from starving to death left the hoarder infested with fleas that she passed on to other people in her home. For weeks another hoarder nursed a dog with a broken pelvis, convinced that the local shelter would immediately destroy it if given the opportunity.

Many hoarders portray themselves as operating shelter or rescue organizations. One hoarder claimed that she performed a "community service by taking in stray animals" and "saved quite a few lives of some of those cats." Several said that they were trying to place some or many of their animals in other homes, only temporarily keeping them until these arrangements could be made. In one case in which eighteen emaciated dogs were seized from a home, the hoarder explained to authorities that she was starting her own humane society. Sometimes they claimed to do this because existing shelters provided poor animal care in their opinion. A hoarder of more than twenty-four dogs told reporters that after she rescues dogs from bad "pounds," she gives them shots and adequate nutrition. Other hoarders specifically use "no-kill" terminology to describe their animal work. When thirty-nine cats were discovered living in horrible conditions, the hoarder said she was trying to establish a no-kill shelter. "I am not a collector, people said I was a collector because I refused to associate with shelters that euthanize." By claiming to be rescue or humane organizations, hoarders frame their acts as kind hearted and benevolent, caring for animals that no one else will help or save. They tell themselves, and others, that their behavior is reasonable or, in some instances, morally admirable.

In keeping with their saintly presentation, hoarders make many sacrifices to rescue animals. In their own eyes, they are what Rosenhan (1970) calls autonomous altruists, or those who, to a much greater degree than others, forgo many things and undergo great labor to aid people, or in this instance animals. Those who believe the hoarders' efforts at self-presentation might view hoarders in a positive light (Heckert 2003) and offer them social approval because hoarding, like the behavior of saints and good neighbors (Sorokin 1950) or the unselfishness of heroes (Scarpitti and McFarlane 1975), involves self-sacrifice and does not threaten society. However, it is more likely that even if hoarders' accounts are believed by others, they will still be regarded negatively because their sacrifices are so extreme.

One hoarder calls such sacrifices her "hardship" and lists not being able to go far from home, never having a clean and neat house or yard, never having undamaged material possessions, and having no social life. Another hoarder laments her inability to travel on vacation because no one can take care of her many animals and because she would never use a kennel; another cites the inability to have a "neat" house and yard because of her animals' habits, another the loss of her antique furniture and hand-knotted rugs because of urine saturation, and yet another the fact that the potent smell of her cats prevents visitors, including her best friend and sister, from entering her home. Indeed, several hoarders say that they miss their human friendships, although animal friendships replace them. In short, they diminish their horizons and forgo their desires, except those related to animals. Like saints, they eschew worldly wants and personal possessions in the name of having many unfettered animals. Spurning worldly or middle-class desires for the greater good of helping animals echoes the belief in communist societies that renouncing the strife for individual property benefits others, though the one benefits animals and the other humans. To hoarders, curtailing everyday pleasures for the sake of their animals is not a political statement, it is just something that is seen as "more worthwhile." As one hoarder says, she would rather spend all of her money on her animals than on herself.

One sacrifice, withdrawing from the social life of the community, is justified as necessary to protect animals from seizure by authorities. Hoarders explain, sometimes accurately, that humane law enforcement agents or animal control officers disapprove of their treatment of animals and want to remove them from their homes. They describe constant attacks by aggressive and insensitive officials, implying that the problem rests with those who seek to take their animals rather than with themselves. "Demonic" was the description of one local humane society. "I give those cats the best food money can buy. Whenever I'm away I have people taking care of the cats. Those people [humane society] are just out to ruin me. . . . All was going well until the humane society moved in." Feeling harassed, one hoarder proclaimed, "Why don't they just leave us alone?" Another hoarder insisted that a humane agent threatened her, "saying he would get me and all of these animals would be euthanized." And another frustrated hoarder said, "They've been on us like locusts. . . . He [a town official] just says anything. I have no sick or miserable animals here. . . . We're doing our level best."

They are victims, according to hoarders and their supporters. Friends of one hoarder considered her to be a "victim of constant hounding from county officials and neighboring ranchers—adversaries who color her strange for devoting her life to helping wayward animals." A neighbor defended another hoarder as someone who is eccentric but loves animals: "He's kind of different and sometimes people try to take advantage of him. In this case, he's kind of getting railroaded. It seems like the humane society is on a witch hunt." Hoarders claimed that officials or humane societies had personal vendettas against them. In a case where more than 150 dogs, 14 cats, 3 monkeys, and a pregnant pot-bellied pig were discovered living in squalid conditions, the hoarder charged that she was being harassed without reason. She

claimed that police bruised her wrists and breasts and treated her elderly mother with no respect. "For 12 hours I sat in jail, treated like a
criminal," she said.

Feeling unfairly persecuted by those who endanger their social world
with animals, hoarders tragically depict what would happen if authorities seized animals. These declarations testify to the importance of keeping their animals and the harm of losing them. A few even threaten to
kill themselves or others if their animals are taken.

In response to perceived persecution hoarders adopt a siege
mentality, hiding from their neighbors and the community at large.
One confided that she erected a seven-foot stockade fence as much to
keep people out as to keep animals in. By having a low profile, they
hope to keep secret the numbers of animals they have and the unsight-
liness of their property. Loss of social life, although psychologically
costly, is one more worthy sacrifice in their eyes, although to some
extent this low profile continues a life-long withdrawal from social
interaction in general.

With an attitude of saintly martyrdom, hoarders bemoan these sacrifices but point out that it is not worth having nice furniture or taking
long vacations if they come at their animals' expense. What they give
up is justified in their opinion because they can do so much for animals.
As one says, her sense of worth and happiness comes from "making
their crummy lives decent." And they claim that animals do so much
for them, even becoming their social life. In the words of a hoarder:
"We just get our friendship from the animals. We don't miss the human
friendship because we are always with the animals."

Hoarders resign themselves to these sacrifices and normalize them
in their lives. Best typifying this attitude is one person who ceded her
kitchen to thirty cats so they could have it as their territory for eating,
playing, and excreting. She, nevertheless, still used the kitchen, at great
inconvenience from an outsider's perspective but not hers. The woman
grew accustomed to—in fact advocated the benefits of—no longer sitting down for meals in the kitchen, and instead merely stood at the
open refrigerator door and quickly grazed on whatever she grabbed
"to get it over with," while her son had grown comfortable taking his
food out of the refrigerator and closing himself in the adjoining bath-
room with a hotplate and a juicer so that their cats would not interrupt
his meals and soil his food, plates, and utensils.

Normalizing sacrifices leads hoarders to relinquish their human identity and become animalized. That their identity can be so profoundly affected is unsurprising, given the importance of animals to hoarders; it shapes who they think they are and how they behave. At one extreme are those who take on animal alters, although this falls short of the alternate animal personalities experienced by individuals with multiple-personality disorders (Hendrickson, McCarty, and Goodwin 1990).

Their animalization inverts the traditional priority placed on human concerns over those of animals, with greater importance placed on the latter. One hoarder showed an awareness of this inversion after a fire in her home killed some of her animals: "I wanted to die because I felt that I just wanted to be with them. It's funny that you would want to be with your pets more than your husband and kids but that's how I felt [near crying]. We lived near a lake. For a long time, I wanted to walk into the lake and drown." She also recalled a dream about another fire that gutted her home and some of the animals in it. "I said to my son, 'Oh thank God the dogs are okay.' You know, most people would say, 'Oh, your house didn't burn down.'" Inversion is also revealed when hoarders weigh the relative importance of human and animal life. Responding to a local tragedy where a woman killed her eighteen-month-old child and pets, the hoarder said: "When people say, 'did you hear about that girl who killed her baby and her dogs,' I would hear about that lady who killed her dogs and her baby. Do you follow me? I've got to watch myself because people who don't understand me might think that I don't value human life, which is not true. But to me, it was more devastating that she killed her dogs." Sometimes this inversion is over more prosaic priorities. For example, one hoarder said: "When I punch the clock at night I don't think I'm going home to see my husband and kids. I think I'm going home and little Betty is going to be there and we're going to go out for a walk. She understands me."

This inversion resets the authority relationship between humans and animals, giving hoarders, compared with most pet owners in American society, much less control over animals. They relinquish some of their autonomy and decision-making ability, indeed a substantial amount in a few cases, for the sake of their animals' needs and whims and because they see their animals as having the right, like humans, to be free and exercise choice. One hoarder goes so far as to say that her animals "run" her life; another asserts that "their needs" determine everything she does.

Hoarders do not train animals and impose few rules on them so their authentic personalities can emerge. As one said: "I give them a lot more freedom than rules. I don't expect them to be something or anything in particular for me. I pretty much let them be who they are." By not regulating the behavior of animals, hoarders compromise the quality of their daily lives from the perspective of general community standards. For example, they might make one or two rooms off-limits to animals, but even these supposedly sequestered rooms are often overrun, disordered, and soiled by animals. Hoarders also hope to confine their animals' elimination to certain rooms, although typically there are scores of dirty litter boxes throughout houses and "mistakes" are common. In some cases, the floors of every room are completely soiled. Animals also may be allowed free run of kitchens, even when humans try to eat, resulting in massive swarming of both people and food. With no effort to train them or control their behavior, some hoarders strive to maintain a "peaceable kingdom" among their animals by monitoring and managing their aggressive behavior so that fellow animals are not harmed.

By not controlling their animals, hoarders challenge the cultural category of pet and the treatment of animals as lesser creatures. In fact, many flatly deny that they regard their animals as pets. As one hoarder maintains, people should not treat their animals as humanlike and "love" only a few. Although some hoarders claim to have a few "favorite" animals, and they can often identify many by name, they tend to relate to their animals as though they have a corporate identity rather than interacting with them as traditional pets. Not surprisingly, some hoarders admit they rarely play with their animals, also blaming this on the volume of animals or the difficulty of interacting with feral cats.

From the hoarders' perspective, having many animals is not a leisure pursuit, distinguishing them from people who collect things as hobbies. Of course, like hoarders, hobbyists can be deeply committed to their activities, but they do not lose sight of the fact that they are pursing leisure. And like hoarders, some hobbyists are involved in morally controversial activities; gun collectors, for example, are forced to develop various accounts and justifications for their interests to deal with public reproach for what they find fun to do (Eddy 1988). But they are hobbies rather than missions; passions rather than obsessions; diversions rather than causes.

According to hoarders, regular pet owners are hobbyists because their involvement with animals is just about "love" rather than part of a larger mission to care for them. Having companions is not the issue for hoarders. Some say that their feelings for animals "go beyond love." "I have a feeling," one said, "that you need to protect them because the need is great. You certainly can't keep them out there by themselves to fend for themselves. You can't do that." As another hoarder says about the dog her sister's family kept: "They have love, it's like their child. There's a lot of people that will love their animals and treat it like a human— there's a distinction, though. I mean, it's just not love, it's a caring, it's something deep."

Far from their image of pet owners, then, hoarders' saintly self-presentations starkly contrast with the press's negative portrayal of them as criminal, mentally ill, or pitiful. No doubt, these contradictory images can confuse more than clarify the reader's understanding of animal hoarding. Readers are likely to react to this inconsistent mix of information with shock and horror, but also with fascination. Understanding why readers might be fascinated points to an unexpected use of news stories about cruelty.

NEWS AS RITUAL MORAL EXERCISE

The allure to readers of the upside-down and out-of-control world of hoarders is similar to the appeal of crime news in general. The value of these stories comes from their ability to raise questions and doubts about the social order rather than from their celebration of society's triumph over deviance and disorder. By raising fundamental questions about everyday existence, these stories can connect to and bear on reader's own lives and problems. They do this by providing material for a "ritual moral exercise" where, according to Katz (1987, 67), readers reflect on and mull over issues of personal competence and sensibilities that are often dramatized in crime news. From this reflection, people develop a moral perspective that can help them deal with the fear of miscalculating their own and others' abilities.

This moral exercise, however, can do more than merely shore up questions of competence. Crime news also raises issues about personal and collective identity that key into everyday fears about how well people fit into their neighborhoods or work scenes, as well as more existential concerns about what makes them any better than anyone else. All of us, not just hoarders, face questions of belonging and identity. While the news will not tell readers who they are or how they are different from others, it provides the fodder to develop a perspective that will do so. This perspective is formed as readers locate themselves within a repertoire of emplotted stories. Such identity work is an ongoing dynamic between individuals and culture, or in this case readers and the news, where people come to know who they are by first comparing themselves with others and then by either excluding or including them in their own group.

Hoarding stories raise doubts about the sanctity of the social order. American values and beliefs that are assumed to be taken for granted cannot be, at least when it comes to hoarders. Thus, through these stories the media does not reproduce the status quo, as do other institutions (e.g., Foley 1990), but challenges it. Readers are reminded that things are not always the "way they ought to be" in society. Specifically, reports about hoarders question the endurance and importance of conventional values regarding human-animal relationships, domestic life, and civil obligation.

For one, news stories detail behaviors that blur interspecies boundaries, with hoarders routinely crossing lines that many people expect and uphold when it comes to presumed differences between humans and other animals. Indeed, their acts often violate taboos about inappropriate behavior toward animals. As they do so, hoarders become animalized, abandoning trappings associated with modern, civilized life. And these boundary crossings are likely to disturb many readers, despite growing interest in according animals ever higher moral status in society, whether by improving welfare standards, acknowledging sentience and intelligence, or granting legal rights (Franklin 1999).

These reports rarely reassure readers about this phylogenetic breech of the social order or reaffirm the traditional place of animals in society by clarifying moral and social distinctions between species. One story that did, however, involved a hoarder who allegedly owned fifty-four starving and dehydrated dogs and cats along with five dead cats, some of which were being consumed by other cats. The article suggests that the court's failure to punish this hoarder was due to the lesser social value of animals compared with that of humans. When the defendant argued that her animals "were like my children," the judge retorted: "If these were your children, you'd be going to jail for a long time." Of course, other reasons could account for this courtroom response; judges' inaction may reflect the fact that animal cruelty is considered only a misdemeanor in many states and that animal hoarding as a psychological problem is poorly understood at present.

Middle-class norms also are commonly violated in news stories about hoarding, assaulting what mainstream America holds dear when it comes to standards of cleanliness and order, friendliness and civic duty, responsibility and moderation (e.g., Tittle and Paternoster 2003; Wolfe 1998). Details of hoarders' life-styles defile what many readers assume is minimally civilized behavior in modern society. Indeed, their denial of middle-class morality is so extreme, readers might have almost a prurient interest in these reports because the behavior of hoarders verges on being a class obscenity.

For example, middle-class expectations dictate that one has the right to privacy and exclusive control of personal items, while still being minimally responsible to oneself, one's dependents, and one's home. However, generally assumed standards of cleanliness and order (Hoy 1996), even when generously defined, are routinely violated in articles about hoarding. Reports also portray hoarders as irresponsible to family members, whether human or animal. Certainly, accusing hoarders of extreme animal neglect and abuse points to their violation of this norm; they have taken advantage of their privacy to harm others. And there are occasional reports of elderly parents or children who suffer neglect as well.

Also, there are middle-class norms for being neighborly and civil. Yet reports show hoarders disregarding the presence of others when it comes to maintaining physical property and the surrounding environment. They infringe on the lifestyles of neighbors, for example, when the dilapidation of their homes and yards spreads next door or their animals' defecation and destruction results in unpleasant sounds, sights, or smells that easily offend those nearby. Hoarders also withdraw from neighborhood social life. Many accounts detail their clandestine ways, describing them as loners or reclusive people. They are guilty of alienation, having no acceptable excuse.

A final example is the middle-class norm that encourages moderation over excessiveness. The numbers of animals kept by hoarders and the disarray of their homes grossly violate public expectations for the prosaic and moderate. Such practices tread on the belief that extremes of any kind are unacceptable. Even their apparent lying seems immoderate; there are middle-class limits for tolerating deceitfulness, including the scale or extent of lying. Cover-ups that involve double lives, especially if the weak and helpless are exploited or harmed, are condemned. The very claim by hoarders that their actions are altruistic if not saintly is itself an affront to the value placed on honesty, and may be seen as an admission of glaring irrationality that does not hold them in better steed.

Throughout these reports of species and class violations there is a lack of closure. Society does not triumph over this form of deviance and restore the social order. There is no great celebration or relief because hoarders have been caught; various authorities seem puzzled about how to deal with them, or even how to categorize them, and sometimes there is public outrage directed at law enforcement agencies or shelters. Reading articles about hoarders gives the impression that they rarely appear in court and those who do are rarely punished, except for having future ownership of animals restricted, being required to undergo counseling, or being forced out of their homes to cleaner and safer locations. In part, this impression is due to the style of reporting crime news. "Breaking" stories that cover the apprehension of deviants and early criminal proceedings are favored over those that report trial outcomes. It also is due to the reluctance to impose sentences on hoarders either because the "crime" or "illness" is thought to be unserious or because court officials and other authorities are unsure how best to manage this problem.

The lack of closure leaves these reports raising more questions about the integrity of the social order than providing a sense of moral consensus or resolution. If they do not reassure readers, then what is their appeal? What is in them that readers find interesting to consider? Certainly, as a form of crime news, there is nothing to be gained. There is no information that can protect readers from harm, since few are likely to live near hoarders; and in the unlikely chance that some do, nothing is provided that can reduce the threat of harm to them. Indeed, it is not clear in the latter case that there is any danger posed other than possible damage to neighborhood aesthetics or real estate values.

Nevertheless, the public finds these news stories interesting at a personal level. There are moral tales within these reports that enable readers to work through existential dilemmas relating to boundaries thought to separate them from other people and animals. These reports provoke readers to ask questions about what it means to be human and civilized, to be a good and responsible neighbor, a fit parent or animal owner—questions far removed from the content of the news stories but close to their own anxieties and worries. How far should I go in trying to befriend the family next door? Am I going a little "overboard" by caring too much for my two cats? Does it really matter if I keep my lawn so well manicured? Why do I want certain things and not others? What do I keep secret and would others care to know? Do any of my actions harm others? And in asking and then answering these questions readers can sustain their belief that their own identities, as well as their place in society, are beyond reproach.

SAINTLINESS AND PERSONAL ORDER

Hoarders, too, are working through dilemmas they face in their everyday lives—dilemmas relating to the need to balance chaos with order, instability with stability. That their saintly presentation provides this balance stems from the nature of animal hoarding as opposed to so-called rational hoarding. Rational hoarding has been observed in periods of uncertainty and scarce resources caused by economic failure or military siege. During the Great Depression in the United States, hoarding was a way to cope with the inability to obtain needed goods. The fear engendered by uncertainty and scarcity even continued among depression-era survivors whose acquisition of material objects was less rational. A similar response to uncertainty and deprivation has been reported among those who withstand prolonged military invasion, like the residents of Stalingrad who faced an extended attack on their city by German soldiers, or those who have been forcibly ghettoized, like the citizens of Warsaw in the Second World War.

Animal hoarding's use is similar to the use of hoarding inanimate objects by people confined in institutions. In such circumstances, acquiring material objects is an identity-creating device that gives order, stability, and continuity to otherwise shapeless identities (Csikszentmihalyi and Rochberg-Halton 1981). People who are uprooted from familiar places, and find themselves powerless, disoriented, and without possessions, can hoard objects to rebuild a new sense of self. Prisoners, for example, go to great lengths to acquire and keep almost anything following their dislocation from the outside world. Some of these acquisitions are rational, for example, if the item can be bartered or refashioned into a useful object, but acquisitions also allow prisoners to reestablish their identities by having something—and all the better if they and others regard the objects as important. Likewise, patients in mental institutions often become "pack rats" as a way to form an identity in a place that strips away their former selves without replacing them with new ones (Goffman 1961). The more possessions one acquires, the more identity one can amass under such deprived and changed circumstances. This is also true for uprooted survivors of natural disasters and for people placed in nursing homes who discover the meaning and use of possessions only after they are lost (e.g., Erikson 1976).

Most hoarders fit this profile, having psychological and social histories beginning in childhood that are chaotic, anomic, and marginal (Worth and Beck 1981). The vast majority report feelings of insecurity and disruptive experiences in early life, including frequent relocations, parental separation and divorce, and isolation from peers. As adults, they tend to be single, employed part-time, and without close ties to friends, neighbors, community organizations, or larger social institutions. Animals are for hoarders their primary or only connection to others, albeit nonhuman.

Amassing large numbers of animals reproduces and reinforces their earlier chaotic and marginal life. The disorder and isolation, however, can provide order and purpose in the personal lives of hoarders only if they define their activities in socially desirable ways. Accounts of saintly behavior toward animals provide a bridge to a larger culture that praises extreme instances of helping others, especially when they come at great cost to the helpers. Consumed by their consumption, hoarders build their saintly self-images in ways that transform what others see as appalling neglect into something that feels more familiar than strange, more comforting than distressing, more kind than cruel.

4   Shelter Workers

Finding Authenticity

Euthanasia did make my day go a little bit easier. My shelter ran very smoothly and efficiently. And then, after the fact just to resolve the cognitive dissonance in your head, you would say, well, it's infinitely better to kill them then to have them confined in cages for months. But if you do this you are needlessly killing animals that could be rehomed. That doesn't feel right to me. We didn't go into this business to be cruel. A shelter worker is not a killer.
—Former "euthanasia technician"

HOW DOES ONE BECOME an authentic person? "We would all like to know," the sociologist Edwin Schur wrote in 1976. "Getting in touch" with one's "true" or "inner" self preoccupied many people in the 1970s era of personal growth and the awareness movement. The standard litany assumed that a real self or true identity exists and can be discovered if only we "take charge of ourselves" and "learn to be real." Pursuing one's inner self offered people excitement and hope of personal change and renewal, leading to a cultlike enthusiasm for authenticity. Yet according to Schur (1976), this hope was illusory because no true self existed; in the end we are but a collection of social roles.

Whether illusory or not, the notion of authenticity survived this age of analysis and became more than simply a cult word. In recent decades, many groups experienced authenticity controversies, believing that their behaviors betrayed how they wanted to see themselves. Racial and ethnic groups have sought to express their "true" selves, aiming to cast off unwanted identities attributed by more powerful groups to those with less power. Nor have questions of authenticity been limited to ethnicity and race. Those asking what it means to be a man, a Christian, or a disabled person also have challenged traditional views of who they are supposed to be. All of these challenges reflect the construction, reconstruction, and deconstruction of identity and community, and the search for "false faces" that preoccupies postmodern society (Nagel 2000).

Throughout much of the twentieth century, a nagging sense of inauthenticity has plagued workers in animal shelters and produced a caring-killing paradox (Arluke 1994b). On one hand, they have a core professional identity of being humane, good-hearted "animal people" who want the very best for their charges. Most have histories of owning multiple pets and of being supernurturers, caring for stray and injured animals while feeling a strong attachment to animals in general (Arluke 2001). Not surprisingly, many choose shelter work to be in the presence of animals, whose companionship they highly value, while pursuing with passion their personal and professional mission to improve the welfare of animals. On the other hand, people in animal shelters destroy millions of animals each year for lack of space or because of ill health. Workers have always detested this work because it seems wrong to euthanize so many animals that could be kept alive if only adopters were found and because the act itself is so antithetical to their "nature." Killing animals, unless they are suffering egregiously, is deeply disturbing and counter-instinctive to shelter workers.

Never actually referred to as inauthenticity, scholars have spoken about the "moral stress" of those who euthanize animals (Rollin 1988) and researchers have documented this tension (Owens, Davis, and Smith 1981; White and Shawhan 1996). First-person reports of this stress are common in magazine articles about shelter workers—sometimes called "euthanasia technicians"—who lament the killing of animals and feel that this act is contrary to their nature as animal lovers. Nonetheless, they learn to live with this unpleasant task as an inevitable feature of their jobs by relying on various institutional coping devices that reduce the stress and normalize killing (Arluke 1994b). Typically, shelter workers see themselves as compassionate people who put animals out of misery in a humane way while blaming the general public for causing the killing (Frommer and Arluke 1999). Most shelter workers deny that their killing or "euthanasia" is cruel and do not see it in the same light as harm rendered to animals in laboratories or farms, even when they euthanize animals that might be adoptable, let alone those that are young, attractive, and healthy. They just see no other option for handling the enormous numbers of animals brought to shelters. Workers are thus able to maintain their humane, animal-person identity, despite their euthanizing animals or even because they do, and thus distinguish themselves from other institutional workers whose humane identities are either suspect or nonexistent.

Until the past decade, shelter workers could sustain their humane image because little if any organized criticism claimed that euthanizing was cruel. When criticism occurred it tended to be case-specific, focusing on which animals were euthanized and how the euthanizing was done. Individuals in the community who were distressed by euthanasia informally communicated their concern to shelter workers. Negative comments came mainly from passing remarks made by friends or strangers who lamented the killing of animals and lauded the "nice" shelters that did not euthanize. Even apparently positive remarks intended to be empathetic, such as "I could never do your job," were often taken as slams against the humaneness of shelter workers. In this context, the dominant paradigm in the shelter community defined euthanasia as a necessary evil because animals were considered unadoptable or there was insufficient space to house them. Although a few shelters offered an alternative to this paradigm by restricting admission of unadoptable animals and billing themselves as "no-kill" shelters, they did not represent a serious threat to the continuation of "open-admission" thinking about euthanasia where virtually all animals were taken but some were euthanized because the shelter lacked sufficient cage space or considered them to be unadoptable.

A change began in 1994 when the Duffield Family Foundation created the Maddie's Fund, which, through the lure of financial support, sought to revolutionize the status and well-being of companion animals by championing the "no-kill" movement. Some shelters have embraced the "no-kill" philosophy and have become the vanguard of this movement, designating entire cities (most notably, San Francisco and Ithaca, New York) or entire states (such as Utah) as "no-kill." No longer possible to ignore or discount as an outrageous idea, this movement has spurred debate at the national level about the proper role of euthanasia in shelter practice.

Criticism of euthanasia has steadily mounted in frequency and fervor from within certain segments of the sheltering community, challenging the idea that euthanasia is humane and raising the suspicion that those doing it might be cruel to animals and themselves. Indeed, more than mere suspicion, 2003 saw the first court case involving a shelter worker charged with cruelty because she euthanized seven cats as part of her job that might have otherwise been adopted. The accused, nicknamed "Killer Kelly" by some of her co-workers, was thought to have been too quick to euthanize these animals, ignoring posted notes by her peers to "not kill the kittens!" In her defense, Kelly said that although overcrowding often left her no choice but to euthanize animals, the decisions were heart-wrenching and made only after supervisors approved them (Murray 2003).

While both open-admission and no-kill advocates abhor euthanasia, their views on killing are different because they rest on different conceptions of the fundamental "problem." Open-admission shelter workers see the problem as an animal problem—one of managing pet overpopulation, and argue that the no-kill approach does not solve this problem but instead shifts the responsibility for euthanasia to another shelter or agency. So the problem still stands. No-kill advocates see the fundamental problem as a person problem—one of changing shelter work so that workers can have a professional identity uncontaminated by the contradictions posed from conducting frequent euthanasia, especially if they are animals seen as potentially adoptable. Evidence of this changing emphasis from animals to people can be seen in the public justifications of shelters that have abandoned their prior open-admission/euthanasia policies for no-kill approaches. When the ASPCA (American Society for the Prevention of Cruelty to Animals) did so, the *New York Times* headline proclaimed: "A.S.P.C.A. Plans to Give Up Job Killing New York Strays." The text elaborated: "Killing stray dogs and cats has obscured its mission—and its image. . . . The society has backed away from killing, which it calls animal control. 'Philosophically, it's a nightmare to kill 30,000 to 40,000 animals a year . . . [and] that's not our mission' [a spokesman for the ASPCA was quoted as saying]. . . . Being perceived as an animal killer has . . . saddled it with an image far different from the one it wants—that of an animal care and adoption agency" (Hicks 1993, B14).

The result is that tension has mounted within the shelter community between two apparent camps advocating either open-admission or no-kill. To be clear, these tensions are not new to the humane community. They always have existed, lurking in the cultural background of shelters and animal control offices everywhere. The difference now is that because of the no-kill movement, these doubts, concerns, and questions have been brought to center stage to be challenged and reconsidered by some, defended and explained by others. To wit, one article about this polarization entitled "Killing Ourselves Over the Euthanasia Debate" catalogues "hurtful criticisms" lobbed by each side "accusing the other of not caring for animals in the 'right' way" (Dowling and Stitely 1997, 4). Although some argue that virtually everyone in this debate is passionately concerned about the welfare of animals, the rift dividing the shelter community over this issue seems to widen daily.

This controversy defies a quick fix because it touches on the defining issue of what it means to be a shelter worker. Identities turn on core themes about how people regard themselves. For shelter workers that core theme is about the importance of being "humane." Nothing defines these workers more powerfully than their interest in and concern for the welfare of animals. Nothing strikes these workers as more contrary to their identities than the accusation that they might be inhumane or cruel to animals.

No-kill followers see themselves as forging or "rediscovering" their humane identity in contrast to open-admission workers who they feel "have forgotten our mission and are lost in the overwhelming job of . . . euthanasia." They talk about coming to the realization that the work of open-admission shelters "is not the work of a 'humane' society'" (*Best Friends Magazine* 2001, 17). Carrying out euthanasia is thought to be an "endlessly demoralizing activity" that stops workers from focusing on their "core purpose: bringing an end to the killing of these animals" (*Best Friends Magazine* 2001, 16). Open-admission shelters, it is argued, need to rethink their mission and identity so they can become no-kill themselves and "get out of the killing business."

No-killers forge this identity by leaving behind euthanasia and suggesting that open-admissionists are cruel for continuing to euthanize. These challenges have strained the ability of conventional shelters and humane organizations to protect workers psychologically from the charge that euthanasia is a form of cruelty. Instead of preventing cruelty, which their mission maintains, they are now seen as causing it. How do no-killers use the implication of cruelty as a way to reclaim emotions long gone and the kind of identity these feelings create? Although the charge that euthanasia is cruel is foremost an animal issue, at another level the charge is about what shelter workers should or should not feel. It is about caring for animals the way animal people ought to in the eyes of no-kill proponents. They are tired of feeling guilty because they kill animals, tired of having so little hope for animals, and tired of holding back their attachments to animals for fear of being hurt. In short, no-killers deny that they are "animal killers" and strive to get back in touch with feelings they consider to be "natural" for anyone who cares about animals and wants desperately to rescue those in need. This chapter focuses on how the accusation of cruelty becomes a stepping stone for no-killers to find and experience their authentic self, and the feelings that go with it.

Escaping Blame

For much of the twentieth century shelter workers felt blamed by the public for euthanizing animals. To reduce their own guilt and uneasiness, workers turned around and blamed society for euthanasia because it created the pet overpopulation problem (Frommer and Arluke 1999). Workers complained that they had to "clean up" after irresponsible pet owners who "surrendered" their animals without good reason, overburdening and overcrowding shelters that were then forced to euthanize animals for reasons of space or economy. In the words of one frustrated staff member: "Society teaches the public that they can throw their animals away. Shelters perform the incredibly difficult and draining task of cleaning up after a society that holds life in low esteem."

No-killers, however, by seeing euthanasia as a form of cruelty, have shifted blame away from themselves to their open-admission peers. They have accomplished this shift by creating oppositional identities that allow them to cling to the implication or assertion that they are not cruel, while open-admissionists are. No-killers fashion oppositional identities out of what for many years was an ambiguous and confused image of shelter workers. One worker's recognition that "open-admission shelters make it possible for limited admission shelters to exist" acknowledges the identity-conferring power of creating an antithetical self. Open-admissionists are what no-killers are not. One kind of shelter worker is cruel, the other humane. One is to be blamed, the other not. To admit otherwise would be to blur distinctions between themselves and open-admissionists, endangering their quest for authenticity.

Making Accusations

One way for no-killers to create oppositional identities is to accuse open-admissionists of cruelty. At one level, the charge is indirect. No-kill workers portray open-admissionists as complicit because they make it "easy" for the public to handle their animals like unwanted consumer goods that can be disposed of without forethought. As one no-kill worker points out: "They [open-admission shelters] are teaching the public they can throw away their animals at the shelter and the shelter will euthanize their problem for them and they aren't to blame because they took the pet to the shelter." This charge insinuates that open-admissionists are cruel because they help to end the lives of animals that should or could be adopted into loving homes.

At another level, the charge is more direct. Certain methods of euthanasia, it is argued, are deemed cruel because they cause animals to suffer. For example, critics of a shelter that uses carbon monoxide to kill animals consider this form of euthanasia to be morally "wrong" and "cruel" because "the animal is crying out in pain or fear," and it sees other animals dying (Gilyard 2001, 6–7). Also branded as cruel is death by lethal injection, the contemporary standard for "humane" euthanasia. Although critics point to instances when animals suffer because of improper injection technique or psychological distress from sensing their own or other animals' deaths, more generally, euthanasia by definition is considered cruel because most animals, it is thought, should and could be kept alive and adopted with proper care.

These accusations, according to open-admissionists, have tainted their identity. As one worker explained, who was feeling morally tainted because she and her co-workers "kill" animals: "We have been devoting years to helping animals, so why am I and my organization now an enemy? Why do we have to defend ourselves now? It used to be the humane societies versus the pounds, who were the baddies. Now we are the baddies." As the "baddies," open-admission workers feel that they have been "looked down upon" (Milani 1997), "discredited" (Bogue 1998b), or "guilty" because they have been labeled as "murderers . . . sadists, or monsters" (R. Caras, personal communications, July 9, August 21, 1997). Moreover, some claim that with the growing popularity of the no-kill concept, the public has joined the bandwagon to castigate them as bad people for euthanizing animals. One open-admission defender had an experience that illustrates this worsening public sentiment. He reported that while marching in a local community's parade, he was shocked when an angry onlooker yelled at him, "You killed my cat!" merely because his sweatshirt bore the name of a well-known "kill" shelter.

Manipulating Language

No-killers reinforce their accusations by manipulating language to suggest that they are humane and that open-admissionists are cruel. "No-kill" is a weighty symbol for what it suggests about shelter workers who "kill." Use of this term can make open admissionists feel "put-down" as killers (Bogue 1998a). Indeed, those who question no-kill are concerned that the terminology itself positions open admissionists as "pro-kill" (P. Paris, New York ASPCA interoffice memo, September 24, 1997), making them uncomfortable if not angry. "Open admission shelters are not 'kill' shelters anymore than 'pro-choicers' are 'pro-abortion,'" one open-admission advocate explained. Unsurprisingly, the open-admission shelters have called for an end to the term "no-kill" by substituting terms such as "low kill" and "limited admission" (Arnold n.d.) or, less seriously, "rarely-kill" (J. Morris and L. Saavedra, personal communication, September 16, 1997) and "you-kill" (Miller n.d.).

No-killers also draw careful linguistic distinctions between euthanasia and killing. One no-kill spokesperson argues that open-admission organizations "kill healthy animals" (Foro 1997, 16) and that in doing so they misrepresent the real meaning of euthanasia. Elaborating, she writes that use of the term euthanasia for "the destruction of healthy animals softens the reality and lessens its impact on the public. Sadly, to mislabel killing as euthanasia for controlling animal overpopulation does not allow society to deal with the tragedy or to accept responsibility for making this happen" (Foro 1997, 17). On one hand, no-killers also claim that euthanasia, if not for population control, is the wrong term for owner-requested "killing." On the other hand, "true," "authentic" or "dictionary-defined" (Foro 1997, 17) euthanasia, as opposed to killing, is mandated for extreme, untreatable, chronic suffering in the lives of animals. Open-admission advocates reject this distinction, claiming that it is mere "semantics."

Language also is used in no-kill rhetoric to blame open-admission shelters for killing animals in ways that evoke "Nazi" cruelties to humans. One such accusation labels the open-admission approach to the pet overpopulation problem as the "final solution," a term fraught with Nazi and holocaust associations. Similarly, highly provocative references to the Nazi era were used during several panel discussions at a national no-kill conference. Stirring the audience's emotions, one presenter spoke about the "holocaust of family members [i.e., shelter animals] being put to death" (No-kill Conference 2001). In another instance, a shelter manager that euthanized animals with carbon monoxide chambers, a method not prohibited in his state, was attacked by no-kill critics who were "outraged" with this "gassing" and called for the "dismantling [of] his little chamber of horrors. . . . Just what kind of people are running this 'humane society?'" (Hindi 2001, 6). To remind this shelter director that he was causing animals to "suffer," some activists rigged a small truck with a video monitor, parked it outside the home of the director and other shelter officials, and played videotapes of animals being fatally gassed. The shelter director said of his critics, "I don't appreciate being called Hitler" (Gilyard 2001). Nor was this particular shelter director alone when it came to such accusations. Another director similarly said, "I've been called a butcher, Hitler, a concentration-camp runner" (Foster 2000). And one shelter was referred to as "Auschwitz" because critics claimed it excessively euthanized potentially adoptable animals (Yaffe 2004).

Drawing on Social Movements

No-killers rely on cultural resources besides language to maintain their humane image and to imply that open admissionists are cruel. To construct an identity that could be both absolute and exceptional in its stance toward killing, no-killers piggyback on two, somewhat opposing, social movements dealing with human issues—one based on an absolutist stance to not "kill" and the other based on the exceptionalist position that some killing is "humane." Large and successful social movements provide an assembly of symbols and ideological trappings—a cultural resource—for groups to fashion their own thinking and model their own actions or to draw emotional power and symbolic coherency.

The absolutism of the no-kill identity resonates with that of the pro-life movement. Although there is no evidence that no-killers subscribe to pro-life beliefs in a greater proportion than does the general population, there are many parallels between the ideologies of these two groups that empower the no-kill movement and emotionally charge the identity of its followers. Like the pro-life movement's campaign to save the "helpless unborn" that should not be "killed," the no-kill movement questions the moral, not just the practical, basis for killing unwanted or undesirable shelter animals. "To me it's *criminal* if a dog with poor manners or who is a little bit standoffish should be euthanized for behavior reasons," one no-kill advocate noted. There are accusations that open admissionists are conducting "mass slaughter of animals" or are "executing" them. For example, when no-killers disavow any notion that their own euthanizing is as a form of killing, they distance themselves from it in their language. One no killer said, referring to a dog kept in a shelter for sixteen months that was highly aggressive, having bitten two staff members and requiring muzzling for walks, "I could not in good conscience *execute* this dog before every treatment avenue has been explored." This explanation suggests that if open-admission workers euthanized this difficult-to-adopt, potentially dangerous dog, they would be wrong, if not cruel, for doing so. In the same spirit, no-killers claim that their shelters do not have "killing rooms" (Foro 1997) or *"execution* chambers." This "killing" of shelter animals signals a moral assault on the fabric of human-animal relationships that is unimaginable to no-killers, much as abortion is to pro-lifers (Ginsburg 1986; Kaufmann 1999). Many no-kill proponents see the open-admissionists' version of "euthanasia" as an act of murder committed by selfish owners and unresourceful shelter workers willing to accept the status quo; in this way they are like pro-life advocates who define abortion as a type of crime approved by a legal system that protects murderers and leaves victims unprotected (Doyle 1982). Like killing a viable fetus, it is killing a viable adoptable, loveable animal.

The exceptionalism of the no-kill identity resonates with the right-to-die movement. Here, social movement piggybacking is necessary to justify euthanasia when it is performed. No-killers often speak of euthanasia as a humane option by comparing the plight of some shelter animals with that of humans in dire straights, where suffering merits death. One worker criticized "sanctuaries" that keep animals alive to the point where they suffer on the grounds that humans do not let that happen to each other. In her words: "If you are not being humane, and the animal is in physical distress, that may be considered a 'sanctuary' (living out their lives until they end naturally). Technically we don't even do that for humans anymore. If someone is in pain, they usually are put on a morphine drip with the dosage slowly increased to reduce their discomfort. The reality is morphine suppresses the respiration." Another proponent argued for euthanasia when animals suffer emotionally: "What happens when you confine humans? What happens when you put humans in mental institutions? You can make it acceptable for some time for some dogs. Some can handle kenneling. Others need the bond . . . something or someone, and sitting in that kennel is not the same for them. They just can't hack it."

These approaches to creating oppositional identities are not completely effective. No-killers become uneasy if they sense that their new-found identity is being blurred. For example, conciliatory gestures by no-kill shelters, when seen as "selling out" to the open-admission perspective, reflect this uneasiness. One such gesture involves modifying language. Aware that the no-kill language hurts or angers others, some in the movement sympathize with this concern and curtail use of such terms. In one instance, the director of a major no-kill shelter publicly acknowledged that use of the term no-kill can be upsetting to others and consciously tried to refrain from its use in such contexts. However, these appeasing gestures, combined with reports that this shelter increased its euthanasia rate, made some question whether no-kill has lost its footing. In another case, the head of the national no-kill conference decided to change the name of this annual meeting to include rather than exclude people and organizations from the open-admission shelter perspective, renaming it in 2002 the "Conference on Homeless Animal Management and Policy." This move distresses some no-killers, who wonder what this change means for the fate of their movement and identity. Although such moves puzzle or even threaten no-killers, they still fiercely cling to what they regard as their authentic selves. Other feelings, crucial to forming their oppositional identity, are there to validate the kind of shelter worker they imagine for themselves.

Rescuing the "Instinct" to Save

Fashioning identity is a complicated social process. For no-killers, establishing what they regard as an authentic identity entails more than dealing with blame and guilt. To escape even the hint that they might be cruel, no-killers identify and own what they regard as positive and "natural" feelings for animals. They want to be hopeful that they can find a loving home for almost every animal that comes to their shelters.

When they talk about what drew them to shelter work, those who first worked in open-admission shelters often say that their passion for helping animals was stifled, that they were unable to act on their "urge" to save shelter animals because there were too many animals to euthanize, too few resources to rehabilitate the impaired, and too little support for thinking and feeling more positively for shelter animals. Hopefulness is something they lost along the way. Yet the theme of losing hopefulness, only to regain it by working in no-kill shelters, is commonly articulated. At a recent San Francisco conference for teaching open-admission shelter staff how to convert to no-kill, the keynote speaker reached out to the audience in his opening remarks by reminding them that they were different from others because they had a strong rescue "instinct" to save lives thwarted in open-admission shelters. As heads nodded enthusiastically, he went on to describe how rescue workers in India went in after an earthquake to find people suffering but alive in the rubble. They found a boy who was so badly trapped they had to cut off his leg to get him out. He compared the actions of these rescue workers, who did not give up trying to save people, to those at the conference who also had this "calling" to save.

Fighting for Animals

No-kill is a way to discover or return to this "instinct," an identity that can shield no-killers from implications of cruelty. In building their new identity, it is important for no-killers to feel they are championing individual animals or, as one advocate pointed out: "We dare to think that every individual life does matter— that that individual's life actually matters." This means they will "fight the good fight" for every animal that comes their way, expending as much time, labor, and money as necessary to ensure that the animal—likely euthanized in open-admission shelter—is cared for, loved, and, hopefully, adopted.

No-killers fight for individual animals by trying to find homes for all animals taken into their shelters. One worker compared this desire to rescue animals to the attitude of emergency room personnel who are trying to save human lives: "That's like giving up on a patient that you know you can save. It's like triage. You are working in an ER and a patient comes in, if he came in ten minutes earlier you would have gotten him. That's how I have to look at what I do. It's very ER-ish. You have to want to save the next one. And that's why we are here and not in an animal care and control facility. We pour everything into an animal. We invest it all." However, it becomes progressively more difficult for no-killers to fight the good fight when they try to rescue animals with increasingly adverse medical and psychological conditions. Yet they remain hopeful. As one worker said, her facility's goal is to try to make ever sicker animals into adoptable ones: "We are raising the bar for what we can handle medically or behaviorally. We've got animals with chronic health conditions. We've got aggressive dogs. We are trying to rehabilitate them so they can be made adoptable."

Workers who violate this rescue ethos are often isolated from their peers, teased, or seriously ridiculed. They are seen as too "rigid" with intake selections, turning away animals that would then be killed, or too "eager" to call for and endorse the euthanasia of shelter animals. In one no-kill shelter, a kennel manager was referred to as "Dr. Kevorkian" by staff members because she "put down" (euthanized) a ten-year-old dog that tried to bite but was regarded as very adoptable by most workers. In a different no-kill shelter, there is strong internal pressure on intake workers to accept as many dogs as possible from the nearby animal control office, regardless of their bad or "spooky" behavior or poor condition; otherwise they likely will be euthanized. For example, after an intake worker refused an aggressive, six-month-old dog offered to her shelter, several coworkers chided her and called her a "murderer"; more politely, some peers criticized her in general for being the "most conservative" temperament tester in the shelter. "I am the bad guy," she noted sadly.

The implication of fighting for individual animals is that shelter workers who do not take this approach are cruel. Open-admissionists, understandably, find this implication to be provocative and make countercharges of cruelty. Open-admissionists think it is wrong to fight for individual animals because doing so misuses limited resources. They argue that if no-killers "rescue" with their hearts, they neglect the "bigger picture." To open-admissionists, it is more important to attack the overpopulation problem by euthanizing unadoptable animals than to indulge one's need to feel hopeful. Attacking overpopulation through euthanasia means taking in all animals brought to shelters, fearing what might happen to those not surrendered. Open-admissionists say that no-killers' rescue ethos causes animals to be turned down because their shelters have insufficient resources to keep taking more animals. To open-admissionists, the no-kill approach is a failure in management— a combination of poor resource allocation and bad judgment that allow workers to be self-indulgent. Such shortsighted policies are thought to benefit workers, offering them emotional gratification at the expense of animal welfare. They say that relating to shelter animals with one's heart makes it harder for no-killers to acknowledge "suffering" in their animals because doing so raises the possibility of euthanasia. Having such a narrow definition of suffering delays what open-admissionists see as necessary euthanasia, in turn causing more suffering.

Open-admissionists also argue that no-killers are cruel because they "warehouse" animals past the point where they should be "humanely euthanized," keeping them in shelters for long periods, sometimes with inadequate care, socialization, and housing. Referring to the "confinement" of shelter animals in "pet warehouses," an open-admissionist said, "The Humane Society of the United States has files of cases on 'no-kill' shelters from which they've had to rescue neurotic, sick animals that were kept in desperate conditions." Another open-admissionist claims that some no-kill shelters keep animals so long they develop "that nervous thing, like dogs spinning, or some of the barking sounds like suffering to me. They are just unhappy or crying." And another critic of warehousing points out after visiting a no-kill shelter: "It was spotless. They had air conditioning, climbing trees, toys and good food. But when you walked in, they were all over you. I had cats attached to my legs and arms, on my shoulders and my head. I had scratch marks for a week after that but not from aggression. These cats were starved for human contact. That's what breaks my heart about these places" (Donald 1991, 4).

Strengthening their allegation of cruelty, open-admissionists hold that warehousing can cause physical harm to shelter animals. This critique is echoed in a popular magazine article that reports the reactions of a 4-H group leader after visiting one no-kill shelter: "Dogs limping around with mange and open sores. Others gasping for air or dragging broken legs, struggling to fight off vicious packs in the large communal pen. I might as well have taken them to a horror show" (Foster 2000). The reporter who wrote this article refers to the "atrocious conditions" at some no-kill facilities and the "luckless inmates" that are "condemned" to "filth" and "suffer" from long-term caging. Indeed, one open-admissionist claimed that the "quality of care of animals is horrific. They [no-killers] need to do it right and have some standard of care." To illustrate, he pointed to a no-kill facility that asked his shelter to take 110 animals to reduce overcrowding. A visit to this no-kill facility alarmed him because he discovered that it was very cold, a mere "semblance" of a building, with dead animals strewn throughout.

Such charges, especially if unanswered, challenge the ability of no-killers to maintain their hope for animals, and without hope, their claim to an authentic identity, free from cruelty, becomes precarious. Charges of warehousing are extremely threatening to the no-kill quest for authenticity because they raise the specter of cruelty. That they continue to be heartened reflects their ability not only to reject but to transform these charges into further hope.

Most no-killers vehemently deny warehousing animals. One advocate spoke of her frustration with people who misconstrue the meaning of no-kill as a preference for keeping animals alive in unpleasant or unhealthy circumstances: "I don't know if there is any sane person who would agree with a warehouse-kind-of-life, like an animal collector, is better than death. I don't think anybody is arguing that except for an extremely small subset of people who are not in the mainstream of the no-kill movement." No-killers say that if adverse "warehousing" exists, it is very rare and at a facility other than their own. Indeed, it is common to point to a few very well-funded no-kills where "lavish" surroundings include "luxury suites for animals, replete with toys, TVs, and playrooms" that are not excessive but "important for the animals" to reduce their stress and make them healthier and happier. "So the toys and playrooms are not frivolous. They're just what the doctor ordered."

Through their language, no-killers redefine these extended stays as hopeful and humane, although "less than ideal" (L. Foro, personal communication, 2001). There is, for example, a lot of talk about maintaining the "quality of life" of animals. As one worker claimed: "[It] is as good if not better than the placements at many open admission shelters. I know a good many dogs in suburbia who don't get walked, have minimal veterinary care, don't get socialized, they don't get patted as much by their owners, they're in the yard." No-killers also find hope in the language used to describe physical and mental problems in animals housed for long periods in shelters. For example, in one such facility, animals with behavior problems, sufficient to justify euthanasia in open-admission shelters, were described as only having "issues." "Issues" conjures up psychological problems in humans that can be lived with and managed, as opposed to more troubling behavior that is difficult to tolerate and control. In one case, a shelter dog had a history of snapping at children was spoken about as "having an issue with children." The solution was to work on ridding the dog of that "issue," while also seeking childless adopters who could keep the dog away from children.

Seeing Viable Pets

To remain true to their mission, no-killers must be able to see all of their charges as viable pets that can be kept and loved in homes, each animal having the potential for a good life for itself and its guardians. The identity forsaken by no-killers is one that turns its back on animals that are less than "perfect," euthanizing many that could be placed in homes if given behavioral or medical attention, as well as time and careful placement. One no-kill worker elaborated this view: "Where do you draw the line? Does everything have to be pristine and perfect, and you kill everything else? We want to give animals a chance that we think ought to be given a chance. I mean, the Blackies and the Willies out there, they would be killed because they are not perfect, and I see this wonderful pet that would make a great companion for someone and I think they are worth investing the resources into." Another no-killer explained: "There are a lot of self-proclaimed experts who will tell you that this or that dog is unadoptable, don't even bother trying. And we don't accept that. You can get terrifically good outcomes. It's a question of when can you and when can't you. The jury is out on our animals until we have exhausted all reasonable attempts."

No-kill trainers believe they can rehabilitate most problem animals, including those exhibiting aggressiveness. One trainer compared this challenge to working with criminals, concluding that both can be rehabilitated if people try hard enough: "If you've gotten people who've committed certain levels of crime, can they be rehabilitated? If you gave them the right counseling, can you turn them around or is it always in them? I would submit that the right kind of effort hasn't been tried." Indeed, the belief that any shelter animal is a viable pet extends deep into no-kill culture. In one shelter, the desire to see animals as viable pets even extends to avoiding certain common words, such as "adoptable," that suggest some might not measure up and make it into a home. A worker explained: "We don't use the word adoptable. We refuse to have that word in any of our literature. A kitten with two legs who is four weeks old is adoptable to a person who wants to adopt her. Adoptability is only about who wants this animal. It is not about you judging, to sit back and say, 'This darling animal is adoptable.' No. Adoptability is only judged by the adopter. We had a dog who was thirteen years old. This one had no front legs. She gets around. She kisses everyone. And she was placed."

Seeing all their charges as viable pets, however, can be difficult in no-kill shelters because some animals are far from the well-behaved, healthy, and attractive pet desired by most adopters. In fact, critics charge that no-kill shelters downplay or conceal problems in animals to get them adopted. "They [counselors and trainers] are soft-peddling the issue. . . . They are couching it in a less scary way for the client," according to one worker. For example, "excuses" are made for the bad behavior of animals, as in the case of a dog whose "guarding behavior" around food was "explained away" by pointing to how little it had been given to eat. Making excuses for bad behavior sometimes is combined with failing to disclose information to adopters about the dangerousness of aggressive animals. Another worker spoke about "the betrayal the public would feel if they were aware that the shelter they trusted has made them the subject of an experiment in placing rehabilitated biting dogs, an experiment with so many failures." Uncomfortable with her own shelter's policy, she reported "incredible feelings of guilt" making it "hard to sleep at night" because she felt "complicity" in adopting out unsafe animals to clients from whom information about these problems was hidden. Upset by this problem, another worker described a shelter that was being sued for adopting out a Rottweiler that was known to have already killed one dog, only to have it subsequently knock down its new owner and kill her pet dog. The same worker also claimed that this shelter did not tell potential adopters that another dog had bitten seven volunteers. In response to such shelter actions, the worker said: "That is the main reason I had to resign from volunteering with the rescue group I was working with. They adopted out any and all dogs, no matter their history and worst of all, did not tell adopting families if the dog had bitten previously."

Finding Perfect Adopters

No-killers believe there is a suitable adopter for every rescued animal. However, the drive to save difficult-to-adopt animals severely reduces the pool of potential adopters, since it takes a very special person to be the right match for an animal with behavioral or veterinary problems, let alone one that is old or unattractive. No-kill workers convince themselves that a perfect adopter exists for virtually every one of their charges. Having this view justifies keeping animals for a long time as adoption staff search for the right person for each animal.

This search can be particularly trying when dogs are highly aggressive, needing to be muzzled and constantly monitored. When a no-kill worker was asked who would be an appropriate adopter for such challenging animals, she said a dog trainer would eventually come to the shelter and take home one of these dogs, adding: "How many dog trainers come through our doors looking for a dog? That's the problem. We can see that. It's not that there is no owner in the world who can do it, it's that there is no owner who wants them or can take them right now. In the right hands they would be okay." She acknowledged, without apparent irony, that no such adopter had visited her shelter since she arrived there three years earlier.

Rescue narratives circulate among workers about shelter animals that make it into good homes and "live happily ever after" because they have been saved, despite many medical or psychological problems. Hopefulness pervades these stories because shelter workers correct the animal's problem and find the right kind of owner. The rescue tale is especially prevalent in no-kills because it speaks to that culture's wish for happy endings and denial of euthanasia. The latter's subtext is that it is wrong to euthanize an animal because, if given a chance, it can find a loving home. Less commonly relayed, but serving to support their hopefulness, are tales about failed or missed rescues, typically at open-admission shelters. These stories describe animals declined at intake because of ill health, bad behavior, or unattractiveness that could have been rehabilitated and adopted if they had been in a no-kill facility.

This culture also helps workers cope with and explain adoptions that apparently fail because animals are returned to the shelter. When this happens, it can be a problem to maintain the belief that animals end up with the right owners and "live happily ever after." These apparent failures, if not addressed, can disillusion workers and question their no-kill identity. In these hope-threatening instances, workers learn to blame adopters for whatever problems they were having with the animals. One adoption counselor bemoaned the use of this strategy, feeling that animals rather than adopters account for these failures: "When animals are returned for the very problems they had, the attitude of the people in the dog division is always anger at the client— they did something stupid, they blame the client. And I often deal with clients who come back here in tears because they wanted to love and bring this animal into their homes. Sometimes they have been with the dog for a month hoping the thing [bad behavior] will improve, but it has gotten worse and worse and worse. Sometimes it's just a day and the dog has bitten somebody in the household. They are very unhappy and they have often been traumatized by the experience. It's amazing that they are not angry. They feel guilty about bringing the dog back. They're apologizing to me. And I gave them a dog that was almost guaranteed to do something like this. But when the dog is brought back and I walk over there [to the training department] and say, 'Gee, Fluffy was returned.' 'Why?' 'Well, he bit the aunt who came over to visit.' 'Well, she must have done something. She must have startled him. Boy, what a jerk.' That's the attitude." In one such case, two dog trainers listened to a visibly shaken adopter who, as she cried, spoke about how she tried to cope with her adopted dog's wide-ranging destruction of furniture, rugs, bedding, and other items as well as its biting when she tried to control its unruly behavior. Distraught, the adopter walked away, talking about how she felt like a failure. After she left, the dog trainers shook their heads, reaffirmed their belief that the dog was a fine and manageable pet, and mused that the adopter was probably unfit to have any dog.

Despite the occasional failed adoption, no-kill shelters claim to have extremely high adoption rates. Open-admissionists challenge the claim that no-kill shelters have a 100 percent adoption rate, calling it a "smart marketing strategy." Instead, they argue that no-killers create high rates by taking only very adoptable animals in the first place, leaving the "burden" of euthanizing rejected animals to open-admission shelters. Critics allege that no-kill shelters "take in the 'movie star' dogs and cats, the pretty ones they know they can place in new homes, and turn away the rest" (Caras 1997, 17). "They are strays, 'too old,' unsocialized, injured, or diseased. They are considered unadoptable by no-kill shelters so they are brought to us" (Bogue 1998b). One person compared this self-serving policy to a private high school that always has impressive SAT scores because it accepts only bright students in the first place. Some no-kill shelters are "pickier," even rejecting animals with extremely minor problems. As one open-admissionist contended: "If an animal has the tiniest patch of flea allergy, dermatitis, which is curable, they say no if they want to. Bad teeth, they say no if they want to. Any animal they can say no to, they are going to say no. They don't take many that need treatment." All of these manipulations, some charged, enable the "no-kill propagandists" through "deception" to produce very high rates of adoption and low rates of euthanizing.

Even after taking an animal, critics charge that no-killers can reclassify its status to maintain a high adoption rate. They claim that no-kill shelters use a "changeable" classification of animals, such that a placeable animal could be reclassified as unplaceable if the animal were not adopted. This strategy enables the no-kill shelter to say that no adoptable animals are killed and to assert that a "huge" percentage of their "placeable" animals are adopted (Stark 1993). Some feel that this classification "game" is so incredibly capricious as to make the very notion of no-kill "a joke." One worker said that even "color" could be used as a reason to classify an animal as "unadoptable" if there are too many similar-looking animals together in a shelter, such as tiger-stripped kittens. "I could make distinctions any way I want . . . their rates are meaningless."

Challenging back, some no-kill shelters contend that their save rates would be higher if they did not have so many difficult and unadoptable animals. Denying that they are "picky," no-killers claim to take many animals that are not the "cream of the crop." As one worker said: "One of the things that gets hurled at us, I mean I become so defensive even if there is no attack, is the charge that we set the bar so high medically or behaviorally, therefore almost anybody can label themselves no-kill." Another no-kill worker concurred: "We get only the worst here, everybody thinks we take only the best dogs here . . . [but] we get the worst of the worst. If you are looking for a behavior case, we are probably the shelter to go to. It's harder for me to find a family dog in our shelter than it is in most because we are taking the ones no one else takes."

No-kill culture makes it possible for workers to feel hopeful. It does so even though some of their very steps to rescue and save animals come perilously close to the antithesis of their identity—cruelty. Despite criticisms that could easily threaten their hope, most no-killers cling tenaciously to the belief that almost every shelter animal, regardless of disability, age, or unattractiveness, can be successfully placed if given sufficient time. The focus on the welfare and fate of individual animals, combined with the knowledge that euthanasia is very unlikely, allows no-killers to indulge their desire to have emotionally deep and complex relationships with shelter animals, even though permanent guardians will probably adopt them. Feelings engendered by these relationships are an essential component of the cruelty-free, humane identity no-killers seek. They experience these sentiments by constructing them as they carry out their everyday shelter jobs.

FREEING "NORMAL" EMOTIONS

No-kill workers want to be attached to animals, without fear of getting hurt, and to grieve their loss without scorn from colleagues. Safe attachment to animals and the expression of grief are thought to be natural for people who love animals, and they should be expected in settings like shelters, according to no-killers, where they are not cruel to animals. Their culture offers them an opportunity to experience these feelings of attachment and grief; indeed they are strongly encouraged to pursue them and are punished for failing to do so. Alternatively, denying these feelings is seen as a violation of their animal-loving nature. No-killers understand, though, that such control of emotions is a necessary coping device for those who carry out euthanasias that they believe are often preventable and unnecessary; or in other words, that are cruel.

Killing as a Job

Because open-admission culture is thought to promote the bottling up feelings and denial of grief, it provides no-killers with a foil or model of inauthenticity. They know or learn about their alter identity—the one linked to cruelty—from working in open-admission shelters or hearing about them through small talk about what work is like in other facilities where the rules surrounding euthanasia and death seem harsh.

While open-admission workers lament having to euthanize animals, they handle it differently than do their no-kill peers. Rather than expressing their emotions about preventing euthanasia or grieving when it occurs, these workers block their emotions. In one typical facility, workers bemoaned that euthanasia had to be done but felt that it was the right thing to do because of the large number of surrendered animals and the limited space and resources available. To make it easier on themselves, they did not form deep and complex relationships with shelter animals. And when it came time to euthanize animals, workers still distanced themselves. For example, there was no "spoiling period" for animals slated to die—an informal practice at many no-kill facilities where special consideration is given to animals after the decision is made to euthanize them. To open-admissionists, these periods are more for the psychological benefit of workers than the animals and place a "huge emotional burden" on the staff members doing the spoiling. With emotion under wrap and attachment minimized, the staff routinely and unceremoniously euthanized animals. As one worker recalled: "I was like a killing machine, a certified euthanasia tech that euthanized sixty to one hundred-plus animals every single day. Some days that's all I did—clean and kill. And go home. You put your feelings on the shelf. You just do your job. You have to deal with that sometime down the line."

To be clear, open-admissionists are not unfeeling when it comes to the death of shelter animals. Their work carries an emotional burden, especially when they euthanize "rejects" that could have been adopted were there more time to keep these animals or money to pay for veterinary help. Workers at open-admission shelters feel drained and distressed when killing animals. This feeling applied not only to dogs and cats thought to be adoptable but also to species ignored by many no-kill programs. For example, one animal control employee lamented killing the various animals sent to her facility by a no-kill shelter because of the "waste" of "wonderful" animals and its emotional effect on her. "It is so frustrating," she explained. "I hated putting down that dog because it is a dog who could have gotten adopted so easily if we had a little more time, which we didn't. The [nearby no-kill shelter] wouldn't take the dog— wonderful dog, but it had pit bull in it, but wonderful temperament. It was a lap dog, but because of that pit-bull quality they wouldn't take him. I was practically in tears putting him down because it was so wasteful, so useless. It would be one thing if he were sick or something. We are killing animals who could have homes if they could have a tiny bit of work— a minor surgery— not to mention the birds, the guinea pigs, the hamsters, the rats— I love them." Despite their emotion management strategies, most open-admissionists only reduce their psychological discomfort rather than eliminate it entirely. Uneasy feelings still slip through the cracks between justifications and excuses (Arluke 1994b). What feels "wrong" to them, no-killers argue, is that they are working closely with animals with whom they cannot bond when alive or mourn when dead and, even worse, they are taking lives without sufficient reason; in short, they are tainting what it really means to be a shelter worker because of the implication of cruelty.

Being with Friends

Many no-kill workers are acutely aware of the psychological benefits of working in an environment where animals are rarely killed. "People are drawn to work here," one said, "because it is less scary." The "scariness" spoken about refers to the loss, guilt, and grief workers experience if they kill animals with which they have established some relationship. A worker explained: "I don't have to worry that I am going to bond with an animal and then have to put him down, which is my perception of what happens in kill shelters—you really like an animal but you already have a number of them at home. You can't take it home but nobody has come in to adopt it and its time is up. So I feel lucky that those are the kinds of emotions I don't have to deal with." When animals are killed, the killing is done for egregious clinical or behavioral problems. Workers can tell themselves that it is the most humane thing to do because it alleviates animal suffering. Knowing that euthanasia will be done only in extreme cases makes it easier for no-killers to feel safely attached to their charges. One worker elaborated this point: "When I started the volunteering thing I was told that no animal would be put down unless it was a very severe medical or behavioral issue—a definite quality of life issue for the animal—and under those conditions I felt I would be able to work. It would be a lot safer [than an open-admission shelter] because if they are going to put a dog down I probably would feel okay about it because I could agree with them or at least see their point and feel very sad. There would be a strong inclination that they would be right anyway, and that would be best for the animal. I thought with that in mind, I would be able to handle it."

The deep attachments fostered in no-kill shelters were dramatized by an incident involving a dog trainer who visits shelters to teach how to evaluate the temperament of dogs for potential adoption or euthanasia. Once when she visited a dog-training school for a demonstration on temperament testing, workers from a nearby no-kill shelter took one of their dogs there hoping she could help them make a decision they had been unable to make about whether to euthanize the dog. The trainer declared, "This is not an adoptable dog" and recommended euthanasia. The no-killers were upset; they found her comments cold, calculated, unsympathetic, and unfair because the dog should not have been tested at a training school where fifty people in a large and unfamiliar room might make the dog behave poorly. In other words, the setting was loaded against the dog's behaving normally and in a way that would show him to be fit for adoption. Some cried when the dog was euthanized; because they did not kill animals, the very act of euthanasia was extremely disturbing to witness or know about, especially when it involved a dog with whom they were so close. Some cried because they came to observe this trainer's demonstration hoping that she would see some redeeming qualities in this dog, only to be disappointed. Others cried because they felt that they could have taken the dog to their own home and worked with him to the point where he would be adoptable. They saw the euthanasia as a "tragedy" and felt that the trainer was "too hard on the dog" and that they would have "gone the extra mile" for him.

In no-kill shelters, euthanizing an animal is rare and involves a weighty decision. One facility has formal guidelines for deciding on all euthanasias (except for emergencies). Signatures approving this act are required from the president, vice president, and initiating department head, and the names of the animals are clearly posted so the staff can note their deaths and no one will be shocked by inadvertently discovering that a "friend" had been euthanized.

Once the decision is made, workers are allowed to show their feelings for animals scheduled to die. At one no-kill shelter, cats slated to be euthanized are given special foods or treats, soft, comfortable, secure bedding, and adequate scratching posts and visits from the staff, while dogs are given similar bedding, a rawhide bone during the day and a beef bone at night, special food and "extra special goodies," a cloth toy, and staff member visits for "quality time" with the animal, including long walks, outdoor play "with their special buddies," or "quiet time." These last days are difficult for workers, as one explained: "I find it very hard to look at a dog carrying on its normal life and knowing that soon it will all be over. I think it helps us to know that our dog's last day or so was really special. It seems to bring peace to the people around the dog who are suffering knowing that the dog is going to get euthanized. It is always such a big deal. I just cannot get used to it."

No-killers can distance themselves from the killing of animals by transforming euthanasia into a clinical, veterinary act performed elsewhere by technicians in animal control agencies or by their own in-house veterinarian and veterinary technicians. Thus, euthanasia is not merely a rare event, it is a task that workers do not have to carry out, allowing them to feel untainted by the killing of animals. By removing themselves at least one step from euthanasia, no-killers can adopt the role of mourner rather than killer of animals being "put down." Euthanasia becomes an infrequent, highly ritualized and emotionally upsetting loss of a "good friend" performed by an in-house veterinarian. As mourners, they can feel comfortable expressing their unhappiness, even on the job, about this loss, whereas most traditional shelters discourage such displays because they "make everyone uncomfortable." To properly mourn their loss, no-killers frame these rare deaths as hopeless situations where there is no ambiguity about the wisdom of the euthanasia. To see these euthanasias otherwise would complicate their grief with guilt that they could have done more to save the animals. These steps make workers comfortable and secure while on the job. They come to see their particular organizational way of life as the best one for animals and themselves.

Their quest to feel like authentic shelter workers, however with no specter of killing cruelly, is challenged when animals—with whom workers have bonded strongly—are to be euthanized for reasons that seem dubious to some. When this happens, workers no longer feel safe and take steps to repair the scene and reduce risk of emotional harm. For example, at one facility, management decided to euthanize several overly aggressive dogs that had been in the shelter for many months. They had become a danger to the staff and to potential adopters and were a liability risk to the shelter. Management held special meetings with different groups of workers and volunteers to deliver this news, calm those upset or in "shock," and raise the organization's "bar" for rehabilitating difficult dogs. During the meetings, senior staff largely blamed external forces (e.g., "our hand has been forced by elements in society") for the need to euthanize these dogs, given unreasonable expectations for the behavior of animals and for being too litigious. Trying to ease distraught and confused listeners, senior staff claimed they "did not have choices" and they "couldn't" do anything else with these dogs.

Lacking the detachment of their open-admission peers, most staff members found it emotionally wrenching to face the euthanasia of these problematic animals and to make rational decisions regarding their fate. They strongly opposed the decision, believing that the dogs' quality of life was satisfactory and their risky behavior was modifiable. A few workers and volunteers demanded meetings with shelter officials to protest the decision, and rumors circulated about leaks to the press and a volunteer protest strike. Real fear existed among workers about how these euthanasias, if carried out, would adversely affect their identities. One employee, for example, was uneasy about what she saw as a slippery slope created by these few euthanasias: "We are in a position now of either becoming like every other shelter and we save only perfect dogs who need nothing or what?" Because of the workers' considerable and continued pressure several dogs were taken off the list and sent to sanctuaries—places where animals can live and be protected for the rest of their lives.

A few dogs were euthanized, despite protests. The most unsettling euthanasia involved Josh, a dog having a history of aggression but with whom several workers, referred to as the animal's "fan club," had intensely bonded. Josh created a "tug of war" between the behavior-and-training group and other departments at the shelter. An opponent of Josh's euthanasia was optimistic that his difficult behavior could be modified enough to make him a good companion, despite his history of biting several people. She commented: "Some people are really pushing to have him euthanized, but we have kept him here a year and we ought to at least try drugs. We haven't even gone down that route. If we keep them here a year, we owe it to them to try everything." The fact that his euthanasia was for behavioral rather than medical reasons made it especially difficult for workers to say that Josh's "suffering" justified his death. Their resistance to euthanasia drew on the need to feel hopeful about the fate of even the most challenging shelter animals. And their anger was fed by the feeling that management had betrayed them; they had been given a green light to get this close; they applauded that permission and now insisted that the existence of such attachments not be taken lightly.

When Josh was euthanized, only his "fan club," the inner circle of caretakers and admirers, was permitted to be present. Lights were strongly dimmed in the dog's quarters, and the mood was extremely solemn if not despondent. Many workers were very distressed by his death; a few chose not to attend the euthanasia because it was too upsetting, one staff member was hospitalized because the event so disturbed her, and several others took "sick days" because of their grief. The shelter closed early that day to avoid interaction with the public at such an extremely delicate and private time. During the hours preceding the euthanasia, as well as the days following it, workers could be seen embracing each other, offering words of comfort, and shedding tears. "People are walking around like zombies," one worker commented sadly about her peers. A wake held the evening of the euthanasia again excluded those outside the inner circle of mourners; a poem in honor of Josh was available, stories were swapped about the animal along with photographs of him, and flowers and wine were there for the occasion. The sentiment was "we love you guys, you did good work but this one just didn't work." Contrary to shelter policy, one worker requested the dog's ashes, though a few staff members thought this was going "overboard."

Ultimately, Josh was one of only a few dogs from the initial euthanasia list that was killed. Workers pressured management to spare most animals on the list, further validating their rescue ethos and securing an emotionally safe setting that would not be cruel to humans. The no-kill shelter's safe organizational context for expressing emotions about animals allowed some workers to position themselves as kind and gentle, despite criticism by open-admissionists or protests from fellow no-killers. Seeking to prevent cruelty to humans was the vehicle these no-killers used to accomplish this positioning.

DIVIDING THE COMMUNITY

Cruelty is a pivotal concept no-killers use to define and assert a new identity. However, the quest for authenticity divides as much as unifies people, creating tension between the no-kill and open-admission camps as well as within the former group. Although Durkheim (1912) and others who followed him (e.g., Heeren 1983) argue that social groups create unity through sharing emotions in group rituals and practices, emotions play an equally important role in separating people from one another. For example, victims of disasters develop a strong unity with fellow victims (Fritz 1961), but experience conflict with outsiders.

Boundaries go along with any shared feeling. Pride can lead to an increase in social cohesion (Retzinger 1991), but a more cohesive group may be more likely to be in conflict with outsiders. Similarly, anger also can unify victims who share that anger, but that emotion may lead to dissociation with others.

By disavowing their own cruelty and seeing it in others, no-killers manage emotions in ways that divide the shelter community; the cost of their pursuit of authenticity is the solidarity of the larger group. One way they pursue authenticity is to transform open-admissionists into dirty workers. No-killers portray the job of open-admissionists as distasteful, if not discrediting, casting a moral pall around those who do this work (Hughes 1964). Those doing it are seen as "less" of a person, morally and emotionally, making them a modern form of untouchables—a caste of people symbolically contaminated and best avoided or pitied because they are associated with unpopular, unpleasant, or unclean tasks. Predictably, open-admissionists resent doing the dirty work. By being forced to euthanize so many animals, they shoulder all the moral, emotional, and aesthetic heartaches that are part of euthanasia. The harm of a no-kill facility, according to an editorial by an open-admissionist (Caras 1997, 17), is that "it punishes shelters that are doing their very best but are stuck with the dirty work. It is demoralizing and disheartening for humane workers who would do almost anything to stop that heartbreaking selection process. Humane workers who are brave enough to accept that dirty work deserve better than that." Open-admission workers deplore dirty-work delegation by no-kill shelters and call for "sharing the burden." As one worker said: "As long as there is euthanasia to be done, our resentment is that we shouldn't be doing it all. We should all be doing the good stuff and the bad stuff." Despite these protests the distinction remains, and open-admissionists are shamed by the stigma that no-killers attach to them.

A second way that no-killers divide the shelter community is to portray open-admissionists as powerful people who defend the status quo and muffle dissent from the powerless who challenge tradition. In their quest for a humane identity, free of any trappings of cruelty, no-killers create a heightened sense of embattlement or even persecution that further cements boundaries between them and open-admissionists. This identity is empowering because it has an outlaw quality that makes it an attractive label for no-kill workers who feel alienated from, and excluded by, the mainstream humane community. In particular, poorly endowed, small no-kill shelters cling to the outlaw image because it symbolically represents their powerlessness and domination by a few large and powerful national organizations. Believing that they are disempowered frames their camp as "anti-establishment," relative to open-admissionists (Foro n.d.). In this tense environment, the latter are sometimes accused by no-killers of ignoring, misunderstanding, or criticizing them. They feel ignored, misunderstood, and criticized at national conferences sponsored by open-admissionists. Angry at the reaction she received at a national conference sponsored by open-admissionists, a no-killer explained: "I don't like being dissed and demonized. So many people there were very resentful of us. We were like getting slammed, shielding ourselves from the rotten vegetables being thrown at us. That feeling was very pervasive [at national meeting]." When it comes to planning and running their own conferences, no-killers feel thwarted in their attempts to get open-admission support and participation. One spokesperson claimed that open-admissionists did not even return her telephone messages inviting them to take part or asking for conference advice.

There also is tension within the no-kill ranks because institutional guile is used to pursue authenticity. Like all workers, no-killers are normatively constrained to display "appropriate" feelings for specific contexts. In shelters, they are guided to feel guiltless, hopeful, and safely attached to animals. Some resist these collective sentiments, however, because they "feel wrong" to them. Instead they value emotions prohibited by their organizational culture (Hochschild 1983; Whittier 2001), and in turn, these sequestered feelings make them question the no-kill identity expected of them; they do not always blame open-admissionists, feel hopeful about their charges' prospects, or enter into deep and complex relationships with them.

Rather than blaming others, at times some no-killers resist the oppositional identities of no-kill versus open-admission. Some no-killers interviewed for this study lowered their political and rhetorical guards enough to admit to more overlap in their identities than they would concede in a public forum. They revealed that they knew the emotional party line about what they were supposed to feel, but it did not resonate with them. With their guard down, they talked about shelter workers in general in ways that were less polarized and more sympathetic than one might expect because of the public rhetoric over the nature of their "real" occupational identities. Clearly, such rhetoric is for public posturing and is not an accurate reflection of the feelings and actions of everyday workers. If they are permitted to air their thoughts, stark and inflammatory distinctions blur or fade. Workers "see through" the collective search for authentic shelter identity by identifying with open-admissionists or feeling as though they are fellow travelers, more alike than not in core values relating to the care of animals. At these times, no-killers acknowledge that they feel like open-admissionists, expressing common rather than conflicting sentiments about basic issues and concerns faced by everyone in the shelter world. Other movements, particularly those whose mission and effectiveness call for crafting just the right emotions for followers, also experience this kind of resistance, as in the case of pro-life and pro-choice supporters; when they are confronted one-on-one, their differences are less pronounced than is their public rhetoric (Dworkin 1993; Kaufman 1999).

To illustrate, some no-killers express solidarity with open-admissionists. These no-kill resistors have sympathy and pity for those who have to euthanize animals, or even work in shelters that do this, because the emotional toll of killing causes staff to "suffer." Furthermore, they identify with open-admissionists who are assumed to have the same compassion as they do for animals but simply work in the wrong place. One no-killer speculated that open-admissionists resent those who work in well-endowed no-kill shelters: "It's a horrible thing to have to euthanize animals every day. I feel fortunate that I am working in an organization where we don't have to do that. They [open admissionists] have the same amount of compassion that we have, but because they have fewer resources, they can't do what we do. I can understand why they are resentful. And that is where this [tension] is coming from."

In addition to not blaming open-admissionists, no-kill resistors are less likely to embrace the rescue ethos expected of them. They oppose fighting for each animal admitted to the shelter and dispute that just the right adopter exists for every shelter animal. Resistors consider even the "best" shelters to be unhealthy if not destructive environments for animals and express feelings for shelter animals that are far from the hope and optimism central to no-killers authentic identity and its feeling rules. In an ideal world, they agree that shelters would not exist or, if they do, serve only as temporary way stations to rehabilitate and home needy animals. In the words of one no-kill worker, even her own "nice" shelter is "still" a shelter: "Don't get me wrong, I don't want to come across as gloom and doom about no-kill. I am pleased that we go the extra mile for older animals or animals with more involved medical needs, like this diabetic cat we just adopted out. But in other cases, I really wonder about their quality of life. I think five hundred days is our longest-term animal right now. They get walked and handled by staff, but I wonder about their quality of life. Granted, we are a nice shelter, but we are still a shelter." Another no-kill worker concurred with this sentiment: "We've had dogs here for a year or two and you look at when they came in versus when they went out or were put to sleep, and they get worse not better. Shelters aren't always great places for dogs. And the longer they are here, the more likely we are to make them worse." And yet another no-kill worker expressed similar misgivings about virtually any shelter confinement, even in the best facilities: "I don't care how wonderful we make it for them, they are still institutionalized. Caretakers are there for thirty minutes to an hour and then you are alone— not able to do any of the innate things that you as a dog are supposed to be doing. None of those needs are being fulfilled." No-kill resistors also stop themselves from forming deep relationships with shelter animals. Like open-admission workers, they refuse to become closely attached to shelter animals and do not openly grieve the loss of individual animals that are euthanized. To these resistors, no-kill has less to do with getting in touch with one's true identity and more to do with indulging certain feelings at the expense of proper animal care.

This resistance creates conflict among workers. Sometimes other workers marginalize dissenters by dismissing their objections and labeling them "problem children," "difficult employees," not "team members," or the like. They are expected to adjust to the job (i.e., accept and play by the rules for expressing no-kill emotions and identity), become silent, or leave, but these expectations may fail. In larger facilities, there are cliques devoted to such dissent. Alienated from their own shelter's feeling rules, resistors outwardly challenge them. Within some no-kill shelters, cliques lead to debates about the appropriateness of their own facility's stance on euthanasia when that issue is raised for certain animals, but this dissent is usually contained to specific cases rather than generalized to broader shelter practice. Nevertheless, some degree of tension permeates these shelters as workers question the propriety of their facility's feeling rules and debate what constitutes cruelty.

Whether the ambiguously provocative notion of cruelty creates tension within the no-kill world or between it and the open-admission camp, the tension is a struggle over the right way to feel about doing shelter work and the proper way to think about one's identity. At a certain level, this struggle goes beyond tensions within individual shelters. The no-killer's pursuit of an authentic identity, and the feelings that go with it, present a crisis to the shelter world akin to the impact of natural disasters on communities (e.g., Erikson 1976). While there is no destruction of physical property, within the shelter community there is destruction of an idea: the long-accepted method of disposing of unwanted animals is now seen as a cruel practice. The no-kill perspective has damaged the community that long existed among shelter workers, changing how they think and feel about each other. The vast majority of shelter workers suddenly are thought of as cruel; five million deaths each year are seen as avoidable rather than inevitable, as previously thought. The no-kill idea created culpability within the shelter world; open-admissionists became the guilty party. When cruelty became an issue for workers—escaping it or being accused of it—their sense of solidarity was dealt a serious blow. Now challenged by two camps, each vying for what constitutes a "true" shelter worker, the unified community that once existed is no more.

Although emotions surrounding cruelty divide the sheltering community, I next examine the power of emotions to unify groups and create social cohesion. Cruelty can heal fractured groups as well as cause their fracturing. As Durkheim (1912) observes, groups shattered by tragedy reintegrate themselves by celebrating shared feelings.

5 Marketers

Celebrating Community

The cat-in-the-dryer case did not have the right ingredients to be picked up by the media. To get really extensive coverage and a strong response from the public you need a victim and a happy ending, and an animal that is saved in some way. Even though the kitten case was really disturbing—someone butchered it alive and threw it in a dryer where a little boy found it—it was not a real good media case. It's disturbing, but unless you can show an actual animal that people can identify with and have this animal helped in some way, it's almost too gory.

—Media affairs staff

USUALLY AFTER TRAGEDY destroys a community there is an outpouring of grief and support from survivors to reestablish social bonds. However, sometimes there are tragedies that have no community to restore a sense of order and meaning after loss of life or property, and the survivors pay for this void (Brison 2001). If there is no community to begin with, tragedy occurs in a social vacuum, as happens when death strikes isolated people. There is no one to reaffirm and support core community beliefs and standards of morality, no one to tell the survivors that their former identities are still honored and respected, no one to mull over the meaning of the death or recall memories of the deceased, and no memorialization—the person or event is forgotten. There is no healing.

This scenario often applies to the humane community when animals are egregiously abused—severely neglected and abandoned, enduring prolonged suffering and an agonizing death, or burned, beaten, crushed, drowned, poisoned, shot, or otherwise intentionally tortured. Few people would deny that these are extreme cases of "cruelty" that go well beyond routine violations of the "food, water, shelter" requirement of the cruelty code or what agents might describe as a bullshit complaint.

Although there is significant harm to animals in these cases, most of the time only a small number of people beyond the complainants and abusers themselves know that something untoward happened.

147

Sometimes severely abused animals have no owners who can try to mend this travesty, and if there are owners, they often do not have community support for the loss they feel; they are alone with their thoughts and emotions. Humane agents might talk about these cases among themselves, but usually other people do not want to hear about such "gory" things. And this silence applies to the veterinarians, hospital technicians, and shelter workers who examine and treat abused animals. They experience a sense of loss when animals have to be euthanized or are brought in dead and have to be disposed of, but this loss is individual, informal, and often private.

Although these cases are not easily forgotten, most people who work for humane organizations or who support their mission never learn about them. There is no mechanism for them to hear about these victims, let alone memorialize and mourn their loss. Thus, there is no public or official recognition that these cases of cruelty, as a group, are the saddest of all animal cases that come into humane societies and their hospitals. There is no grief or mourning that is openly ritualized and that would permit the honoring of these animals. In short, animal abuse is a tragedy in search of community.

Occasionally, there are "big" cruelty cases whose unique features address these problems. Word about them travels throughout humane societies because they involve every department of these organizations. In addition to law enforcement agents who seize animals or bring in dead ones suspected of abuse, veterinary pathologists examine dead animals for clinical signs of abuse, internists or surgeons treat their sicknesses or injuries, veterinary technicians help them through recovery, and shelter workers nurture them and try to find them new homes.

The public hears about big cases through humane society marketers— the media affairs and development departments. The former covers these cases as part of public education, while the latter uses these them to make their financial appeals more effective. Images of abused animals appear on the outside of direct mailings and their abuse is described inside with grisly details of cruelty that elicit the reader's anger, horror, sadness, uneasiness, and frustration. However, most of the thousands of cruelty complaints made each year to large, urban humane societies are never considered for such use; only a few are the egregious sort, and most of these are not suitable for mass mailing and pubic education.

When the right kind of case does come up, it is regarded as an enormous opportunity; failing to capitalize on it is considered a mistake.

Despite their small number, big cases are just what are needed by both the concerned public and staff within humane organizations. Cruelty, especially the blatant, sadistic sort, is a deep shock to these people. In its aftermath, they are horrified by the harm done, perplexed about its cause, and angry with abusers. They feel shaken morally and emotionally, just as are people when unexpected violence strikes others, particularly so when the victims are innocent and defenseless. Big cases are particularly valuable because through them the institution, its staff, and its supportive public come to terms with cruelty. It is acknowledged, grieved, and memorialized, and in the process, the humane community's solidarity is enhanced. Finding and shaping these cases, however, is no easy matter.

THE "BEAUTIFUL" CASE

Not all incidents of egregious cruelty can qualify and be transformed into beautiful cases that achieve high visibility in the general community. A case must possess a number of characteristics to make it what some staff call "beautiful." To capture the hearts and minds of the public, media experts scour new cases in search of the right mix of ingredients, just as do journalists. Walter Goodman of the *New York Times* calls it "prettifying reality," a point elaborated by Bernard Goldberg (2002, 71) to describe the press's distortion of homeless people in the news. To arouse sympathy for the homeless and build support for programs, documentaries focus on otherwise hard-working couples or attractive teenagers rather than "off-putting specimens." Making cruelty appealing to the public is an equally challenging task.

Acceptable Suffering

Properly depicted cruelty is the most important part of a beautiful case. A media affairs staff member explains the value of such cases: "If there is something graphic about an animal's abuse, we want to show it because you want people to care about that animal, you want them to be moved." Staff believe that when people are so "moved" they will more likely provide information, donate, or adopt. Only certain images of abuse or neglect are thought to so effectively mobilize emotions.

To start with, cruelty needs to be visible and disturbing to viewers. In one case, a dog was neglected for many months and developed several veterinary problems. The most graphic abuse—the dog's heavy coat of extremely matted hair—would easily photograph to dramatically highlight the "before" and "after" scenario used in presenting these cases to the public. But this was not a beautiful case. Some veterinary problems the dog suffered, including "terrible skin problems and other issues involving its well-being," would not be apparent in photographs and would remain hidden from the public. Moreover, badly matted hair and serious skin problems were not "sexy" forms of cruelty that could pull the heartstrings of viewers, but they were, nevertheless, real and vexing problems for the animal.

Cruelty, however, according to development and media affairs staff, should not be too disturbing. They feel that the challenge to marketing egregious abuse is that it must be perceived as sufficiently "bad" to elicit sympathy and perhaps even identification by the public but not be so upsetting that people turn away from the solicitation because they are appalled or grief stricken. If people are "horrified" by pictures of cruelty, they might not read the material or donate, staff members claim, so "in the pictures we were very careful not to show how bad it really is. You want to show cruelty, but it is too much when people start not wanting to open their mail."

The institutional practice of "going light" with cruelty is based more on informal custom and political posturing than on sound market research. Within humane organizations and among its supporters, cruelty is an unseemly or uncomfortable topic for some people to face, despite the fact that combating and preventing it was the impetus for the organizations' creation and is the heart of its current mission. Many employees want someone else to deal with cruelty because it is so horrible; they know abuse happens but do not want it "in our faces." The organization also is "conservative" compared with other animal groups in that they do not want to be "sensationalistic" or "political" when dealing with issues like cruelty. Their public base of support is different from the supporters of animal rights organizations that are more willing to describe in text and picture the stark reality of extreme cases of cruelty. As one person in development noted, its audience is uncomfortable with graphic and ugly portrayals of cruelty: "Over the years, we have gotten letters. The public has made the line clear to us—our public—the one we target, which may be different than PETA's [People for the Ethical Treatment of Animals] or HSUS's [Humane Society of the United States]."

To avoid offending people, the media affairs staff rejects the use of photographs showing extreme abuse. One staff member explained how they screen animals for use in photographs: "We go see what they look like because we don't want an animal that is just so awful that people are going to be horrified and angry at you for pushing this awful thing in their face." For example, according to a humane agent, in one particularly violent and hideous case, media affairs failed to pursue press attention because the cruelty was too "icky": "These two kids who took a cat and threw it off the roof of an apartment building, hung it up on a wrought iron gate fence, crucified it by tying its arms to the fence. They took the intestines out and stretched it out in a crucifixion type manner with the intestines, and then took one of the eyes and stuck it in the mouth—just as sick as you can imagine. We locked them up, gave them counseling. That happened some months ago, but that got no coverage. It never made the papers only because our media relations director felt it was too icky for the papers. It's got to be cute cruelty."

Photographs from other, perhaps equally disturbing cases, might be used, but only after careful selection of easier-to-see pictures, or perhaps even uplifting ones of abused animals in recovery. Staff members might, for example, reject the most shocking pictures in favor of showing "after" ones. In a case involving tar-covered puppies found in a sewer, "before shots" could not be used because, according to one staff member, "they would have been too hideous, too horrible to a lot of people. We have to be so careful." Instead, photographs were used of the dogs after they were washed. Sometimes "before pictures" are taken that avoid showing potentially disturbing details. In this regard, the head of development spoke about Fluffy, a terribly abused dog, who was used in one humane society's mass mailings: "We will take 'before pictures'—in the case of Fluffy who had had one of her hind legs severed by her owner—the story was that her owner had chained her by her leg to a post for so long that the leg had severed right around where your thighbone would be. And it was really horrific when she came in. She was emaciated, covered in hundreds of ticks, and she had short hair so you could see all the ticks, huge engorged ticks all over her, and you could see a bit of bone this big—an inch or two—sticking out of the stump on her leg. It was just horrible in every way imaginable. You could see her suffering, it was beautiful. The only thing we had to do when we took our 'before pictures,' and even our after pictures, you had to be careful not to show too much of the stumpy, bloody, horrible leg because you didn't want to horrify people." The Fluffy case, while beautiful, was difficult to manage because of the concern that her cruelty—if fully shown—would be too much for the concerned public to handle.

Not offending people also means carefully wording descriptions of cruelty. Media experts choose the correct language to move readers while not shocking them. Creating an acceptable narrative of abuse means sidestepping the use of certain terms. In one case involving "degloving," press releases avoided this term and instead spoke of skin being removed from the animal without describing in detail what this meant. A staff member explained: "That was one of the tough things about the Mandy story. She was degloved. And when I first heard that I wasn't sure what it meant. It means that all the skin was removed on her arm. It's pretty horrible. It was difficult to figure out how to write degloving and explain what that meant without making it sound so hideous. Sometimes it is ugly." This staff member added that animal rights organizations might not have downplayed degloving if they had used it in their promotions.

Descriptions are also carefully worded to avoid offending the media and organizations important to humane societies. A media affairs staff member spoke about the need to be "conservative" rather than "sensational" when writing about cruelty: "We have a fine line that we have to walk on. You have to grab the media's attention but you don't want to appear too fanatical as far as the language that you are using. You are a little bit more conservative with the language. I mean put powerful language but not over the top. We always try to keep that respect that the media and other agencies have for us, so we need to be truthful and present the severity of it yet without sensational language. I think when you get a letter from PETA or ALF [Animal Liberation Front] the language and pictures hit you over the head, I mean there is no mincing of words. We have to be respectful of the person who is reading it and mindful of the image we are presenting." To avoid politicizing the issue, then, language is softened in press releases and solicitations. Instead of using words like *torture* or *maim* that are used in the direct mailings of more politically inclined animal organizations, humane societies use wording that is more dispassionate.

Appealing Animals

In addition to the right amount of graphic cruelty, beautiful cases have appealing victims that can easily evoke sympathy. Certain kinds of animals are automatically excluded, although they can represent some of the most brutal cases. As one media affairs director said: "I would never take pictures of dead animals and put those in press releases. That would cross the line." Abused farm animals, too, rarely appear in cruelty promotions, since most of the target audience would find it harder to identify with them than with domestic or wild animals that are harmed.

Companion animals, when in just the right condition and pose, are thought to be the most effective type of animal to elicit support from the public. By far, dogs are most commonly featured, and small dogs are considered the best for promotion. Tiny, a deliberately burned dog, was described by a staff member as a potentially beautiful case for this reason: "It was a big case because the violence was so graphic, but I also think there's a species issue too. I think people react differently to a small dog [or] puppy. [They get a] peak reaction. Tiny was a small dog with very graphic pictures that showed burns. It was a defenseless little dog intentionally hurt, and the way Tiny looked—you couldn't look at him without wanting to cry."

An abused animal's age can affect its appeal. Although any small dog or puppy is thought to be a perfect victim for presentation to the public, a dog that is too young is problematic. As one society staff member pointed out: "From the start, Buster was very young. Not quite a puppy, but very young. Not so puppy-like to be disturbing to see how crippled and injured he was. Seeing a very young puppy that crippled would have been very disturbing." A development staff member illustrated this problem with the example of Susie, a dog whose leg was chopped off and was used in one society's direct mailings: "You walk up to this dog and her tail starts wagging like mad and she's good natured and has this beautiful face. She was a dog who, right from the start, had a natural visual connection to you. Just telling the story itself was emotional. If Susie had been a six-week-old puppy missing a leg, I don't think we would have used her because that would have been way too horrific for people to handle."

An animal's expressions can also affect its appeal. As one staff member remarked: "You have to think about every little thing—Does the dog have its tag on? How does it look? Does it look happy? Does it look angry? If it's a pit bull you want to be sure it's got a sweet, sensitive face. You don't want it to have an aggressive face." Indeed, showing behavior like aggressiveness is carefully avoided when animal victims are photographed or taped for television. In one case, for example, the abused dog, off camera, was worrisome because "it had warning signs." As a staff member explained: "He had to be anesthetized to have anything done to him because he was ready to bite off the staff's fingers. He was a biter. We wouldn't let anybody get close enough to see if he really would bite. He was fine with his owner and people he knows, but with strangers could be aggressive." The public also does not want to see expressions on animals that could be construed as suffering. As a media affairs expert observed, "They don't really want to see a dog show pain." However, abused animals can "look bad" if they still show some sort of appealing expression. For example, in one case of a badly beaten dog, the media affairs director noted that she referred to it as "Little Frankenstein because it had black stitches across its face." She explained: "On the TV coverage, almost all the commentators warned people that this might be graphic. But despite the wounds, he still looked like a happy-to-be-alive dog."

Even appealing names are thought to help market beautiful cases. It is thought that the names of abused animals should be fitting— inoffensive and uplifting. In one case, staff members changed an animal's name from Lusty to Hope so that the development literature would be more appealing. They explained their action: "Actually we changed her name. The officer at the time, or someone in the shelter or hospital, had named her when she came in and it wasn't sellable. It was a horrible name. It was just awful. I don't know what they were thinking, but they weren't marketing people. So Susie and I sat for a while trying to think of a good name—something that was uplifting and sweet and feminine—and just reflected what we thought her personality was. That's how Hope came to be. It's a female name but it has a different meaning. At the time we were desperately looking for the right story for a mailed solicitation, and pop, she appeared just in time for us to do this mailing and just in time to put one photo of her in that brochure." At some societies, names become identified with particularly successful marketing campaigns and are retained long after the animal dies. The

Dusty Fund, for instance, features a "new" Dusty about once a year, even though the breed and abuse are different from the original dog used in this campaign to raise money to fight cruelty.

The search for appealing abused animals means that the best cases will eventually be trumped by even more appealing cases, making them all, in the end, replaceable. Addressing this matter, one staff member said of a particularly effective case: "Sunshine is timeless but I have no doubt that in six months I will have another horrifying Sunshine story, just as bad, and just as good at the same time, and I may never have to use Sunshine again. But I have her. That's the sad truth of this awful business—there's going to be another Sunshine in six months. I am sure of it, as sure as I am sitting here."

Since beautiful cases can become "boring" to the public, marketing campaign star-victims are rotated. One development staff member likened this rotation to the change of characters in a popular television show: "I am hitting up most of the animal lovers and I don't want them to get bored. So you rotate—whether it be in advertisements, mailings, stories in newsletters. If you use the same animal month after month eventually it gets boring. It's like the TV show *Law and Order*. It's been on TV for ten years and people still love it. Part of the success of *Law and Order* in my opinion—a marketing perspective—is that the characters change. They've been through three or four detectives. There are two sets of detectives, which are the law—they are the cops. And the order is like these DAs. In the ten years they have changed the DAs and cops numerous times. And in other shows, you change the main character and the show goes to pot. But they made it part of their thing so the show is always fresh. Sometimes they focus more on the cops and sometimes more on the DAs. That keeps it fresh too. And I think that's what's going to hopefully keep the Buster Fund fresh. You change the stories, you change the faces, you rotate things." Species victims also are rotated to keep things "fresh." One staff member described this rotation: "We do dozens of mailings throughout the year, so we'll rotate them throughout, rotating dogs and cats. So if you are a cat person—you've got a cat story and maybe the next quarter of the year we'll use a dog story to mix it up."

Distraught Owners

Owners can be shown as victims too—revealing further damage from cruelty. Although both development and media affairs concentrate on

the animal's side of the story, owners—if they are known and not themselves the abusers—can have a small but important part in beautiful
cases. Indeed, by the time newspapers and television programs craft
their own abuse stories, owners are given center stage to provide some
human interest to cruelty stories. Owners express a range of strong
emotions, running from being distraught to being furious, thereby dem-
onstrating that they too are victims. These displays of emotion match
the reactions of people who are featured in news stories about children
who are harmed, abducted, or killed. As one media affairs expert noted,
"We definitely want people to act like they care and are concerned
about this."

Owners who speak for their animals can generate public outrage. As
one staff member explained: "When they were interviewing Kim, Little's owner, they kept asking her, 'How do you think Little feels?' and,
'What would you say to Little if Little could understand?' They were
trying to get an emotional story. They definitely want to ask those questions that will turn the story on its emotional edge." When owners are
asked such questions, viewers are indirectly asked to imagine the
answer—by putting themselves in the place of the animal—and to
accept that getting an answer to such a question is reasonable and possible. Having an owner speak thus serves a transferential function if the
statements prompt or facilitate identification by outsiders with the
owner's position. A media affairs staff member underscored this point
when she described the public's reaction to an owner who expressed
great lament over his abused dog. This reaction aroused sympathy in
viewers, who saw a kindred spirit—a fellow animal lover in distress—
felt his suffering, and offered support. "This case, since I've been here,
generated the most phone calls from the public. I lost count how many
calls were from people who have small dogs too who identified with
this dog's owner, saying 'I have a little dog. I can't imagine someone
doing that to my dog.'"

Owners, if they are in the picture, need to be appealing, just as do
animal victims. For cases to be beautiful, owners must be upset over
the mistreatment of their animals and be responsible caretakers. Public affairs personnel closely monitor "celebrity owners" to ensure that
they project the right image. In one case, the dog Blacky had been brutally abused, but media affairs was not confident that his owner would
appear to be a good caretaker. The staff considered downplaying or

excluding Blacky's owner in newspaper and television reports because she was somewhat "shady" and did not fit the standard profile of a good owner; they feared that on air she might talk about wanting to breed her abused dog, use inappropriate language, not show sufficient feelings for her animal, or accuse someone of animal abuse. Unfortunately, on the first newscast, which the society did not orchestrate, the abuser and her family came across as hardly ideal owner-victims. A staff member compared Blacky's owner to "Mickey's," the latter being perfect owners: "Blacky's owner was challenging to manage because she was on the edge. The perfect owner would be someone like Mickey's owner. They were a couple in their mid-fifties, they had grandchildren and children, who absolutely loved their dog and were articulate and responsible and dependable in terms of what they said publicly about the case. Blacky's owner actually turned out to be publicly quite good. The media asked her the same question ten different ways to try to get her to publicly cry on camera— 'If you could talk to Blacky . . . ? If Blacky were a child, what would you tell him?' They were really pushing the envelope to try to get her to show emotion. I was concerned because in person she was the kind of person who had trouble completing a sentence without swearing. She also wasn't a stable woman, but she truly loved her dog and on camera, she was fine. And she was very grateful. I mean, off camera, her sister told me, 'If you don't get him [the abuser], we're going to get him.' I told her to please not say that on TV. She did have other members of her family in the background shouting inappropriate things. On the first piece of news coverage you will see that they actually pointed a finger at someone they truly believed did it who turned out not to have done it. But they were positive he did it and channel nine was questioning him on camera, basically asking him why would they say you did this if you didn't do it?"

Shadowy Abusers

Beautiful cases also feature abusers. Indeed, without a "perp" or "respondent," there is a lingering sense that justice has not been rendered as the criminal roams free. The ideal abuser, if included, has no motive to harm animals other than sadistic pleasure—evil intent is clear. More important, the abuser is arrested, charged with cruelty, convicted, and sentenced.

When direct mailings or press releases include abusers, they are portrayed as dangerous and guilty of aggression toward animals. A media affairs staff member recounts one such case: "I wrote a piece about a woman in the Southend housing project who had an argument with her neighbor. She attacked her neighbor and her dog. Her neighbor went back into her apartment, but the dog was outside. She used a box cutter to slice up the dog—mainly superficial wounds—but ones that looked pretty bad. We went and arrested her for animal cruelty because she attacked the animal."

More commonly, the abuser's presence in a case and the court outcome are only implied. For example, one humane society's newsletter often reports cruelty cases that are still under investigation, so there are no criminal justice outcomes to disappoint readers. However, the city where the abuse takes place might be listed and articles routinely note the current maximum penalty for cruelty, indicating to readers that the humane law enforcement department has some idea about who harmed the animal and that the abuse will be pursued and taken to court.

Although beautiful cases might include arrest and successful prosecution, they rarely do because so few egregious cases have an abuser who is arrested, let alone found guilty and punished. In one case of an animal that was doused with gasoline and set on fire, no abuser was found, making it difficult to elevate this incident to a perfect one, although in every other regard it "qualified." The victim was a small, cute dog that did not die. Her abuse was graphic and violent but suitable for photographing in ways that de-horrified the cruelty. And she had a loving owner who spoke openly about the tragedy and the distress she felt. As one administrator said of this case, it was over without an abuser: "It depends on what happens now. The chances of us identifying who did this are pretty small. The story is kind of over unless they find the abuser."

Most abusers fail to go to jail or receive much punishment, and certainly it is impossible to ensure that the abuse will not be repeated. As one staff member complained: "The public wants closure on these high-profile cases. They want to know that the person who did it to them is going to go to jail or be punished some way and that that person is never going to do that again. We all want the person who did this to be brought to justice, but it is a difficult thing." Another society representative added: "I wish the stories had an ending of, 'Here's the conviction and this man is going to jail for doing this.' And maybe that would get the message across that this is unacceptable and will be punished. I don't see the punishment component out there." And yet another staff member said: "I would love a case with a conviction to announce, but that has never happened since I've been here— like 'torturer gets five years' would be great. It just hasn't happened. That would be great, but I'm not optimistic. It is sad."

Like cruelty that is too gory to report in detail, the judicial experience with abusers, if reported completely, might appall the public. Media experts dodge the fact that abusers get away with these heinous crimes by focusing on other aspects about them. For example, one development officer explained that she focuses on the counseling abusers receive because they all go unpunished—an outcome that she would like to report: "In the end, I would only choose to talk about the process of improving them [abusers] and how the society might participate in that, for example, with counseling. The abuser is not the story. The story is the animal. You use the abuser only when you need to support the animal's story but not to focus in any way on the abuser. If the sentence wasn't satisfactory to me, then I can't believe it would be satisfactory to our donors. We have unfortunately not reported any sentences in our mailings. I can always pray, but right now we haven't had a good sentence to publish." One case was considered beautiful because the abuser was convicted, but the society's handling of the case ignored time served to prevent the reader's "horror." As a staff member pointed out, "Every angle you look at it, it is beautiful—the guy eventually did get convicted, although we didn't state the sentence because most people would be horrified at how little it is—it was like time served."

Perfect stories also ignore abusers when their behavior is considered too bizarre: "crazy" or unseemly actions are thought to detract from the animal focus. One officer described a grotesque case of cruelty that was not used for promotion because of the abuser's loathsome character. Officers investigating the case found several pit bull puppies that had been used as bait: one had half of its face missing, another had gangrene from a chain collar grown into its neck, and a third had hundreds of bites and an eye entirely closed: "The individual who owned these dogs had quite a reputation in the neighborhood. They were all scared of him. I could see why people were scared of him— two hundred and sixty pounds and about five feet nine inches, with a Nazi tattoo on his back. Crazy as a loon to boot. I knew it would be one of those things where we would be rolling on the ground with him. We got cuffs on him. He of course was charged with animal cruelty and he had quite an extensive arrest record. It was almost like these were junkyard dogs and this individual didn't care. In fact we found one skull in the back. He bragged that he killed a number of dogs and buried them in the back of that yard. This individual is about as sick as you can get. But this case has not gotten any publicity. These kinds of cases in general don't get into the papers."

Because there are so few examples of prosecuted and punished abusers whose behavior is not too disturbing, most press releases and direct mailings about cruelty ignore the judicial component. Public relations experts delicately sidestep the entire issue of justice in extreme cruelty incidents because they believe that reporting courtroom reality detracts from what are otherwise beautiful cases. Indeed, not being able to include some happy judicial ending in the reporting of these cases is a sore point for all staff members, who are disappointed and frustrated because abusers are not apprehended or punished for their crimes. As one public relations director said: "Since I've been here, the one really frustrating thing for me in dealing with the public and the media on these cases, and I am sure a hundred times more frustrating for law enforcement, is that we generally don't get the people who did it. It's very, very difficult to make an arrest and even if you do make an arrest, they tend to get off. It is very frustrating because you talk to people who are really moved to want to donate to the reward fund, to want to help with this, and really respect what our officers do, but you very rarely are ever able to bring someone to justice for these cases."

Happy Endings

To move the public, media experts believe that beautiful cases should have "happy endings" where animals do not die but have healthy and robust futures. In the words of one senior administrator at the society: "It hurts if the animal dies. Then the case is over. It doesn't have a continuing life because the dog didn't survive. There's nothing like having a happy ending, from a marketing perspective. A happy ending is just a wonderful thing. Who wants a dog dying? That's a bad story." Although happy endings are very important and are featured in direct mailings, in reality, unhappy endings are far more common. Many animals found by agents are either dead or are in such poor veterinary health they must be euthanized, as happened in the case of a dog suffering from a severe skin disease that left it with no fur and eyes practically closed from swelling. "You look at it— like I don't want to touch that animal. That animal should be put down now. There is no hope for it," one public relations staff member said.

Nevertheless, choosing or creating the right "after-photographs" can produce happy endings. An animal that appears responsive to humans, perhaps even playful, is a crucial ingredient, as a development staff member pointed out in one beautiful case: "We have a great after-picture of Tina [an abuse victim] that we use in solicitation where she is happy and her tail is wagging and she is licking the face of the officer that rescued her. She was a really sweet dog, a really wonderful dog. She was in my opinion the epitome of what a really fabulous story is. Tina in every way is perfect. You see her happy. You see her healthy. You see that she is capable of leading a good life." Some after photographs are staged in exterior settings that transcend the adversity of cruelty and further imply a happy ending because of their shear beauty and tranquility. In one beautiful case, the featured victim was posed for pictures in an outdoor setting hundreds of miles from the city where its abuse occurred. A member of the development staff talked about how these photographs featured a brilliant blue sky above a healthy-looking former victim standing alertly on a sand dune: "This photo was chosen because the animal is out, and it is beautiful, and it's happy and free— you know, it is glorious. That is what people want to hang. They don't want to hang a picture of a dog emaciated and covered with ticks and with a paw missing. The first couple of times we worked with the photographer, we sat with him you know, "this is what we are looking for," and now John really knows, and I might say over the phone, 'I want black and white, or color, or be sure to get one where she is doing this or that.' These little details are important."

Happy endings also mean that animals end up in good homes or are returned to their owners, if the owner is not the abuser. Many animals in big cases have no owners because they have been abandoned or their owners are irresponsible or even criminal. In these cases, adopters serve as proxy guardians and contribute to the case's perfection. In one such case, over thirty puppies in "horrible condition" were rescued by officers from a deplorable "puppy mill." After being nursed back to health by the society's hospital workers, these animals were farmed out to shelters and all found adoptive homes. The society's newsletter covered these "happy" adoptions: "After they [the abused animals] recovered, they went to the shelter where they were over-whelmed with people who wanted to adopt them. One of the dogs was adopted out to a nice family with two little boys that were featured in a video we did. And it even had the little boy writing a letter to the shel-ter saying, 'Please let me adopt this dog and I'll take him to the vet, I'll take good care of him.' That's really the ideal story."

Constructing happy endings, however, means ignoring cases where adopted animals have demanding behavioral or medical problems or leaving out these details in direct mailings or press releases. Indeed, some animals in beautiful cases would not be put up for adoption were they "normal" shelter charges because of the problems they present to adopters. Yet the notoriety they receive often generates many offers for adoption. For example, one case involved a dog whose unpublicized behavior was at times difficult and challenging for his new owner to manage, even though she was a very experienced shelter manager. According to a senior administrator familiar with the situation: "We want the beautiful cases to be neat and clean and the happy endings to be wonderful, but sometimes all is not what it seems. Sometimes peo-ple are cruel to animals because they are angry because the dog bit them or snarled at them. And so they did an incredibly cruel act, and it became highly public and we fixed the animal up, but the reality is that this is not a very nice dog. We end up with an animal that has a slew of problems associated with it, not just as the result of the cruelty, but because it is a behavior-problem dog. So what do you do now with this dog that is not beautiful cruelty? It can be a big case, but all of a sud-den you are dealing with an animal that is hard to deal with. Gigi is an example. She has a slew of behavior-related problems associated with her. She hates men. And she is also into everything. I mean, Gigi's sec-ond trip to the hospital was when she chewed up Betty's [the adopter's] purse and ate a bottle of Ibuprofen, plastic and all. This is a dog with a lot of problems who was very lucky to have been a dog that Betty fell in love with." When Gigi appeared in the society's public relations material, no mention was made of the many difficulties she posed to her new owner. She was just one more beautiful case.

THE PERFECT MESS

The disorder of the 1968 Chicago Democratic Convention was a "perfect mess," according to the social critic Abbie Hoffman (1968). Despite the chaos and violence at the convention, all parties involved in the scene—from the mayor to the police to the Yippies—had a chance to show the world that what they were doing was right. Everybody tried to manipulate the media to advance their version of reality and the ugliness surrounding the convention provided this chance. "Everyone gets what he wants," Hoffman writes (p. 122). To some groups, it "proved" conspiracy; to other groups it "proved" the need for law and order. "There was enough of a perfect mess for everyone to get a share of the garbage" (p.123). What Hoffman saw so clearly was the desire and ability of various groups to make sense of the same tragedy in different ways to advance their own agenda or meet their own needs. Even in the worst situations, there lies opportunity.

Extreme cases of animal cruelty also are perfect messes, and though they are of a very different sort from what Hoffman observed at the 1968 Democratic Convention, they are both chaotic and violent and, as Hoffman perceived disruption at political conventions, they pose serious trouble to humane societies. Although these organizations purport to fight cruelty, why should their followers continue to believe in the organizations and their mission if there are no victories over animal abuse? For the same reason, why should their staff members not suffer a serious blow to morale? There are no easy answers to explain away these troubles and, without proper addressing, they can challenge an institution's core beliefs, lessen the zeal of its followers or proponents, and tarnish the robustness of its vision. Left unaddressed, extreme cruelty cases can only remind humane societies, their staff, and their public, that some people blatantly disregard dearly held values about the proper treatment of animals. Left unexamined, these cases can blunt confidence in the institution. Left unanalyzed, these cases can extinguish hope for a better world for animals.

Like Hoffman's observation that political disruptions created opportunities for various groups, the tragedy of cruelty has the same potential. In fact, beautiful cruelty cases are seen as "opportunities" by humane societies—far greater ones than stories about other activities or services, such as their hospitals and shelters. Speaking about the significance of these cases, a staff member said: "They are the most compelling news stories we have for the media and the public. We want them to *do* something." It is the work of development and media affairs to create narratives about these cases, so they can do something. Their stories explain the society's work with cruelty—why it is so horrible, how humane agents carry out thorough investigations of it, what kind of criminal penalty is appropriate for abusers, how skillful veterinarians work with animal victims, and how sensitive shelter staff care for them.

Officially, humane societies want these stories to raise money and public awareness. To say, however, that these cases are good because they result in donations or provide public service messages does not give full credit to their value, although fund raising and general education are vital concerns for humane organizations. Actually, beautiful cruelty cases "do" quite a bit more. In the face of untoward events, unmanageable problems, unremitting uncertainties, and inexplicable actions—and cruelty is all of these—humane societies must rely on the narrative power of their stories about cruelty to make understandable, orderly, and meaningful something that is not. In reality, the events surrounding abuse are disjointed and fragmented, full of ambiguities and muddled with contradictions. At a different level than fund raising and education, creating and telling stories about cruelty is a process by which humane societies make sense out of what it considers to be a tragedy. This organizational sensemaking (Choo 1998) produces moral tales that distinguish right from wrong and draw boundaries between good and evil. Such tales enable the organization to sustain its battle against cruelty because they remind the public at large and the staff members of humane societies what is important, who they are, and why they should believe.

Reaffirming Values

Extreme cases of cruelty are major blows to humane societies and their followers. These tragedies cry out for recognition, they provoke mulling, and they demand meaning. In other words, they prompt memorialization of animal victims—just as do human tragedies for survivors who mourn the dead and injured. Memorials have many important functions, perhaps none so important as the extraction of "lessons" from concrete events that find something of value in what are otherwise meaningless, untoward situations. Communicating lessons about cruelty gives humane societies a significant opportunity to promote their view of cruelty and increase awareness of their mission.

There is however, a different opinion in the United States that it is frivolous to be too concerned about animals. At times the media seems to encourage this sentiment. The *Boston Globe*, for example, ran a front-page article and photograph called "Paws and Smile" that talks about "ruff days for canine commuters" (Arnold 2000). The human interest article, whose photograph showed well-behaved dogs strapped to the seats of a school bus, described the dogs' drive to "doggie day care" as the "lap of luxury." The $325 monthly fee, however, did not include lunch; dogs had to bring their own because "some are picky eaters." "You've got to love dogs to do this," the manager of the program said. Soon after this article appeared, several hostile letters to the editor ridiculed it as further evidence of the silliness with which humans approach animals and the waste of resources spent on them. By establishing that humane treatment of animals is normative and that cruelty is norm violating, beautiful cases contest such perceptions.

As a vehicle for mass moral education, beautiful cases convey the notion that the mistreatment of animals is reprehensible—whether this is a novel view for some people or redundant to others. The first and simplest way media experts use beautiful cases to communicate the seriousness of cruelty, as one expert pointed out, is to make clear that "cruelty is wrong. That cruelty is bad. That it is not acceptable. And that something needs to change. I have been here so long, I sometimes take it for granted that people know that, but not everyone knows that. We still need to get out the general message that cruelty is wrong and it shouldn't be tolerated." And staff members believe that this basic message is effective; one media affairs director praised the ability of beautiful cases to change people's thinking and action toward animals: "We use examples of people doing the wrong thing so that people out there will understand, 'Oh, this is wrong, this is bad, this is not something that should be done,' whether they are going to do it themselves and it will stop them from a potential action or it simply makes them humane ambassadors so that when they see it, they know it's wrong."

The second way media experts use beautiful cases to underscore the seriousness of cruelty is to emphasize that such cases are commonplace, even though they are rare. The direct mailings or press releases of humane societies often try to put individual cases into a bigger context by noting the large number of investigations each year and the fact that this number is probably much larger because many witnesses do not report these crimes. As one brochure notes, "I am gravely concerned about how rampant animal cruelty is right now. Last year, the Society's Law Enforcement received more than 4,300 complaints of animal abuse or neglect. . . . At the risk of alarming you, however, I must state that the problem is even more serious than these figures indicate . . . there is a lot more violence being inflicted on animals . . . than we know about." In truth, the total number of yearly abuse complaints to the society has remained fairly constant over the past decade, and the vast majority of these do not involve incidents of active cruelty. Nevertheless, by featuring extreme cruelty, rather than everyday neglect, promotional pieces like this one give readers an exaggerated picture of the frequency of cruelty.

Third, to portray cruelty as a serious crime, beautiful cases have just the right kind of animal victim at their symbolic core and dramatic center. In a process Majone (1988) refers to as norm-using, they rely on broadly accepted social standards to give these images added legitimacy and currency. Thus, the narratives underlying beautiful cases seem reasonable if not conventional because they tap into existing attitudes that people readily appreciate and endorse. For example, the child protection movement gained power when its ideas were connected to broadly respected norms about defending children from harm (Sinclair 1995). Beautiful cases also put forth a victim that is childlike in its innocence and helplessness. Animal victims, then, attach to dominant cultural norms specifying appropriate response to human victims. By implicitly suggesting that animals are like children, beautiful cases suggest a breach of fundamental social values similar to that suggested in media reports of murdered children (Grabosky and Wilson 1989), in turn providing an opportunity for the concerned public to share its outrage over these incidents and reaffirm "fundamental" values they hold regarding the proper treatment of animals. Moral education most effectively happens when tragedy is appropriately staged.

Fourth, media experts communicate the seriousness of cruelty by making frequent references to the "scientifically" established connection between cruelty and other violent crimes. The mailings of humane societies speak of the "link" between animal abuse and violence toward humans, as though it were a proven fact. As one letter proclaims, "We now have scientific proof . . . that people who abuse animals are far more likely to commit acts of violence toward people . . . 70% of animal abusers also had criminal records for other serious crimes. This is alarming!" Interestingly, the study from which these statistics were extracted reported that animal abuse rarely leads to later violent behavior against humans (Arluke et al. 1999). However, by invoking the "link," humane societies can upgrade or broaden their case for the gravity of cruelty.

Fifth, media experts emphasize the "law and order" theme in beautiful cases to underscore the seriousness of cruelty. They rely on a "vocabulary of justice" (Kidder 1983) that makes sense to the public and reflects social norms about what is thought to be just. By emphasizing the value of law and order in general, these cases resonate with well-established, legitimate social goals and send the message that the expectations of humane societies for law enforcement policy are reasonable, that cruelty is a crime, and that humane law enforcement agents are to be supported in their pursuit of abusers. Even though most abusers are not caught, and those who are rarely get convicted and punished, beautiful cases project a strong image of agents as fighters of abuse and guardians of humane treatment of animals. To showcase agents to the public, one society names celebrity "uniformed officers" in mailings and press releases or on television news. "The uniform is a presence," one media relations staff member explained: "We want people to know that we are investigating cruelty cases and that they can come to us if they have a concern about another animal. A lot of people don't realize that we do law enforcement. Out of a city of nearly ten million people, we only have ten agents doing law enforcement. A lot of cruelty goes undetected."

To complete this vocabulary, the society, in its promotion of beautiful cases, asks sympathetic individuals to report information, often with a reward, that might lead to the arrest and conviction of abusers. By offering "a reward for information leading to the arrest and conviction of suspects," the narrative creates a criminal drama where the public is made to think about their role in apprehending abusers and bringing them to justice. Even if this is more of a symbolic gesture than one that can produce real results, the concerned public can feel as though they are contributing to a larger effort to apprehend abusers. Although these requests for information rarely lead to arrests or convictions, they also tell the public that action is being taken to catch abusers and presumably to punish them, serving as another reminder that abuse is a form of criminal behavior—on a par with serious crimes committed against humans—because the request and reward for information leading to arrest and conviction is the same language used to summon information about suspects in other crimes. There is, then, a high symbolic value in making this request.

In the end, beautiful cases are moral tales. They have bad people who take advantage of and violate the love and trust given so easily by innocent animals, dedicated and caring agents who work to apprehend abusers and bring them to justice for their crimes, tragic victims who end up happy and healthy while abusers pay the price, and a humane society whose battle against cruelty is slowly but surely being won. These tales challenge the public to think about what constitutes the proper treatment of animals and their abusers. To the extent that they do this, beautiful cases are an opportunity for humane societies to establish social norms that support the prevention of animal cruelty and the punishment of abusers. Of course, trying to change legal and social responses to animals is a slow process because social attitudes must change, but beautiful cases are a platform to pursue this end.

That these tales say nothing new to those who support or work for humane societies is exactly the point. Rather, this "education" is a restatement of core norms and beliefs that are at the moral center of the concerned animal community. They need the right issues to rally around—those that endorse and articulate their central values, long-term dreams, and heart-felt sentiments. Egregious cruelty is exactly the right kind of issue. It can be a trigger for the amorphous animal community to step out of its isolation and express these beliefs, hopes, and concerns. Beautiful stories are a vehicle to elicit these feelings—to "move" people—and those who write them consciously create emotionally charged narratives, even if their tone is reportorial and unsensational. As one media expert admitted, "Your emotional side will come through when you are telling a story, and sometimes that will help to have a bigger impact because people can see that it is a moving case."

Validating Identities

Hearing or reading about extreme cases of cruelty can deeply disturb people who have strong sympathy for and identification with animals, even though the victims are not their own. These cases pull at the heartstrings of the public as well as the staff of humane societies because they are unusual enough to provide comparisons, yet universal enough to evoke identification. "Narratives unfold with flesh and blood," encouraging empathy and humanizing content (Ellis and Bochner 1992, 98). It is easy to imagine how people who care a great deal about animals will be moved by these stories, but those who lack special feelings for animals also can be moved if these stories touch on themes—such as the loss of a child—that most people readily appreciate.

Things about these cases shake up people's core beliefs and values. For one, they can feel unsure about their own identities as animal guardians and what they assume are fundamental ingredients in human relationships with domestic animals. Extreme cruelty is a stark reminder that not everyone shares their view that these animals should be loved and protected. For another, these cases may make them feel less assured that the world is a safe and just place for animals. They reveal that some animals were not protected from harm, that similar threats to other animals might occur, and that abusers are often not caught and, if caught, rarely punished.

Clearly, the friends, donors, and supporters of humane societies need to have their identities validated and supported after they hear about extreme cases of cruelty, but this is difficult to accomplish because most are isolated in the general community. Many are regarded as "animal people," an inexact but nevertheless commonly used folk term that labels those who are strongly concerned about the welfare of animals without necessarily being heavily involved in the animal right movement. Unlike activists, members of the concerned animal public belong to an amorphous group; they do not have frequent meetings to attend, rallies to cheer at, products to boycott, or petitions to sign. They have few if any animal-related events that make them feel part of a larger, defined group. To be effective, however, humane societies need a "cult" of dedicated followers because their work needs to occur in an atmosphere of compassion, encouragement, and support. An audience, especially of the laity, that shares the sorrow over cruelty and anger toward abusers validates the sentiment of humane societies and helps myth making take on an air of authenticity and relevance.

Beautiful cases can bolster and validate these battered identities by creating a sense that "we" are in a battle together to fight cruelty. They do this by opening a channel for expressing sentiment about cruelty, since the public can be particularly interested in and concerned about the victimization of animals, especially when it is extreme. Because they see humane societies as having compatible values, some people telephone or write to these organizations and "vent" their concerns about cruelty, express their affection and pride for their own animals, and communicate their views about human-animal relationships in general. A media expert explained that her job is to listen to these people and reassure them that abused animals are being helped: "I got dozens of calls from people after the fact wanting to know how Sparky was doing. You know, 'Is he okay, I haven't heard anything? Did you catch the guy?' A lot of it is that they just want to vent. Some of this venting is anger— we get calls generally from young men who want to go out there and get the guy themselves and also want to donate money to help. But mostly, it's just emotion, that people are really moved by these cases and want to talk about them. They just want a sympathetic ear to tell how they feel about this and to hear someone say to them, 'We feel the same way and that it was so kind of you to send a contribution. Thank you.'" Once opened, this channel allows supporters to express their empathy for abused animals and their owners. It was common, for example, to see letters addressed to the abused animal and "signed" by the letter-writer's pet. At a deeper level, these responses make it possible for people to feel connected to the victim's owner as well as to the larger animal community, as one staff member speculated: "These cases do things for us—for animal lovers—they reinforce the way we feel about our animals. It says, 'I am not the only one who loves my dog as much as she loves her dog.' People really do identify with the cases. I can't tell you how many people call me and start telling me that they are moved by Sparky's case [a dog beating] but then they get into their own dogs— all about their dogs and how important their dogs are to them and how they couldn't imagine anyone doing anything like this to their little puppies or whatever. You really get a lot of that."

More tangible support also is offered. An outpouring of donations come in after these reports hit the news. For example, the press picked up one of these cases: a cat that had been badly abused needed a thousand dollars' worth of medical treatment and a home. After this article appeared, donations poured into the society that paid for veterinary care, and several offers were made to provide homes for the cat. In another more dramatic case, television exposure resulted in donations to help pay for a burned dog's expensive reconstructive skin grafts.

And in yet another case, a direct mailing that described a horrific case of cruelty was mailed to twenty thousand people and brought in over sixty-five thousand dollars—an average of about eighty dollars per gift— "and that's about as good as you could possibly get," one staff member explained. People also donated money when the society offered a reward for information leading to an arrest and conviction, often wanting to increase the reward through their pledges. Nor is it unusual for donations to continue to come in for months after a perfect cruelty case appears in the news. Those who donate get a thank-you letter signed by the society's president, which serves as a way to "reach out" and create new relationships as well as reaffirm old ones.

The meaning of these monetary gifts goes beyond the dollar amount. Raising money for animal victims is similar to raising funds in human tragedies, where unusual efforts or sacrifices are made to give donations. In one beautiful case, for example, a personal trainer was giving free sessions to his customers if they donated. So much money came in that the dog's bills were paid and surplus money, with donors' consent, went to help other animals through the society's general reward fund and its pet assistance program. Those who respond often offer more than just money; their special sentiment shows they regard cruelty as a true tragedy. They want to console the owners for their grief, validate their anger, and share their frustration. In rare, but telling moments, they just want to be in the company of these owners and their animals, as if paying their respects at a funeral of a loved one. A society employee recalls an unusual expression of support: "People do really extraordinary things. A woman in New Hampshire who makes custom dog beds insisted on being put in touch with one dog's owner and actually drove down from New Hampshire to bring a custom-made dog bed to this dog and its owner as a gift. She brought her whole family with her and was thrilled to meet the owner and the dog. She really wanted to see the dog and to meet Shelly [the owner]. She wanted to help this dog, she was so moved by the story. She liked Shelly and was very happy with the visit." Others responded to this particular case by mailing toys for the dog. The victim's owner said that her "phone was ringing off the hook with people calling to offer help and wanting to know how her dog was doing." At such times, people feel they are comforting both animal and human victims of abuse, experiencing a sense of community as they do so.

Beautiful cases also bolster identities by creating enemies—those who are deplored because they mistreat animals. Enemies are useful for communities for building identities and creating boundaries, telling people who or what they are not like. Enemies form an inverse reference group that allows people to say, "I am this type of person because I do not belong to that group." The essence of a community's identity can be found by discovering its deep or core imagery— things it holds most sacred, things it most fears, things it sees as most evil and unforgivable. Beautiful cases bring home this imagery and identification of both the enemy and "me."

Having an enemy elicits and focuses outrage. Although some Americans are not outraged by animal cruelty, they do respond to media reports of child abuse, which often elicit strong arguments for harsh criminal justice responses. These articles have banner headlines like "Hang the Bastard" and sometimes discuss "wild protests" erupting outside court houses by concerned members of the public calling for the death penalty (Wilczynski and Sinclair 1999). Beautiful cases elicit the same passionate response but more privately in letters and telephone calls to humane societies. Some people become incensed when they read or see a report about animal cruelty that notes the weak maximum penalty for this crime and vent their anger by contacting these societies to proclaim, for example, "The penalty is much too weak, it should be increased." Even if sentences are imposed, abusers rarely get sufficient punishment in the concerned public's eyes. In this regard, readers are upset by the fact that the newsletter does not name abusers, noting only the town or city where the abuse occurs. Although the editor cannot report names, readers are nevertheless disturbed that abusers remain anonymous, neither formally sanctioned by the courts nor informally sanctioned by the animal community. Those offering help are sometimes given guidance about what they can do, such as contacting their legislative representatives to support a bill that increases penalties for cruelty.

In short, beautiful cases are moral emergencies for animal people that inspire them to articulate deeply felt but rarely sanctioned sentiments about animals. As people respond to these cases by calling, writing, or donating money or gifts to humane societies, they also articulate their place in a larger animal community, showing how they think and feel about animals. Beautiful cases, then, ignite identity-generating emotions by providing an opportunity for people to offer their help and support to animals, their owners, and humane societies more generally.

Strengthening Morale

Most extreme cruelty cases are not beautiful—animals are crucified or have their eyes gouged out; many are dead, and those that are alive are not particularly cute; many abusers are not found and of those who are, most go unpunished. These cases rattle the sensibilities of everyone who works for humane societies, including the most experienced. Although they are in the animal welfare "business," staff members never get used to these disturbing cases. They are horrified when they encounter them and have strong feelings of anger and sometimes rage toward abusers, just as do animal people in the community. Sadistic cruelty is usually seen only in photographs. When extreme cases are directly confronted, even seasoned employees find their faith shaken in humanity. As one twenty-year shelter veteran admitted: "It is upsetting to see what mankind is capable of— embedded chains in necks, a puppy with amputated legs that somebody has chopped off with a cleaver, another dog with wire wrapped around its leg for a long period of time that grew into its skin, so it chewed off its own leg. Things like that are so horrific. Horrific things that make you not want to be a person. How can you do this? I would tell law enforcement, don't ever give me a gun if you take me out on the road because I would shoot everybody. I know that's the extreme, but to me, to inflict such horrible harm on a defenseless creature who has no defense is the lowest. To do this, how sick do you have to be?" These cases can make the most seasoned worker doubt their mission's effectiveness.

Beautiful cases help shore up these doubts. For one, they remind staff members that their core mission is to prevent and fight animal abuse. Although humane societies were created in the nineteenth century to deal with exactly this problem—the mistreatment of animals—few employees handle cruelty regularly and most never do. Managing, investigating, prosecuting, and promoting beautiful cruelty cases symbolically link humane societies to their historic mission. Indeed, as people describe their involvement with beautiful cases, they refer to the cruelty-fighting efforts of Henry Bergh, the founder of the American Society for the Prevention of Cruelty to Animals, and George Angell, the founder of the Massachusetts Society for the Prevention of Cruelty to

Animals. For example, one development director drew on this history in her efforts to publicize a case of a dog brutally chained by its leg: "That's my job—telling people that these horrible things happen and that by supporting us they can work slowly toward making those things not happen. Henry Bergh went to this socialite type dinner back in the 1800s and there was this fantastic centerpiece. It was gorgeous, alive with color. And on closer inspection, he realized it was live butterflies pinned to this ball as the centerpiece. And the flutter of their wings was all this live color. Now you and I today would be horrified. It may only be an insect, but that's disgusting, that's horrible. But it was acceptable to everyone except for Henry who said, 'Wait a second, hold on here. Is that right?' I don't know if he made a scene at the dinner, but I know he did later write the woman and say that was horrible, how could you do that? I don't think that, overnight, that changed. But I know today, one hundred years later, we wouldn't think of doing it. Maybe overnight, people aren't going to chain their dogs until their legs are severed, but hopefully a hundred years from now they will have better sense than to do that." Especially when employees see beautiful cases in the news, they "feel good" about working for humane societies—particularly those outside of law enforcement—because everyone can feel as though they are "on the front lines stopping animal cruelty." As one worker said: "In public affairs you can go days just doing the office work you do, and you may not make a dent, and then a law enforcement case will break, and it really just brings everything home. It reminds you, oh my god this is the work we are doing. This is what is really making a difference."

Most important, beautiful cases provide hope to staff members who do not feel that cruelty is being prevented or dealt with effectively. Although this pessimism resonates throughout humane societies, workers feel constrained not to go public with their sentiment, at least in an official capacity, for fear that such bleakness would hurt the organization's image and effort in this area. One media affairs staff member, for example, recounted her despair after one egregious case: "This was the most disturbing cruelty case that I have ever seen. I still have difficulty thinking about. I just can remember the look of this dog. It was a dog that we believe was being raised for bait in dogfights. It was called Wishbone. This dog had been abandoned in a lot. It was clearly neglected. It was severely malnourished. It had been in many fights. There were scars all over its body. Wishbone had a lot of scars, but he didn't have any gaping wounds. It is just the demeanor of this animal— these sad eyes. You just felt like all the joy had gone out of this dog's life. It was just the saddest thing, the ugliest thing I've ever seen. That was not an easy case in the sense that it was a disgusting, tragic case. And this dog was euthanized. That was the most humane thing. I get very sad, disgusted, and angry because sometimes you get like, Is what we are doing even working? Are we making a difference? You are just faced with something so disturbing and you can't believe that things have gotten better in the last ten years or however long you've been in the business." A beautiful case remedies this pessimism, if only briefly, because it furnishes hope that even in the most tragic episodes of cruelty, sometimes things turn out well. Happy endings can happen after animals are seriously harmed—they recover, they find good homes with loving owners, and they live out contented lives. Beautiful cases, then, help to restore faith in the institution for those whose belief and spirit are flagging.

Providing Heroes

Hope for a happy ending is essential for the morale of workers, but sometimes it feels like an illusion because happy endings are rare. Most abused or neglected animals seized by humane agents have no doting owner, are in poor veterinary health, and cry out for nurturing because of the miserable treatment they received. These animals provide opportunities for "rescuing" in a setting devoted to helping animals in need. By coming to their aid, humane agents are saying that people will help animals but with personal sacrifice and commitment. When staff members make this sacrifice, they keep hope alive by providing flesh-and-blood heroes who embody the finest qualities valued by a group. These heroes can restore confidence in institutions by showing that good things can happen after untoward events.

One way to become a hero is to show special interest in seized animals. For example, most humane agents end their involvement with these animals after giving them to veterinary technicians or shelter workers. They return to the field to conduct new investigations. However, some agents continue to be involved with the animals, taking an active interest in their welfare and outcome. A few visit and "keep track" of what's happening with the ones they bring into the hospital or shelter. For their unusual effort and compassion, employees praise these agents: "They don't just drop them off, like it's over. Todd worked on the Annie case and he was up here [fund raising] once a week just talking about her, talking to Tina [the shelter manager], talking to Mary [a hospital employee], about the progress of the case. Any information he could give us— he wanted to help in any way he could. Todd cares a lot." These agents develop reputations within humane societies for following cruelty cases, when animals survive, all the way to adoption, even to the point of checking out the suitability of adopters—tasks far exceeding their job requirements. One such agent reflected on a "high visibility" case from two decades earlier: "I remember everything about Natasha. Maybe I remember Natasha so well because it felt so violent and so unfair to this little puppy. I developed a personal relationship to this dog. I was the person who basically interceded and took control of this dog. And the protection of this animal undergoing this terrible painful thing was my responsibility. I visited her a lot in the shelter. And then I ended up knowing the person who adopted her. And I saw that dog for the rest of its life."

Others become heroes by spreading the word about seized animals, so people throughout humane societies learn about their history and abuse, veterinary welfare and progress, and fitness for adoption. More important for the fate of victims, these champions make the animals (and themselves) in-house celebrities. One senior administrator gave the example of an employee in the accounting department who is known to make it a personal mission to get involved with egregious cruelty cases: "Maybe people in accounting won't get involved in an HLE [humane law enforcement] case hands on, but they all know about them. If a big case comes through they hear about them. Very few people don't know about them. They know about them because a lot of people go down and visit the shelter. They visit the dogs. They talk to other people. Like Lauren Smith in accounting knows a lot about the HLE cases— she really loves the animals and loves her dog. There are a couple of others in there, but if somebody in there is going to talk about an animal case, it's probably going to be Lauren." The more who know about these cases, the more likely these animals will receive constant attention and care, support for legal prosecution, and offers of adoption by society workers.

Others become heroes by interceding on behalf of seized animals that have long shelter stays because they are being held as "evidence" for pending court cases. Many empathize with them because they have been subjected to abuse or neglect and are still in the "current and continuing plight of being in a cage." In response, these employees rally around the animals and become their "ambassadors," agitating to get something done for them. They may, for example, express dissatisfaction with the animal's plight to humane law enforcement. One department head described this problem, as it led to the fostering of a seized dog: "Buster was there [in the shelter] for more than a year. People were very upset that he was here that long. They identified with his continuous confinement. I mean they were walking him all the time. But they were really upset with us but they don't understand our situation. There is a tendency in some people to believe that we are not doing as much as we could or should. It is not realistic. There is a need to blame someone and who better or who else to blame than the people who brought the animal in and stuck the animal in a cage. I never had calls in which people were nasty, but they appealed to us to do something about it. What can be done about it? It was frustrating and demoralizing to me and the staff because they were painted with the same brush. This accusatory brush—basically, that we were ineffective."

Finally, some become heroes by adopting seized animals, creating real-life happy endings. These adopters become well known throughout humane societies, as happened in one organization. Jane, in shelter operations, adopted Susie—a shepherd severely beaten with a club. Barbara, in public affairs, adopted Sheldon—a badly burned cat. Tim, in law enforcement, adopted Spot—a Beagle deliberately run over by a car. Helen has photographs of her adopted law enforcement dog prominently displayed in her office along with copies of newspaper articles about the case. And there are many other animal victims adopted by staff members who gain institutional notoriety for their acts. As one media expert said: "Some cases stand out more than others, especially if you have someone who champions that case— where someone will really fall in love with the case and they will do whatever it takes to help that animal to the very end get adopted, fostered. Chi was adopted by his champion, which was Susie Snow. Tina Louise was adopted by Mary." These special partnerships become moral badges of caring for the staff members of humane societies. They are the final act of compassion that can be offered to victims—taking them home, despite veterinary or behavioral problems. Everyone knows about these special adoptions and applauds those who step up to end the suffering of victims by providing them with loving homes. They are local heroes who make beautiful cases believable enough to give life to the myth of happy endings. Amid cruelty's perfect mess lies sociological opportunity.

THE IMPERFECT VOICE

Beautiful cases do not portray the gritty reality of animal cruelty. That is not their goal. Like other traumatic events that the media memorializes (Peri 1999), they need to distort reality. Memorialization requires that events be simplified, people's achievements be highlighted, and their foibles be forgotten. If cases were presented more accurately, with all of their contradictions and complexities, it would be difficult to create myths, followers, and heroes—the stuff that makes a memorial.

Some humane society members who have face-to-face contact with cruelty—agents, shelter workers, hospital staff—believe, however, that people inside and outside the organization should see the dark, unsavory side of human-animal interaction so they can understand what it feels like to investigate, treat, and nurture severely abused or neglected animals. More important, cruelty workers think that if others see what they see, there would be greater support for combating this problem. In other words, they want a voice that accurately and fully represents their efforts to better fight cruelty.

These workers are not sanguine about this possibility. They feel that many of their fellow staff members, let alone the public, do not want to know much about cruelty and certainly not in the way that those on the "front lines" do. For example, people manning the telephones, overseeing the budget, or hiring or firing workers will become sickened and saddened if they see severely abused animals, but their reaction is to turn away and let others "take care of it." One public relations director described how two of his workers reacted to a big case in the hospital: "People don't want to face cruelty and they want someone else to take care of it. You show people neglected animals and there are some that are shocked. We had one case where a guy neglected his dog and decided to kill it. It was a Rottweiler. He wanted to get rid of it. And he shot it in the head three times. Either he was a bad shot or Rottweilers have really good skulls because this animal was shot in the head and three days later he still wasn't dead. It came into the hospital and *Newsday* was covering the story and my two press people who had not been exposed to a lot of cruelty and animals in hideous condition had to see this. And they were like, 'oh my god, get us out of here,' they were just ready to cry and throw up." Such reactions make cruelty workers think that others want them to take care of abuse so they never have to directly face and be shocked by animal suffering. In fact, the director of a humane law enforcement department was rebuffed when he wanted to make a slide presentation to the board of directors to show them, in uncensored and brutal detail, what humane agents see when they investigate the worst cases. A senior administrator asked the director not to show slides of grotesque abuse— "Don't get too ugly because it's dinner time." Although the director initially resisted cleaning up his slide presentation because he felt that agents' work was "messy" and wanted board members to have empathy for their work, he finally agreed to tailor his presentation so that the dinner could remain a "cordial" affair.

Memorializing a few beautiful cases reinforces rather than remedies cruelty workers' concern that their voice is unheard. The fact that "real" animal abuse and neglect, and the problems dealing with them, are not fully and accurately communicated to other people makes them uneasy with the "reality" presented by beautiful cases. Most of what they experience, according to one law enforcement director, are "negative, disturbing cases, not the happy ending cases. The animal didn't survive. People in this business avoid sharing those cases. They're downers. They are too disturbing. They are too upsetting. But in the process of withholding them you get a very distorted picture of reality. It's not reality." Beautiful cases prevent people from grasping and appreciating the severity and ugliness of extreme incidents of abuse.

The focus on beautiful cases also ignores other things considered important for the public to know, according to cruelty workers. For one, they resent that the vast majority of harmed animals—the more everyday cases—are passed over for beautiful cases. These animals, it is thought, also deserve to have their story told to the public, even though the abuse in these cases is less dramatic. Also, there is some resentment that because only the rare case is picked for publicity, the vast majority of cruelty work—routine law enforcement investigations, veterinary intervention, and shelter care—get no acknowledgment or praise. In other words, beautiful cases fail to capture the plight of most harmed animals and the efforts of most cruelty workers; the institution is guilty of neglect. One worker summarized this sentiment: "Sometimes when you are involved in these things day in and day out, it's like— so I investigate 500 cases a year and because one of them involved a cute little puppy you're interested in that one? What about the other 499 that are just grunt day by day, talking with people, working my way through problems, trying to resolve something which is really a fight between neighbors in which the cow is being shot at, but the guts of my work is this. I think sometimes individual officers will react by saying, 'I've never heard from you media people—the only time you want to talk to me is about big cases. Why aren't you interested in the rest of my life?'" Their everyday work is thought to be too "mundane" and not "sexy" enough for the media. As one agent explained: "There is a large amount of work that we do all week long that doesn't get pitched to the media simply because it's fairly standard. We probably get seventy-five to a hundred neglected dog and cat cases a week and we follow up on a lot of them—either there is no violation or there is some violation and a summons is written and two or three days later they go back and check to make sure something is done. It's all mundane work. It's not sexy."

Patently, beautiful cases will not satisfy humane workers' desire for a more effective voice. As proxies, these reports cannot equal the reality of face-to-face encounters with extreme or everyday cruelty, whether people hear about them from humane society employees, read about them in newspapers or direct mailings, or watch them on television. However, that beautiful cases are done at the expense of reality is exactly why they serve so many useful functions for the society. Their value lies in venting and validating the emotions of staff members and the concerned public.

In the end, our institutions of mass communication are ultimately responsible for conveying the sober details of social problems like animal abuse to the laity. Imperfect, or ugly, cases do sometimes get covered by the news media. Indeed, for much of the general public—many of whom never read humane society promotional material—this is how they learn about egregious cruelty. Such coverage might address the lament of cruelty workers—that despite its mission, the society tiptoes around the issue of cruelty, such that its civility all but ignores abuse and neglect or sugar coats them in a way that leaves fellow society employees and the concerned public unenlightened about the nature and significance of this problem. Yet what people learn from ugly cases is as much a reflection of their own anxieties and concerns as it is a "factual" report of harm to animals. The result is that the overall picture of cruelty in the mass media is more confused and conflicted than clear and consistent.

Conclusion

Cruelty Is Good to Think

"We need Westy to become the new Democratic mascot. Everybody loves Westy. I'm going to take him on tour with me." Senate President Stan Matsunaka—who's also running for governor—commenting on Westy the cat, who survived being set on fire by two teenagers last year and who was at the Capitol on Tuesday to help pass an anti-animal cruelty bill.
—*Denver Post*, January 31, 2002

WHEN CLAUDE LEVI-STRAUSS (1963) observed, "animals are good to think," meaning that they are food for symbolic thought, he inspired anthropologists to examine how different groups think about animals (Shanklin 1985). While some sought to discover the principles of classification involved in this thinking, and how these principles compose logical systems of belief and action (e.g., Tyler 1969), others explored the metaphorical use of animals in nonwestern cultures (e.g., Leach 1964). More recent anthropological work extends this tradition by examining the symbolic and practical value of animals in Western societies (e.g., Lawrence 1984; Marvin and Mullen 1999; Noske 1997).

This thinking about animals is shot through with contradictions, as is our thinking about their mistreatment. On one hand, it is hardly surprising that people disagree about whether certain acts constitute cruelty. The most common explanation is that suffering's subjectivity guarantees a struggle over what it means. Since animals cannot speak for themselves, people must guess their inner states, opening the doors to a flood of divergent interpretations. And the very notion of suffering, whether in animals or humans, is inherently unclear.

These explanations are problematic because they blame our confusion on the inability of animals to articulate, in human terms, their suffering or on the inherent ambiguity of suffering itself. Our confusion about which acts constitute cruelty, and how much we care if they qualify, can better be explained by the symbolic interactionist approach underlying *Just a Dog* that sees the meanings of objects and events—and cruelty is certainly one—as products of people's interpretations of them. Since this process of human sense-making is social, we should look to explain our contradictory stance toward cruelty by focusing on the inter-personal context that embeds it.

As the discussion and examples throughout *Just a Dog* make clear, the situational nature of cruelty causes confusion over its meaning and significance. The same treatment of the same species in one context can be regarded as cruel, while in another it can be considered culturally acceptable. We saw this confusion when complaints were reported to and managed by humane law enforcement agencies. While dispatch-ers were quick to see suffering in debatable situations, agents were not; certainly, complainants and respondents were miles apart in their per-ception of what constituted cruelty and whether it was acceptable to treat animals in certain ways. There also was confusion when adoles-cents thought about their abusive behavior; some felt substantial guilt because they caused animals to suffer; others seemed indifferent and unwilling to acknowledge much if any animal suffering. We also observed rancorous division among shelter workers about what it meant to be cruel to animals in their charge. No-kill workers saw the euthanasia of adoptable animals as a form of cruelty, while their more traditional peers saw the warehousing of animals as cruel. A different kind of conflict over cruelty existed among hoarders and their support-ers who ignored or denied suffering, while various authorities had no problem labeling their behavior as neglect. And finally, humane mar-keters did not deny suffering but hid from and avoided the most ghastly incidents of it, fearing charges of incivility or sensationalism. Such situational definitions explain at least some of our conflict over the meaning of cruelty.

Just a Dog also reveals that the ability of cruelty to confer identity causes confusion over its meaning and significance. As groups define the meaning of cruelty, they are able simultaneously to use this definition to create their own image or project one for others. Because the ambiguity of cruelty invites many groups to find their own identity, multiple and sometimes conflicting definitions of cruelty can result, col-oring whether and how strongly we think certain acts are acceptable or not. We saw how images of cruelty can address the shared concerns or interests of group members—whether they were law enforcement agents, adolescents, hoarders, shelter workers, or humane society employees and supporters. For each of these groups, harming animals was a symbolic device that allowed them to spin off conceptions of self or other. Humane agents narrowly interpreted potential cruelty to preserve their dignity as law enforcers, while at other times they liberally interpreted it to appear to have more authority than respondents willingly granted; adolescents saw their dirty play with animals as a sign that, though briefly, they had become adultlike; hoarders defined their extreme neglect of animals as evidence of saintly behavior, while readers of news stories about hoarders could feel beyond reproach; shelter workers could reject some of their former tasks, now considered to be cruel, as a way to rediscover their true identities; and humane society marketers could use the most egregious cases of cruelty to give coherence and hope to staff members and supporters.

Finally, this chapter adds cultural anxieties as one more cause of our confusion. These concerns are not limited to a few discrete groups struggling over ambiguous cases of animal mistreatment but exist throughout society. There are collective worries and fears that affect how society thinks about the suffering of animals and that lead to this confusion. These shared concerns act as a cultural filter for how people describe and understand cruelty. Because of this filtering, descriptions of cruelty are not conventionally "objective" or "factual"; they are narratives or stories with many meanings and purposes, not all directly related to the harmed animal's experience. They can, instead, tell a story about the kind of people we are, the nature of our society, and the sort of qualities that make us unique as living creatures. Nor are they always simple and consistent stories, because part of our shared identity is made up of modern apprehensions, doubts, and conflicts. These concerns, however inconsistent they may be, must be teased out of the mix to better expose how we think and feel about the abuse and neglect of animals.

It is reasonable to argue that such concerns affect our interpretations of and reactions to cruelty when it is very ambiguous, inviting wide-ranging opinions and feelings about whether suffering occurred and, if so, to what degree. In other words, when the nature and extent of suffering is most easily contested, there is plenty of room for conflict and confusion. Conversely, it might be argued that our collective concerns and fears would be least intrusive in cases of cruelty that are apparently clear-cut and extreme; here, it would seem, there is little room for debate over moral impropriety. If there is confusion, it cannot be so easily written off to the "inevitable" ambiguity of suffering. Yet, on closer inspection, there is confusion even with what on the surface seem to be incontestable cases of extreme cruelty. This is all the more evidence for the intrusiveness of our identities onto a playing field that narrowly pits abusers against animals, and that alone.

Understanding Ugly Cases

Beautiful cases of abuse, described in the preceding chapter, are not the way that most people learn about extreme cruelty. More commonly, they hear and read about it when the media reports ugly cases. These tell a different tale about harming animals than do beautiful ones. They expose the general public to the unseemly, sordid, and hopeless side of cruelty. Animal victims are not always cute and appealing—less-than-movie-star pets and unpopular wild animals get tortured or killed. Happy endings almost never occur—abusers are rarely found and their victims usually do not end up healthy and adopted. Most important, abuse is often ghastly, even unimaginable—cats are mutilated with knives, then chopped up with an ax (Oppenheimer 2002), a pet llama is beaten to death with a golf club (Quioco 2001), and a family cat has industrial-sized staples driven into its head (Henry 2000). And in addition to egregiously harming animals, people may be victims too.

Ugly cases create alienation and tension. People feel uneasy after they hear about these cases because the abuse is gruesome, the crime, if unresolved, is threatening, and the human victims are distraught. Because these acts are extreme, they make transparent the social forces behind our society's confusion and conflict over cruelty. These forces are evident in three tragic cases extensively covered by the local and national media.

The first case happened in 2001. Two adolescent males in a Colorado parking lot set fire to a tabby cat, called Westy because he was found in the town of Westminster. A veterinary nurse described his condition: "He had third-degree burns over forty percent of his body, which smelled of smoke and charred fur. His pepper coat had mostly melted onto his body, his hindquarters were burned to the muscle and his whiskers singed away from the heat." He was not expected to survive his massive injuries. Veterinarians considered putting him down to end his suffering. Westy was hospitalized for four months, enduring five operations, including two skin grafts. He eventually lost one rear leg, his tail, and both his ears. Media attention turned Westy into a celebrity and a cause célèbre against animal cruelty. The hospital was flooded with telephone calls from as far away as Germany and France with offers of support, money, and adoption. Financial support poured in from sources that ranged from children raising a few dollars selling lemonade (Robinson 2001) to larger donors, whose contributions totaled thirty thousand dollars. Some of the donations covered the five thousand dollar Westy reward fund. After failing to find his owner, one of the veterinary technicians on Westy's case adopted him, edging out hundreds of people who had come forward to do the same. On June 8, 2001, Westminster police arrested two boys on animal cruelty charges who were turned in by their parents. The boys, ages sixteen and seventeen, who harmed the cat did so, according to the prosecutor, because they were curious about what would happen if the cat's tail were set afire "like the cartoons" (*Channelone.com* 2002). The boys served two days in jail, paid a five hundred dollar fine, and received an eighteen-month probation after pleading guilty to the charges.

The second case occurred in 1992. Three young men in Boston "lured" a black Labrador-shepherd named Kelly onto train tracks, where the dog was crushed. The boys had thrown the dog over a fence bordering the tracks, trapping her and making escape from the oncoming train impossible (Cullen 1992b). It was said that the boys had been drinking beer and laughing as they coaxed the dog so that she would be in the middle of the tracks when the train came. The dog's leg was severed and much of her skin was ripped from her body by the impact; she died soon after. Two girls who regularly played with Kelly watched in horror as these events unfolded. They saw the dog suffer enormously before she died. The three young men were acquitted because of insufficient evidence, leaving the dog's owner outraged (Schutz 1992).

And the third case took place in 1997. Two teenaged males broke into Noah's Ark animal shelter in Fairfield, Iowa, and beat twenty-four cats with baseball bats, killing sixteen of them. The cofounder of the shelter described what he saw: "It was like a mad scene out of some horror movie. What must have gone on was beyond comprehension—there were pools of blood everywhere. It's a nightmare" (Dalbey 1997a). He went on to say: "Most of the cats must have been trapped and unable to escape. They had broken legs and jaws and skulls" (Greco 1997). A veterinarian said that injuries included severe head trauma, damage to the eyes, broken jaws, broken limbs, and multiple fractures causing severe pain and shock. Media attention generated financial and volunteer support for the shelter and put animal cruelty in the spotlight, though briefly (Dalbey 1997b). In the weeks following the incident, thousands of telephone calls and letters poured into the shelter and, in the years that followed, hundreds of Web pages provided information about the case and memorials to the lost animals. The trial drew national attention in the media, including coverage by television programs such as *48 Hours*, *The Today Show*, and *Court TV*, among others. Most of the state's evidence, including photographs of the injured and dead cats, and a suspect's bumper sticker reading "Missing your cat? Look under my tires," were thrown out because the defendants admitted their guilt. The jury found the adolescents guilty of felony charges because they broke into and burglarized the shelter, but the charges were reduced to a misdemeanor violation; the teens were sentenced to twenty-three days in jail, twenty-five hundred dollars in fines, four years in a youthful offender program, and three years' probation.

Why is there confusion and conflict about the nature and importance of suffering even when it is egregious? Examination of these three incidents, along with other extreme cases, can help us understand what complicates our thinking about animal suffering and cruelty. Because these cases are reported in the media, reaction to them becomes a collective experience involving thousands and even millions of people who tune in and perhaps identify with abused animals and saddened owners they never met or, alternatively, disapprove of the "flap" over them. The extent of their alarm or indifference about these reports has roots deeper than sheer sympathy for or disinterest in animals.

Our understanding of social problems is shaped by abstract and invisible social forces. Consequently, most people are unaware of these influences on their thinking and behavior. For one, collective fears and anxieties color our thinking about social problems, and this is true for animal cruelty, too. Reports of egregious cruelty describe more than the "facts" of each case. In addition to detailing the kinds and numbers of animals harmed, how they were mistreated, the background of known abusers, and the circumstances surrounding the abuse, these incidents reveal as much about ourselves as they do about animals. Through them, as others have observed (e.g., Granfield 2005), we express our modern concerns and worries.

Being Vulnerable

A sense of vulnerability permeates everyday life in western societies (Furedi 2004). Many people believe that life is riskier than ever—that we live in dangerous times when unpredictable violence threatens us all. Fear of being victimized is high, causing widespread feelings of insecurity. Yet we enjoy an unprecedented level of safety (Furedi 2002). Evidence suggests that only a few will become targets of violence and the rates of violent crimes are dropping. For example, rates of youth homicide have dropped noticeably over the past decade (Glassner 2000). Despite this reality, feelings of vulnerability are built into our culture, influencing our attitudes and behaviors at every turn, including how people tell the story of cruelty.

A sense of vulnerability informs the coverage of ugly cruelty cases. For one, cultural anxiety about violence by male teenagers, in this case toward animals, colors news reports, even though humane societies claim that teens annually account for only 20 percent of cruelty cases, and there is no evidence that this percentage is increasing. Articles establish that individual incidents of cruelty are not isolated pranks or occasional lapses in good judgment but part of a larger pattern of disturbed and "violent [male] teenagers" (*Catsinthenews.com* 2002) who deliberately harm animals. Speaking of the Westy case, one author concludes that he is not "surprised to learn that police suspected the criminals to be young and male." Brutality to Westy, he claimed, was just one more instance of what havoc can be wreaked by "deranged" adolescent boys. After establishing that the perpetrators of specific incidents are troubled young men, articles often report other attacks on animals to reinforce the idea that these crimes are part of a larger pattern. For example, some articles about Westy focus on this cat but remind readers of unprovoked, egregious attacks on helpless animals by other young men. Other articles focus less on the Westy case in particular and more on other cases of adolescent-male attacks on animals. By clumping individual cases, the press creates the impression of a trend or growing social problem. Articles with titles like "Teens Attract Attention for Animal Cruelty" (*ChannelOne.com* 2002), "Grisly Animal Abuse Cases Puzzle Colorado Police" (*Planet Ark* 2002), and "Aggression Against

Animals: Teen Acts of Violence Getting Increased Attention" (*Holland [Michigan] Sentinel* 2002) describe the gruesome, unprovoked crimes of teenagers against animals.

What makes people feel vulnerable is the perception not just that male teens are becoming more violent but that their violence is unpredictable and senseless. And this, too, is emphasized in reports of ugly cases, even though the perspective of abusers, no matter how unsavory, is ignored. Articles stress the gratuitous violence of young men run amok, harming, torturing, or killing animals without reason. Kelly, Westy, and the animals at Noah's Ark were all intentionally tortured or brutally killed by young men who burned, beat, or crushed them. The abusers offered no self-defense that the animals were threatening or attacking them, or even harming their property. For example, in the Boston case, the dog Kelly was lured to railway tracks by three adolescent boys looking for fun. Their intent was clear, according to news reports: trick the dog to cross the tracks just as a train was approaching so that it would be crushed to death in front of the horrified girls. In the reports, the striking innocence of both the dog and the girls is contrasted to the reckless and wanton sadism of the boys. The casualness, indeed moral indifference, of the boys particularly outraged the public. Of particular note in the news was the degree of "callousness police say the suspects displayed even after they were arrested" (Cullen 1992a). A local police officer said that the boys "thought this was entertainment. They thought it was funny. In fact, when we arrested them, they were still laughing. . . . The poor thing was really suffering. And these guys walked away, drinking beer and laughing" (Cullen 1992a). And in the Westy case, one outraged citizen speculated that Westy's abusers were "intentionally tormenting animals for their own sick pleasures. . . . It's very pathetic that these teens have to take their problems out on innocent animals that have done nothing wrong. To think the United States is always talking about children being the future, well look at our 'children' now" (*Channelone.com* 2002). Their senseless cruelty was portrayed as evidence of moral depravity, as highlighted in one article that compares Westy the cat's "braveness" with his abusers' "cowardice" (Green 2001).

At the core of this vulnerability is the fear that random acts of violence against animals will eventually be redirected toward humans. This concern influences how ugly cases are presented to the public, despite mixed evidence for the link. Discussions of specific cases often include dire warnings that abusers will eventually harm people, repeating the same shock-biographies of a few serial killers who allegedly abused animals in their youth. For example, reports of the brutality inflicted against Westy were indistinguishable from other ruthless acts of "carnage and mayhem" by humans who "inflict pain and suffering" (Salazar 2001, J5). One letter to the editor accepts the link as fact: "Even those who aren't animal lovers should be concerned. . . . Mental-health professionals, crime researchers and law enforcement officials have proven that people who abuse animals are likely to be violent toward other people" (Rohde 2001). Shortly after the capture of Westy's abusers, an article quoted a state representative who seems also to accept the link: "These people later go on to murder. These people really need to be put away . . . and taken off the streets." A few sentences after noting that teenagers served two days in jail for Westy's injuries, the article says: "As a child, serial killer Jeffrey Dahmer decapitated a dog and David Berkowitz, New York City's 'Son of Sam' murderer, killed a number of his neighbor's pets" (Hamilton 2001).

To strengthen this connection, some reports characterize animal abusers in a language normally reserved for particularly viscous killers of humans. Abusers, for instance, can be called "serial killers." Perhaps intended as tongue and cheek, the front-page headline of a Manhattan tabloid featured a story about a pigeon serial killer. There was little real danger to humans, but the article's emphasis on a serial killer on the loose could certainly resonate with readers' fears of the human equivalent. The reality was far less dramatic: an exterminator made two known sprayings after being hired by a building superintendent to rid window ledges of pigeons. While this spraying was illegal and unlikely to get rid of the pigeons, the choice of the banner headline made more of this individual incident than was justified by the case's raw details. Similarly, other reports express the public's anxiety about "psycho killers." This anxiety was apparent in one media-instigated story. Television reporters contacted the state humane society about an apparently extreme case—two animals found dead, with parts of their legs cut off; one dog had its front paws cut off, the other dog was missing its back legs. According to the society's media affairs representative, the reporter's theory was that "a psycho" was roaming around a small Massachusetts town cutting off dogs' legs, and the story was filed, even though the society's agents had not completed their investigation and had warned the reporter that animals in this rural part of the state sometimes are harmed or killed accidentally by farm equipment. A number of television stations picked up the story and calls came into the society about people wanting to know about the "psychopath who was cutting off dogs' legs." It turned out that one animal's rear legs had been surgically amputated by a veterinarian and the other dog lost its paws in a train accident. "It wasn't a psycho out there endangering people's pets and yet the media jumped all over that because it was so sensational," the media affairs staff member claimed.

To ensure that readers make the link, reports of ugly cruelty anthropomorphize animal victims, according them status akin to that of human targets of violence. Interspecies boundaries are blurred as the victims are given the status of children, mates, and others humans who are significant in our lives. These metaphors make it easy for readers to identify with these victims. For instance, some people saw Westy, or at least his public image, as akin to that of a human child by highlighting his innocence and vulnerability. His owners were never found, suggesting that he was possibly unloved, abandoned, and alone. One article referred to him as "helpless" and looking like "a victim of warfare" (*Catsinthenews.com* 2002). Another likened Westy's brutalization to "murder, another baby left in a back-alley dumpster, or children killed in a bombing in the Middle East." And yet another likened Westy to an infant by describing him, minus his ears, tail, and one leg, as "swaddled in a baby sleeper on a blanket inside an incubator" (Hamilton 2001). Some articles even diminished Westy's size to make it easier to think of him as a kitten or infant. For example, one article described him as a "little cat," even though veterinary reports referred to Westy as a large tabby.

Once cruelty victims are anthropomorphized, readers can easily identify with the animals and their suffering or death can be transformed into something positive. It becomes a sacrifice for a greater good rather than a senseless crime (Bakan 1968). In Westy's case, his death first led to calls for severer punishment of abusers. Although people were thankful for the arrest of Westy's abusers, many feared they would "walk away with only a slap on the wrist." For example, one Web site that lists cruelty incidents said: "It breaks my heart to post yet another case where a defenseless cat was set on fire . . . the boys accused are charged with only misdemeanor animal cruelty. If they are convicted, their only punishment will be a $400 fine and mandatory anger management" (Lovecats4x.tripod.com n.d.). Stronger penalties, it was argued, would make the point that cruelty to animals needs to be taken seriously as a form of violence (Ridge 2001).

These calls snowballed into a drive to rewrite and improve existing anti-cruelty laws in Colorado, in the name of Westy. One article about him refers explicitly to this symbolic transformation, saying that his "sacrifice ensured that any animal-torturing bonehead in the state of Colorado must now make a nice long visit to a concrete jail cell . . . where he/she belongs!" Passage of Westy's Law upped the possible punishment of animal abusers, accomplished after considerable lobbying in the name of Westy and other animals. Westy, in fact, made an appearance in the Colorado legislature after enduring a "painful ordeal" and "four grueling months of care and operations." This appearance, plus all the other attention Westy garnered, put him at the head of a furious statewide campaign to change the law. The article pointed out that when Westy is not playing with his toys, he is promoting animal rights. It quoted Senate President Stan Matsunaka, after Westy appeared at the Capitol to help pass an anti-animal-cruelty bill: "We need Westy to become the new Democratic mascot. I'm going to take him on tour with me" (*Catsinthenews.com* 2002).

As these cases demonstrate, our feelings about violence cannot be easily separated from how the news reports cruelty. When the way we understand cruelty becomes inexorably intertwined with our own anxieties and fears, it is more likely that animal mistreatment will be thought to constitute cruelty, reflect significant suffering, and merit serious criminal punishment than to be construed as a fleeting indiscretion where cruelty and suffering are doubted and criminal penalties seem excessive.

Being Human

Issues plaguing our identities do not always create heightened sympathy for abused animals or concern for preventing future cruelty. Sometimes our collective anxieties and fears resist seeing them as victims. When cultural worries prevent abused animals from being anthropomorphized or accorded victim status, cruelty will be regarded as a less serious, even trivial matter.

Rather than focusing on an individual animal's plight, cruelty discussions can become a battle to defend what it means to be human and to guard centuries-old moral distinctions between people and animals. Crossing the boundaries between humans and animals is taboo in Western societies. "When boundaries intersect, many fear that the 'primary' category may be influenced, changed, corrupted, or co-opted by the 'other' category. It is believed that if this occurs, there would be a loss of control, which produces anxiety and fear in those who are aligned with the 'primary" category" (Greene 1995). Those who are particularly anxious over such boundary blurring are likely to diminish the significance of cruelty, arguing that if taken too seriously, let alone on a level with violent crimes against people, it will degrade what it means to be human.

In the Westy case, some construed the incident as an example of how people have greater interest or compassion for animals than they do for humans. Inflamed reactions to this cat's abuse pricked the sensitivities of those who argued that it is immoral to care so much about the plight of animals. To make this point, they drew, for comparison, on dire situations facing the most helpless humans. One opinion piece, "Is Dead Baby Less Important Than Cat?" criticized those who called for Westy's abusers to suffer everything from probation to the death penalty. The author claimed that there should be equal or greater outrage over a recent case of a brain-injured baby allowed to die: "Where is the same outrage for Tanner Dowler? A cat has some defenses like scratching, biting and running, but baby Tanner did not. This helpless, tiny, precious boy suffered in a way no one should. Yet the voices of Boulder County have remained, for the most part, silent. We should be asking how we failed baby Tanner. We should demand an investigation into how our local government allowed a 34-year-old man and a 19-year-old girl, living in cars, to take that baby out of the hospital, especially after being warned by the grandparents. Where are the cries for justice? Where are the tears, outrage and sorrow for the families? Will the same people who screamed about animal cruelty display an equal if not louder response to the death of a baby boy?" (Peters 2002). Others expressed moral unease with the outrage over Westy. A district attorney who commented on the emotional stir of the case said that if extra prison beds were available either for those who are cruel to animals or for those who sexually assault children, "I'm going to take the latter" (Hamilton 2001).

Apparent dismissal of human concerns over those of animals also concerned people in the Boston cruelty case. Some were offended that the death of a dog provoked such fury when headlines about violence against people often generate little response. The presiding judge did not understand why this incident disturbed people so much more than any of his prior murder cases (WCVB-TV 1992). He received more than one hundred letters, three hundred phone calls, and several petitions about the case demanding that he mete out justice (Cullen 1992c). "I find it very disturbing that I received more phone calls and letters about the death of an animal than any homicide case that's come before this court in my twenty years on the bench. . . . . A black man was chased onto the tracks by a gang of whites. He was struck and killed. Not a word. Not a call. I heard from no one" (Cullen 1992c). One well-known columnist picked up on the judge's irony, writing a column about the case entitled "Society Skews the Value of Life" (Barnicle 1992). To show the moral mistake of people deeply troubled by the murdered dog and the acquittal of charges against the accused, the author lists many examples of human misery and crime that drew no attention, including no telephone calls to the court house regarding any of the sixty murders during the preceding year, a baby girl who had been smashed against a wall by her mother's boyfriend (who "must be as traumatized as those children who saw the dog get hit by the train"), and a young boy who witnessed a murder and was sodomized by his stepfather, who also raped the boy's sister. The columnist's not so subtle message was that there were other, more important victims being overlooked, and that public outrage over the animal cruelty case was misdirected.

Coverage of these cases reinforces traditional boundaries between the species when the news reminds readers that the law regards animals as property. When so classified, they are denied victim status, at least in an official capacity. In the Noah's Ark case, readers were reminded of the lesser status of animals by the testimony, verdict, and sentence imposed on the teens. Lawyers defending the teens admitted that they were guilty of intentionally entering the shelter with baseball bats to kill cats but framed their actions as a "stupid, teenage mistake." Admittedly, the abusers' attorneys were forced to take this perspective to represent their clients, but it nevertheless articulated a view of animals that resonates with some people. In other words, it was a freak one-time event; the boys posed no further threat of violence to animals, let alone to people. Although they were initially found guilty of a felony crime, this charge was for breaking, entering, and burglarizing the shelter, rather than for harming animals. Human property, not animal lives, was more important under the law. The jury was required to find the value of the animals in excess of five hundred dollars to uphold the felony charges, but the defense argued that a stray cat's life was basically "worthless." Despite the prosecution's response that a great deal of money had been spent on veterinary bills for the injured animals and the care and medical procedures the cats received prior to their abuse, as well as lost potential adoption fees from cats that were killed, the jury failed to find sufficient monetary value in the animals and the charges were reduced from a felony crime to a misdemeanor violation. Such court decisions reaffirm the belief that animals are lawfully different from humans, thereby preserving the sociozoologic order that culturally separates species from one another (Arluke and Sanders 1996).

Nor is it only strays that the media reports as property. Owned companion animals, too, are sometimes classified this way, providing a justification to minimize or ignore their mistreatment to those readers so inclined. In one well-publicized case in 2001, an irate California driver threw a Bichon Frise to its death in traffic because he was upset by a minor car collision. Although many people were horrified by this road-rage abuse and readily defined this dog as a victim whose mistreatment called for serious criminal penalties, there were some who did so only grudgingly, if at all. On a radio program in Boston callers discussing this case thought there was too much fuss over the incident. One caller said that the owner should adopt another dog from an animal shelter and get on with her life; another said that if there were veterinary bills, perhaps they should be paid for but mused that damage to a car is an equally important issue. Underlying these reactions was the notion that animals occupy a lesser moral status to humans, and that because of this lower status, cruelty should not be taken so seriously.

When anxieties about boundary blurring are expressed in reports of ugly cases, both sides of the issue are often presented together, emphasizing the controversy. Often vehement in response, those more comfortable with such blurring lash out at those who decry it. When this occurs, the exchanges focus less on the specifics of individual ugly cases than on general concerns about the moral distinctions, or lack thereof, between humans and animals.

For example, reactions throughout the country to the Westy case were so intense and alarming that one newspaper cartoonist spoofed the cottage industries that often follow major media crimes. Entitled "A Full Line of Blazing Westy Souvenirs," the Denver newspaper *Westword* published a cartoon that many readers understood as an endorsement of pet-burnings. This "humor" offended them because they believe that suffering, regardless of species, should be taken seriously. One reader made this point by expressing the hope that the person behind this insensitive and tasteless cartoonist might "experience the pain that Westy suffered and still is suffering." And yet another was disturbed that the newspaper's "flippancy" and "trivialization" made "light of such a heinous crime and the horrendous suffering of an innocent animal." Others elevated the moral significance of the Westy case by analogizing it to senseless crimes against helpless and powerless humans. As one claimed, the cartoonist's "sickness" was as morally offensive as running cartoons on the "rapes of women in Boulder, or the shooting of high school students, or the Sudan slave trade."

A profound issue underlies the exchange between the cartoonist and these readers. Being outraged and eschewing outrage are two predictable counterpoints in the larger cultural debate over how alike or unalike we are from other animals and, consequently, the nature and significance of their suffering. The Westy case merely provided fodder to express this opposition and continue the debate. Those who responded to the case drew liberally from our culture for the substance and power of their thinking about cruelty and in turn about themselves. Some drew from our culture's trivialization of animal abuse, while others tapped into our culture's growing sensitivity to the proper treatment of animals and their moral and emotional importance. In short, individual cases, and our responses to them, are not just about the facts and circumstances surrounding the harm of animals; they are reflections or symptoms of wider concerns about how different we are, or are not, from other species, and how these boundaries should affect our perception and management of cruelty.

As long as these underlying questions continue to be answered in different ways, we will continue to have different thoughts and feelings about cruelty. The multivocality and ambiguity of modernity precludes our ever reaching consensus on the meaning of cruelty. In this modern context, different and sometimes conflicting voices will continue to use cruelty as a metaphor to express interests and identities. As a metaphor, cruelty invests events, situations, and people with purpose and meaning, inextricably linking how we think about ourselves to how we think about animals. Cruelty becomes a way to tell a story about the kind of people we are and the kind of society we live in, just as cockfighting in Asian cultures provides a tool for people to define their social order (Geertz 1972). The harmed animal's raw experience is transformed as we think about and make sense of cruelty in human terms. And this thinking will be colored—whether it is impassioned or disinterested—by larger cultural concerns and anxieties. We are all, in the end, as much a part of our mistreatment of animals as are animals themselves. Cruelty is good to think.

RETHINKING CRUELTY

Just a Dog examines how humans think about, define, and use animal cruelty. Because my sociological perspective dictates a descriptive rather than a normative stance, the book does not decry such treatment. Nonetheless, discourse about cruelty, including my own, is moral. We therefore must question how we arrive at these descriptions and understandings; our thinking will have real-world consequences for animals. I am particularly concerned about the glossing of cruelty's meaning by policy makers, activists, law enforcement agents, lawyers, journalists, and social scientists. Of course, some of the reasons why we obscure or bury the suffering of animals may not be easily remedied, if at all, but being aware of these constraints can inform, and perhaps elevate, dialogue and debate about this issue.

Ironically, there is one area where attempts to prevent the glossing of cruelty can do a disservice. There are frequent calls to better specify existing "antiquated" cruelty codes that can, if rewritten, inadvertently prevent the identification of certain forms of abuse and neglect. While most efforts to revamp these codes focus on strengthening penalties or reclassifying animals to change their property status, others lament the vagueness and subjectivity of the wording of these laws that cause discomfort for those trying to interpret and apply them (Patronek 1997). Indeed, even when laws are fairly specific, language may still be so vague it requires substantial interpretation, as in the use of the phrase "unnecessary physical pain or suffering." Some believe that humane law enforcement agents are one group, in addition to veterinarians, lawyers, and court officials, that could benefit from clarifying legal codes by reducing the amount of interpretation needed to determine whether or not certain acts qualify as legally defined cruelty. These pleas are well intentioned but must be cautiously approached, at least with regard to humane agents. Rewriting current codes can expunge old-fashioned terms and modernize the language, but ever-greater legal specification will not remedy the need to interpret and apply law. In practice, all police find that laws—regardless of attempts to rid them of ambiguity— can never specify in sufficient detail every situation that they encounter on the streets. Agents use cruelty codes as a general guide to interpret what constitutes abuse or neglect case by case; assessing situations for potential suffering requires their discretion. Well-intentioned efforts to improve and update the legal definition of cruelty can inhibit the informal and discretionary powers of agents, thereby limiting their ability to extend the meaning and scope of this problem as they see fit and as our society grows increasingly intolerant to the harm of animals. Ambiguity, in this instance, may be useful.

In other areas, however, glossing the meaning of cruelty is more problematic. For example, the age-old distinction between abuse and neglect that is built into the Western tradition of jurisprudence creates the idea that some forms of harm are more serious than others, based on the actor's intent and on the immediate and dramatic nature of the crime. Abuse is done deliberately, while neglect is unintentional or even accidental; abuse results in tragic injury to animals, while neglect only creates a hardship for them. Some have even suggested that the term *cruelty* should be reserved for a subset of abuse cases where the offender gains satisfaction from causing harm (Rowan 1993). This "deliberate bad actor" approach (Berry, Patronek, and Lockwood 2005) focuses on human motivation rather than animal suffering, thereby privileging abuse over neglect in terms of imputing seriousness and resulting criminal penalties. However, neglect can result in more prolonged suffering, as in cases of hoarding where animals endure weeks or months of starvation and painful disease. And neglect is far more common than abuse, representing about 90 percent of all cruelty cases (Solot 1997) and being the kind of mistreatment most often encountered by humane agents, shelter workers, and veterinarians. To upgrade the seriousness with which we regard severe neglect, some have proposed calling it "indirect" or "passive" cruelty, although this language may just perpetuate our confused thinking about the harm of animals. When discussing penalties, then, it may be more useful to focus on the consequences or omissions of human acts rather than on the motivations behind them.

Media thinking about abuse and neglect has limitations too because it glosses cruelty, first by not detailing it, then by exceptionalizing it. In the name of civility, reports even of ugly cruelty cases are strangely silent about the presumed suffering of cruelty victims. They stop short after describing the basic information behind each case. We learn about the victim's species, breed, or appearance, and we learn how the victim was tortured, killed, or left to suffer slowly, but the animal's subsequent experience is left to the reader's imagination. By editing cases to make them more civil or by focusing on the human side, these reports gloss the primal experience of cruelty, leaving it cleaned up, overshadowed, or otherwise diminished. Palatable versions, then, of cruelty can be read, but with less emotional clout than would be possible with more detail and description. The result is that the public's stock of knowledge about cruelty is significantly curtailed, as happens with other social problems such as wife abuse (Loseke 1987). Equally important for what the public learns is the fact that by covering extreme cases of abuse and neglect the media ignores more routine cruelty.

The media also glosses stories about cruelty by presenting them as very rare and unique events, just as stories about child abusers describe only the most immediate details of each incident (Nelson 1984; Wilczynski and Sinclair 1999). This focus on bizarre one-of-a-kind episodes prevents readers from seeing or thinking about them as part of a larger pattern of such cases or as part of animal cruelty in general. In the absence of reports about more routine, less dramatic kinds of abuse or neglect, the public comes to regard unacceptable behavior toward animals in fairly narrow terms, limited to situations in which animals are egregiously tortured and killed or are kept in horrendous conditions for long periods, when in fact the vast majority of anti-cruelty code violations involve animals in less dramatic situations.

Glossing prevents moral indignation. When not glossed, social problems can benefit from press attention. The power of the news media derives from its ability to elicit emotions in readers that not only draw their attention but promote action on certain issues by helping "new" social problems gain support and momentum (Spector and Kituse 1977).

For example, publication of child-abuse horror stories has played a prominent role in the success of the child maltreatment movement during the past twenty-five years (Johnson 1995). The news made it quite clear to readers that child abuse is indisputably wrong by presenting a consistent picture of this act as a serious crime and those who commit it as serious criminals. Journalistic conventions used to report these stories angered readers by detailing horrible injuries or gruesome circumstances and by showing that abusers were "bad" people who were solely responsible for intentionally and heinously harming their victims. Some have even referred to the "moral panic" created by these cases as part of the media's sensational approach to child abuse. This process also included the orchestration of expert opinion that contributed to increased demand for state intervention and the formation of popular consensus.

Instead of moral panic, the press has created moral confusion when it comes to those who harm animals. This is not to argue that they should be demonized, as the news has done to child abusers, but the comparison sheds light on just what the public and professionals do or do not learn about cruelty. And what is learned does little to mobilize effective public support for dealing with it. With extreme abuse, public indignation is balanced by equal amounts of dismissal of these cases as overblown or trivial. With extreme neglect, public scorn is curtailed by more frequent expressions of sympathy. The result is that community outrage—so common in reports of child abuse—is either curbed or absent in stories about animals being harmed. Indeed, with hoarding, the press often reports help from the community in terms of food and cash for hoarders and their surviving animals, in one case amounting to forty thousand dollars, as well as interest in adopting the animal victims. Until the press consistently deplores animal abuse and neglect as serious crimes along the lines of its treatment of child abuse, the public will be unsure how to morally categorize and approach these acts.

Although the press's handling of animal cruelty helps to sell newspapers by appealing to the public's anxiety and concerns or by pandering to the public's curiosity for the bizarre or their sympathy for the pitiful, it does not encourage an in-depth understanding of animal abuse and neglect. Without such understanding, society is ill-equipped to deal with cruelty and those who behave inappropriately to animals. Assumptions about what is "real" abuse and neglect will remain unchallenged, and in this context public policy debates about the proper treatment of animals and those who mistreat them will continue to be played out in trivial and distorted terms.

Finally, some might argue that sociologists gloss cruelty by giving a voice to abusers and neglecters. Such humanizing, critics claim, does a disservice to animals that are mistreated because it indirectly forgives such acts by making them understandable. Moreover, these critics allege that it is not the right image to give the public; in their view, society would be better served by a more one-dimensional portrayal of these people that says in no uncertain terms that harming animals is indefensible and that those doing it should be punished. *Just a Dog* does humanize its research subjects, if humanizing means their voices are sought and taken seriously, no matter how contradictory or offensive they might be. For example, some of the people I interviewed did make cruelty into ordinary behavior by ordinary people. In one case, students who had no criminal record remembered being cruel as a particular form of play that was just part of growing up, something that most of their peers did at "that stage of life." These recollections permitted cruelty to vanish beneath their constructed horizon of unacceptable violence toward animals. Limitations they claimed to have imposed on torture and killing set this horizon, beyond which their identities would be suspect as disturbed if not evil people. This ideological work enabled them to define their prior acts as ordinary cruelty, an interpretive process also done by those who are cruel to humans (Knox 2001), leaving some completely untroubled and others just momentarily guilty when pressed to talk about what they had done. This finding might disturb those who mistakenly understand it as saying that harming animals is acceptable if it is not linked to other criminal behavior. Understanding rather than glossing perspectives does not mean that we are forgiving or excusing people who harm animals. Rather, it is a way to better inform the public and professionals who must weigh in on new policies and programs to deal with cruelty.

Yet it is unavoidable that sociological thinking and writing glosses cruelty, and my work is no exception. This problem stems, in part, from the rhetoric of objectivity that constrains social scientists to use arguments and images that are not overly dramatic or outlandish (Cheyne and Tarulli 1989). Even if they are not so constrained, there are very real limits to language's ability to convey the inchoate psychological experience of suffering. I certainly struggled for the right words to describe the mistreatment of animals, but no matter how I expressed my thinking, it always fell short of what I suspected was the reality. Finally, sociological conventions to understand and describe our subjects' worlds take the pathos out of cruelty because they distance analysts— and subsequently their readers—from whatever topic is being addressed. Once I began to capture and interpret my subjects' perspectives, my own thinking and writing moved me one more step away from the abuse or neglect under consideration. However, this glossing—which represents another transformation in the meaning of cruelty—has practical value because it sanitizes the unthinkable in ways that make most readers comfortable enough to consider the suffering of animals, though briefly and with regret. As sociologists unpack why cruelty is good to think, we will not only stimulate further discussion and debate about the nature and impact of cruelty but prompt the public and professionals alike to consider broader concerns about the origin and meaning of our disconnected relationships with animals.

References

Adler, Patricia A., and Peter Adler. 1998. *Peer Power: Preadolescent Culture and Identity*. New Brunswick, NJ: Rutgers University Press.

Agnew, Robert. 1998. "The Causes of Animal Abuse: A Social-Psychological Analysis." *Theoretical Criminology* 2:177–209.

Alexander, Lloyd. 1963. *Fifty Years in the Doghouse: The Adventures of William Michael Ryan, Special Agent No. 1 of the ASPCA*. New York: G. P. Putnam's Sons.

American Psychiatric Association (APA). 1994. *Diagnostic and Statistical Manual of Mental Disorders*. 4th ed. Washington, DC: APA.

Arluke, Arnold. 1988. "Sacrificial Symbolism in Animal Experimentation: Object or Pet?" *Anthrozoos* 2:98–117.

———. 1989. "Living with Contradictions." *Anthrozoos* 3:90–99.

———. 1991. "Going Into the Closet with Science: Information Control Among Animal Experimenters." *Journal of Contemporary Ethnography* 20:306–30.

———. 1994a. "The Ethical Socialization of Animal Researchers." *Lab Animal* 23(6):30–35.

———. 1994b. "Managing Emotions in an Animal Shelter." In A. Manning and J. Serpell, eds., *Animals and Human Society*, 145–65. London: Routledge.

———. 1999. "Uneasiness of Laboratory Technicians." In R. Langley, ed., *Occupational Medicine: Animal Handlers*, 305–16. Philadelphia: Hanley & Belfus.

———. 2001. "Childhood Origins of Supernurturance: The Social Context of Early Humane Behavior." *Anthrozoos* 16:3–27.

———. 2003. "Ethnozoology and the Future of Sociology." *International Journal of Sociology and Social Policy* 23:26–45.

———. 2004. *Brute Force: Animal Police and the Challenge of Cruelty*. West Lafayette, IN: Purdue University Press.

Arluke, Arnold, and Julian Groves. 1998. "Pushing the Boundaries: Scientists in the Public Arena." In Lynette Hart, ed., *Responsible Conduct with Animals in Research*, 145–64. New York: Oxford University Press.

Arluke, Arnold, and Frederic Hafferty. 1996. "From Apprehension to Fascination with 'Dog Lab': The Uses of Absolutions by Medical Students." *Journal of Contemporary Ethnography* 25:201–25.

Arluke, Arnold, Jack Levin, Carter Luke, and Frank Ascione. 1999. "The Relationship of Animal Abuse to Violence and Other Forms of Antisocial Behavior." *Journal of Interpersonal Violence* 14:963–75.

Arluke, Arnold, and Carter Luke, 1997. "Physical Cruelty Toward Animals in Massachusetts, 1975–1996." *Society and Animals* 5:195–204.

Arluke, Arnold, and Clinton Sanders. 1996. *Regarding Animals*. Philadelphia. Temple University Press.

Arnold, C. n.d. "Open-Door Versus No-Kill Shelters." *Humane Society of Santa Clara News*, Spring, 2.

Arnold, David. 2000. "Paws and Smile." *Boston Globe*, May 10, A1

Ascione, Frank, and Phil Arkow, eds. 1999. *Child Abuse, Domestic Violence, and Animal Abuse: Linking the Circles of Compassion for Prevention and Intervention.* West Lafayette, IN: Purdue University Press.

Athens, Lonnie. 1989. *The Creation of Dangerous Violent Criminals.* London: Routledge.

Babyak, Jolene. 1994. *Birdman: The Many Faces of Robert Stroud.* Berkeley, CA: Ariel Vamp Press.

Bakan, David. 1968. *Disease, Pain, and Sacrifice.* Chicago: University of Chicago Press.

Barnicle, Mike. 1992. "Society Skews the Value of Life." *Boston Globe*, April 12.

Baumeister, Roy. 1997. *Evil: Inside Human Violence and Cruelty.* New York: W. H. Freeman.

Becker, Howard. 1970. *Sociological Work: Method and Substance.* New Brunswick, NJ: Transaction Books.

Becker, Howard, Blanche Geer, Everett Hughes, and Anselem Strauss. 1961. *Boys in White: Student Culture in Medical School.* Chicago: University of Chicago Press.

Beirne, Piers. 1997. "Rethinking Bestiality: Towards a Sociology of Interpersonal Sexual Assault." *Theoretical Criminology* 1:317–40.

Berry, Colin, Gary Patronek, and Randall Lockwood. 2005. "Long-Term Outcomes in Animal Hoarding Cases." *Animal Law* 11:167–94.

Best, Joel. 1995. *Images of Issues: Typifying Contemporary Social Problems.* New York: Aldine De Gruyter.

Best Friends Magazine. 2001. "Grace Under Fire: Navigating the Tricky Road to a No-kill Community." September/October, 16–18.

Blumer, Herbert. 1969. *Symbolic Interactionism.* Englewood Cliffs, NJ: Prentice Hall.

Bogue, Gary. 1998a. "Readers Climbing on the No-kill Bandwagon." *Contra Costa Times* (Walnut Creek, CA), September 1, A2.

———. 1998b. "Shelters Need to Join Forces to Stop Killing." *Contra Costa Times* (Walnut Creek, CA), August 30, A2.

Bok, Sissela. 1982. *Secrets: On the Ethics of Concealment and Revelation.* New York: Pantheon.

Borman, Kathyrn, and N. Lippincott. 1982. "Cognition and Culture: Two Perspectives on 'Free Play.'" In K. Borman, ed., *The Social Life of Children in a Changing Society*, 123–42. Hillsdale, NJ: Lawrence Erlbaum.

Bosk, Charles. 1985. "The Fieldworker as Watcher and Witness." *Hastings Center Reports* 15:10–14.

Bossard, James, and E. Boll. 1966. *The Sociology of Child Development.* 4th ed. New York: Harper and Row.

Brison, Susan. 2001. *Aftermath: Violence and the Remaking of a Self.* Princeton, NJ: Princeton University Press.

Bryan, James. 1966. "Occupational Ideologies and Individual Attitudes of Call Girls." *Social Problems* 13:441–50.

Campbell, Carol, and James Robinson. 2001. "Animal Hoarding." In Clifton Bryant, ed., *Encyclopedia of Criminology and Deviant Behavior*, 2:11–15. Philadelphia: Brummer-Routledge.

Caras, Roger. 1997. "Viewpoints." *Animal Sheltering*, September–October, 16–17.

Catsinthenews.com. 2002. "Tabby Cat Rocks the Animal Cruelty Vote and Wins!" June 10.

CBS News. 2001. "Road Rage Dog Killer Found Guilty." June 19.

ChannelOne.com. 2002. "Teens Attract Attention for Animal Cruelty." June 11.

Cheyne, Allan, and Donato Tarulli. 1989. "Reconciling Rhetoric and Image in Psychology." Department of Psychology, University of Waterloo, Waterloo, Ontario.

Chick, Garry, and Jon Donlon. 1992. "Going Out on a Limn: Geertz's 'Deep Play: Notes on the Balinese Cockfight' and the Anthropological Study of Play." *Play and Culture* 5:233–45.

Choo, Chun. 1998. *The Knowing Organization.* New York: Oxford University Press.

Clifford, James. 1992. "Traveling Cultures." In L. Grossberg, C. Nelson, and P. Treichler, eds., *Cultural Studies*, 96–117. New York: Routledge.

Climent, Carlos, and Frank Ervin. 1972. "Historical Data in the Evaluation of Violent Subjects: A Hypothesis Generating Study." *Archives of General Psychiatry* 27:621–24.

Cooley, Charles Horton. 1902. *Human Nature and the Social Order.* New York: Scribner's

Corsaro, William. 1992. "Interpretive Reproduction in Children's Peer Cultures." *Social Psychology Quarterly* 55:160–77.

———. 1997. *The Sociology of Childhood.* Thousand Oaks, CA: Sage.

Csikszentmihalyi, Mihaly, and Eugene Rochberg-Halton. 1981. *The Meaning of Things: Domestic Symbols and the Self.* New York: Cambridge University Press.

Cullen, Kevin. 1992a. "Dog Death Stirs Human Response." *Boston Globe*, April 10, 21.

———. 1992b. "Dog's Killing Stirs Outrage," *Boston Globe*, April 9, 24.

———. 1992c. "No Way to Treat a Dog or. . . ." *Boston Globe*, June 26, 17.

Dalbey, Beth. 1997a. "Brutal Cat Killings at Noah's Ark Stun Local, State Animal Protection Groups." *Fairfield (IA) Ledger*, March 10.

———. 1997b. "No Firm Leads in Cat Killings." *Fairfield (IA) Ledger*, March 11.

Davis, David. 1984. "Good People Doing Dirty Work: A Study of Social Isolation." *Symbolic Interaction* 7:233–47.

Derber, Charles. 1996. *The Wilding of America: How Greed and Violence Are Eroding Our Native Character.* New York: St. Martin's Press.

Diamond, Cora. 1981. "Experimenting with Animals: A Problem in Ethics." In David Sperlinger, ed., *Animals in Research: New Perspectives in Animal Experimentation*, 337–62. New York: Wiley.

Donald, R. 1991. "The No-Kill Controversy." *Shelter Sense*, September, 3–6.

Dowling, Julie, and Cynthia Stitely. 1997. "Killing Ourselves Over the Euthanasia Debate." *Animal Sheltering*, September–October, 4–15.

Doyle, M. 1982. *In-House Rhetoric of Pro-life and Pro-choice Special Interest Groups in Minnesota: Motivation and Alienation.* Dissertation Abstracts International, 43 (11), 3454. University Microfilms No. AAC83-08038.

Durkheim, Emile. 1912. *The Elementary Forms of Religious Life*. Paris: F. Alcan.

Dworkin, Ronald. 1993. *Life's Dominion: An Argument About Abortion, Euthanasia, and Individual Freedom*. New York: Alfred A. Knopf.

Ellis, Carolyn, and A. Bochner. 1992. "Telling and Performing Personal Stories." In C. Ellis and M Flaherty, eds., *Investigating Subjectivity: Research on Lived Experience*, 79–101. Newbury Park, CA: Sage.

Ericson, R. V. 1995. *Crime and the Media*. Brookfield, VT: Dartmouth.

Erikson, Kai. 1976. *Everything in Its Path*. New York: Simon and Schuster.

Favre, D., and V. Tsang. 1993. "The Development of Anti-Cruelty Laws During the 1800s." *Detroit College of Law Review* 1:1–35.

Felthous, Alan. 1980. "Childhood Antecedents of Aggressive Behaviors in Male Psychiatric Patients." *Bulletin of the American Academy of Psychiatry and Law* 8:104–10.

Felthous, Alan, and Stephen Kellert. 1987. "Childhood Cruelty to Animals and Later Aggression Against People: A Review." *American Journal of Psychiatry* 144:711–17.

Felthous, Alan, and B. Yudowitz. 1977. "Approaching a Comparative Typology of Female Offenders." *Psychiatry* 40:270–76.

Fine, Gary Alan. 1986. "The Dirty Play of Little Boys." *Society* 24:63–67.

———. 1988. "Good Children and Dirty Play." *Play and Culture* 1:43–56.

———. 1991. "Justifying Fun: Why We Do Not Teach Exotic Dance in High School." *Play and Culture* 4:87–99.

———.1992. "The Depths of Deep Play: The Rhetoric and Resources of Morally Controversial Leisure." *Play and Culture* 5:246–51.

Fine, Gary Alan, and Kent Sandstrom. 1988. *Knowing Children: Participant Observation with Children*. Newbury Park, CA: Sage.

Fishman, M. 1995. "Police News: Constructing an Image of Crime." In R. Ericson, ed., *Crime and the Media*, 119–42. Brookfield, VT: Dartmouth.

Flynn, Clifton. 1999. "Perpetuating Animal Abuse in Childhood and Later Support for Interpersonal Violence Against Women and Children in Families." *Society and Animals* 7:161–72.

Foley, Douglas. 1990. "The Great American Football Ritual: reproducing Race, Class, and Gender Inequality." *Sociology of Sport Journal* 7:111–35.

Foro, Linda. 1997. "Viewpoints." *Animal Sheltering*, September–October, 16–17.

———. n.d. "Know the Thrill of No-kill–Retreat, Hell! or, How the No-kill Movement from a Conference Grew." www.maddiesfund.org/index/html

Foster, J. T. 2000. "A Fate Worse than Death: Are 'No-Kill' Shelters Truly Humane?" *Reader's Digest*, July 20.

Francione, Gary. 1995. *Animals, Property, and the Law*. Philadelphia: Temple University Press.

Franklin, Adrian. 1999. *Animals and Modern Cultures: A Sociology of Human-Animal Relations in Modernity*. Thousand Oaks, CA: Sage.

Freud, Anna. 1981. "A Psychoanalytic Developmental Psychopathology. In *The Writings of Anna Freud*, vol. 8. New York: International Universities Press.

Fritz, Charles. 1961. "Disasters." In Robert Merton and Robert Nisbet, eds. *Contemporary Social Problems*, 651–94. Beverly Hills, CA: Sage.

Frommer, Stephanie, and Arnold Arluke. 1999. "Loving Them to Death: Blame-Displacing Strategies of Animal Shelter Workers and Surrenderers." *Society and Animals* 7:1–16.

Furedi, Frank. 2002. *Culture of Fear*. New York: Continuum.

———. 2004. *Therapy Culture*. New York: Routledge.

Geertz, Clifford. 1972. "Deep Play: Notes on the Balinese Cockfight." *Daedalus* 101:1–37.

Gerbner, George, 1995. *Animal Issues in the Media*. Universal City, CA: Ark Trust.

Gilyard, B. 2001. "Out of Gas." *Showing Animals Respect and Kindness*, August, 6–7.

Ginsburg, Faye. 1986. *Contested Lives: The Abortion Debate in the American Community*. Berkeley and Los Angeles: University of California Press.

Glassner, Barry. 2000. *The Culture of Fear*. New York: Basic Books.

Goffman, Erving. 1959. *The Presentation of Self in Everyday Life*. Garden City, NY: Anchor.

———. 1961. *Asylums*. Garden City, NY: Anchor.

———. 1967. *Interaction Ritual*. Garden City, NY: Anchor.

Gold, R. 1964. "In the Basement: The Apartment-Building Janitor." In Peter Berger, ed., *The Human Shape of Work*, 1–49. New York: Macmillan.

Goldschalk, J. 1979. "Foreign Labour and Dirty Work." *The Netherlands' Journal of Sociology* 15:1–11.

Goodney, Suzanne. 1997. "Animal Abuse and Personal Histories." Paper presented at the annual meetings of the American Sociological Association, Toronto, Canada, August.

Graber, Doris. 1980. *Crime News and the Public*. New York: Praeger.

Grabosky, Peter, and Paul Wilson. 1989. *Journalism and Justice: How Crime Is Reported*. Sydney: Photo Press.

Granfield, Robert. 2005. "Paradise Lost: The Transformation of Wildlife Law in the Vanishing Wilderness." In Ann Herda-Rapp and Theresa Goedeke, eds. *Mad About Wildlife: Looking at Social Conflict over Wildlife*, 147–69. Leiden: Brill Academic Publishers.

Greco, Jean. 1997. "Cats Killed in Brutal Fairfield Attack." *The Ottumwa (IA) Courier*, March 11.

Green, Chuck. 2001. "Abusers Not as Brave as Westy." *Denver Post*, June 4.

Greene, Eric. 1995. "Ethnocategories, Social Intercourse, Fear and Redemption: Comment on Laurent." *Society and Animals* 3:79–88.

Gritzer, Glenn, and Arnold Arluke. 1995. *The Making of Rehabilitation: A Political Economy of Medical Specialization, 1890–1980*. Berkeley, CA: University of California Press.

Hamilton, Jennifer. 2001. "Treatment of Cat Draws Calls for Stiffer Cruelty Law." *North County (CA) Times*, September 28.

Hartnett, C. 1981. "The Pawnbroker: Banker of the Poor?" In Israel Barak-Glantz and C. Ronald Huff, eds., *The Mad, the Bad, and the Different*, 149–55. Lexington, MA: Lexington Books.

Heckert, Druann. 2003. "Positive Deviance." In Patricia Adler and Peter Adler, eds., *Constructions of Deviance: Social Power, Context, and Interaction*, 30–42. Belmont, CA: Wadsworth/Thomson.

Heeren, John. 1983. "Emotional Simultaneity and the Construction of Victim Unity." *Symbolic Interaction* 22:163–79.

Heinsler, Janet, Sherryl Kleinman, and Barbara Stenross. 1990. "Making Work Matter: Satisfied Detectives and Dissatisfied Campus Police." *Qualitative Sociology* 13:235–50.

Hendrickson, Kate, Teresita McCarty, and Jean Goodwin. 1990. "Animal Alters: Case Reports." *Dissociation* 8:218–21.

Henry, Lindsey. 2000. "Cat-Stapling Costs Man Year in Jail." *DesMoinesRegister.com*. September 8.

Herzog, Harold. 1988. "The Moral Status of Mice." *American Psychologist* 43:473–74.

Hewitt, John. 2000. *Self and Society: A Symbolic Interactionist Social Psychology.* Boston: Allyn and Bacon.

Hickrod, Lucy, and Raymond Schmitt. 1982. "A Naturalistic Study of Interaction and Frame: The Pet as 'Family Member.'" *Urban Life* 11:55–77.

Hicks, J. 1993. "A.S.P.C.A. Plans to Give Up Job Killing New York Strays." *New York Times*, March 26, B14.

Hindi, S. 2001. "Animal 'Humane Society' of Golden Valley Continues Gassing." *Showing Animals Respect and Kindness*, August, 6.

Hoarding of Animals Research Consortium (HARC). 2000. "People Who Hoard Animals." *Psychiatric Times* 17(4):25–29.

Hochschild, Arlie. 1983. *The Managed Heart: Commercialization of Human Feeling.* Berkeley: University of California Press.

Hoffman, Abbie. 1968. *Revolution for the Hell of It.* New York: Dial Press.

Holland (MI) Sentinel. 2002. "Aggression Against Animals: Teen Acts of Violence Getting Increased Attention." June 10.

Hoy, Suellen. 1996. *Chasing Dirt: The American Pursuit of Cleanliness.* New York: Oxford University Press.

Hughes, Everett. 1958. *Men and Their Work.* Glencoe, IL: Free Press.

———. 1964. "Good People and Dirty Work." In Howard Becker, ed., *The Other Side*, 23–26. New York: Free Press.

Humane Society of the United States. 1996. Telephone Survey. Denver, CO: Penn and Sehoen, December 21–23.

Irvine, Leslie. 2004. *If You Tame Me: Understanding Our Connection with Animals.* Philadelphia: Temple University Press.

Jackman, Norman, Richard O'Toole, and Gilbert Geis. 1963. "The Self-Image of the Prostitute." *Sociological Quarterly* 4:150–60.

James, Allison, and Alan Prout, eds. 1990. *Constructing and Reconstructing Childhood.* London: Falmer.

Johnson, John. 1995. "Horror Stories and the Construction of Child Abuse." In J. Best, ed., *Images of Issues: Typifying Contemporary Social Problems*, 17–31. New York: Aldine De Gruyter.

Jordan, James. 1975. "An Ambivalent Relationship: Dog and Human in the Folk Culture of the South." *Appalachian Journal* 2:238–48.

Karp, David, 1996. *Speaking of Sadness: Depression, Disconnection, and the Meanings of Illness.* New York: Oxford University Press.

Katz, Jack. 1987. "What Makes Crime 'News'?" *Media, Culture, and Society* 9:47–75.

———. 1988. *Seduction of Crime*. New York: Basic Books.

Kaufmann, Adrianne. 1999. "The Pro-Choice/Pro-Life Conflict: An Exploratory Study to Understand the Nature of the Conflict and to Develop Constructive Conflict Intervention Designs." Ph.D. diss., George Mason University.

Kellert, Stephen, and Alan Felthous. 1985. "Childhood Cruelty Toward Animals Among Criminals and Noncriminals." *Human Relations* 38:1113–29.

Kidder, Robert. 1983. *Connecting Law and Society: An Introduction to Research and Theory*. Englewood Cliffs, NJ: Prentice Hall.

King, Stephen. 2000. *On Writing: A Memoir of the Craft*. New York: Pocket Books.

Knox, Sara. 2001. "The Productive Power of Confessions of Cruelty." *Postmodern Culture* 11:3.

Koller, Marvin. 1988. *Humor and Society: Explorations in the Sociology of Humor*. Houston: Cap and Gown.

Kraybill, Donald. 2001. *The Riddle of Amish Culture*. Baltimore: Johns Hopkins University Press.

Langley, Gill, ed. 1989. *Animal Experimentation: The Consensus Changes*. London: Macmillan.

Lawrence, Elizabeth. 1984. *Rodeo: An Anthropologist Looks at the Wild and the Tame*. Chicago: University of Chicago Press.

Leach, Edmund. 1964. "Anthropological Aspects of Language: Animal Categories and Verbal Abuse." In E. Lenneberg, ed., *New Direction in the Study of Language*, 23–63. Cambridge, MA: MIT Press.

Levi-Strauss, Claude. 1963. *Totemism*. Boston: Beacon.

Levin, Jack, and Arnold Arluke. 1986. *Gossip: The Inside Scoop*. New York: Plenum.

Levin, Jack, and James Fox. 1985. *Mass Murder: America's Growing Menace*. New York: Plenum Press.

Lightfoot, Cynthia. 1997. *The Culture of Adolescent Risk Taking*. New York: Guilford.

Lively, Kathryn. 2001. "Occupational Claims to Professionalism: The Case of Paralegals." *Symbolic Interaction* 24:343–66.

Locke, John. 1693. "Some Thoughts Concerning Education." In *The Works of John Locke*. London: W. Otridge and Son, 1812.

Lockwood, Randall. 1994. "The Psychology of Animal Collectors." *American Animal Hospital Association Trends Magazine* 9(6):18–21.

Loseke, Donileen. 1987. "Lived Realities and the Construction of Social Problems: The Case of Wife Abuse." *Symbolic Interaction* 10:229–43.

Lovecats4x.tripod.com/abuse.html. n.d. "Stop Abuse!"

Lyman, Stanford, and Marvin Scott. 1970. *A Sociology of the Absurd*. New York: Appleton-Century-Crofts.

Macdonald, John. 1961. *The Murderer and His Victim*. Springfield, IL: Charles C. Thomas.

———. 1968. *Homicidal Threats*. Springfield, IL: Charles C. Thomas.

Majone, Giandomenico. 1988. In Robert Reich, ed., *The Power of Public Ideas*, 157–78. Cambridge: Harvard University Press.

Marvin, Garry, and Bob Mullen. 1999. *Zoo Culture*. Urbana: University of Illinois Press.

McCaghy, Charles, and James Skipper Jr. 1969. "Lesbian Behavior as an Adaptation to the Occupation of Stripping." *Social Problems* 17:262–70.

Mead, George Herbert. 1934. *Mind, Self, and Society*. Chicago: University of Chicago Press.

———. 1938. *The Philosophy of the Act*. Chicago: University of Chicago Press.

Mead, Margaret. 1964. "Cultural Factors in the Cause and Prevention of Pathological Homicide." *Bulletin of the Menninger Clinic* 28:11–22.

Mechling, Jay. 1989. "'Banana Canon' and Other Folk Traditions Between Human and Nonhuman Animals." *Western Folklore* 48:312–23.

Meehan, Albert. 1992. "'I Don't Prevent Crime, I Prevent Calls': Policing as a Negotiated Order." *Symbolic Interaction* 15:455–80.

Melson, Gail. 2001. *Why the Wild Things Are: Animals in the Lives of Children*. Cambridge: Harvard University Press.

Merz-Perez, Linda, and Kathleen Heide. 2004. *Animal Cruelty: Pathway to Violence Against People*. Walnut Creek, CA: Altamira.

Michalko, Rod. 1999. *The Two in One: Walking with Smokie, Walking with Blindness*. Philadelphia: Temple University Press.

Milani, Myrna. 1997. "The No-Kill Controversy," *Journal of the American Veterinary Medical Association* 210:26–27.

Milgram, Stanley. 1974. *Obedience to Authority*. New York: Harper and Row.

Miller, Arthur, Anne Gordon, and Amy Buddie. 1999. "Accounting for Evil and Cruelty: Is to Explain to Condone?" *Personality and Social Psychology Review* 3:254–68.

Miller, Karla, and John Knutson. 1997. "Reports of Severe Physical Punishment and Exposure to Animal Cruelty by Inmates Convicted of Felonies and by University Students." *Child Abuse and Neglect* 21:59–82.

Miller, P. n.d. "Chain Reaction: 'No-Kill . . .' or 'You Kill?'" *California Humane Action and Information Network Letter* 4 (Fall).

Mills, C. Wright. 1940. "Situated Actions and Vocabularies of Motive." *American Sociological Review* 5:904–13.

———. 1959. *The Sociological Imagination*. New York: Oxford University Press.

Morrow, Virginia. 1998. "My Animals and Other Family: Children's Perspectives on Their Relationships with Companion Animals." *Anthrozoos* 11:218–26.

Moulton, Carol, Michael Kaufman, and Judee Filip, eds. 1991. *Report on the Summit on Violence Towards Children and Animals*. Denver: American Humane Association.

Murray, Brian. 2003. "Ex-animal Shelter Worker on Trial for Killing 7 Cats." *Newark (NJ) Star Ledger*, April 11.

Nagel, Joane. 2000. "False Faces: Ethnic Identity, Authenticity, and Fraud in Native American Discourse and Politics." In Joseph Davis, ed., *Identity and Social Change*, 81–106. New Brunswick, NJ: Transaction.

National Inquirer. 2002. "Drugged-out Ozzy Went Crazy and Shot 17 Pet Cats," April 24.

Nelson, Barbara. 1984. *Making an Issue of Child Abuse: Political Agenda Setting for Social Problems*. Chicago: University of Chicago Press.

Nelson, James. 1989. "Symbol and Sensibility." *Anthrozoos* 3:86–88.

Niederhoffer, Arthur. 1969. *Behind the Shield: The Police in Urban Society*. Garden City, NY: Anchor Books.

Noske, Barbara. 1997. *Beyond Boundaries: Humans and Animals.* Montreal: Black Rose Books.

Olmsted, A. D. 1988. "Morally Controversial Leisure: The Social World of Gun Collectors." *Symbolic Interaction* 11:277–87.

Oppenheimer, Dan. 2002. "Kill, Kill Again." *Metroland Online* 25 (30) (July 25). www.metroland.net

Owens, E., R. Davis, and B. Smith. 1981. "The Psychology of Euthanizing Animals: The Emotional Components." *International Journal for the Study of Animal Problems* 2:19–25.

Palmer, C. Eddie.1978. "Dog Catchers: A Descriptive Study." *Qualitative Sociology* 1:79–107.

Patronek, Gary. 1997. "Issues for Veterinarians." *Society and Animals* 5:267–80.

Peri, Yoram. 1999. "The Media and Collective Memory of Yitzhak Rabin's Remembrance." *Journal of Communication* 49:106–24.

Perry, Stewart. 1978. *San Francisco Scavengers: Dirty Work and the Pride of Ownership.* Berkeley and Los Angeles: University of California Press.

Peters, Lori, 2002. "Is Dead Baby Boy Less Important than Cat?" Letter to the editor. *RockyMountainNews.com,* October 23.

Piaget, Jean. 1962. *Play, Dreams, and Imitation in Childhood.* New York: Norton.

Pine, Vanderlyn. 1977. *Caretaker of the Dead: The American Funeral Director.* New York: Irvington.

Piper, Heather. 2003. "The Linkage of Animal Abuse with Interpersonal Violence: A Sheep in Wolf's Clothing?" *Journal of Social Work* 3: 161–77.

Planet Ark. 2002. "Grisly Animal Abuse Cases Puzzle Colorado Police." July 12.

Prus, Robert. 1997. *Subcultural Mosaics and Intersubjective Realities: An Ethnographic Research Agenda for Pragmatizing the Social Sciences.* Albany: State University of New York Press.

Quioco, E. 2001. "Llama Attack Shakes Idyllic Neighborhood." *St. Petersburg (Fla.) Times.* February 14.

Retzinger, Suzanne. 1991. *Violent Emotions: Shame and Rage in Destructive Conflicts.* Newbury Park, CA: Sage.

Robinson, Marilyn. 2001. "Lemonade Stand Helps Burned Cat." *Denver Post,* June 2.

Rohde, Bob. 2001. "Make Fun of the Crime, Do the Time." Letter to the Editor. *Westword* (Denver, CO), June 14.

Rollin, Bernard. 1988. "Animal Euthanasia and Moral Stress." In W. Kay, A. H. Kutscher, and S. P. Cohen, eds., *Euthanasia of the Companion Animal,* 31–41. Philadelphia: Charles Press.

Rosenhan, David. 1970. "The Natural Socialization of Altruistic Autonomy," In J. Macaulay and L. Berkowitz (Eds.). *Altruism and Helping Behavior.* New York: Academic Press.

Roth, Julius. 1994. *Animal Health Care.* Davis, CA: By the author.

Rowan, Andrew. 1992. "The Dark Side of the Force." *Anthrozoos* 5:4–5.

———. 1993. "Cruelty to Animals." *Anthrozoos* 6:218–20.

Rupke, Nicolaas. 1987. *Vivisection in Historical Perspective.* London: Routledge.

Sacco, Vincent. 1995. "Media Constructions of Crime." *Annals of the American Academy of Political and Social Science* 539:141–54.

Sanders, Clinton. 1999. *Understanding Dogs: Living and Working with Canine Companions*. Philadelphia: Temple University Press.

Sandstrom, Kent, Daniel Martin, and Gary Fine. 2003. *Symbols, Selves, and Social Identity: A Symbolic Interactionist Approach to Social Psychology and Sociology*. Los Angeles: Roxbury.

Scarpitti, Frank, and Paul McFarlane. 1975. *Deviance: Action, Reaction, Interaction*. Reading, MA: Addison-Wesley.

Schaef, Anne, and Diane Fassel. 1988. *The Addictive Organization*. New York: Harper and Row.

Scheff, Thomas. 1990. *Microsociology: Discourse, Emotion, and Social Structure*. Chicago: University of Chicago Press.

Schneider, Joseph, and Peter Conrad. 1992. *Deviance and Medicalization: From Badness to Sickness*. Philadelphia: Temple University Press.

Schur, Edwin. 1976. *The Awareness Trap*. New York: McGraw-Hill.

Schutz, David. 1992. "3 Accused of Luring Dog to Death on T Track are Acquitted." *Boston Globe*, June 24.

Sendi, Ismail, and Paul Blomgren. 1975. "A Comparative Study of Predictive Criteria in the Predisposition of Homicidal Adolescents." *American Journal of Psychiatry* 132:423–27.

Serpell, James. 1996. *In the Company of Animals: A Study of Human-Animal Relationships*. New York: Basil Blackwell.

Shanklin, Eugenia. 1985. "Sustenance and Symbol: Anthropological Studies of Domesticated Animals." *Annual Review of Anthropology* 14:375–403.

Sharpe, Robert. 1988. *The Cruel Deception: The Use of Animals in Medical Research*. Wellingborough, U.K.: Thorsons.

Sherizen, Sanford. 1978. "Social Creation of Crime News." In Charles Winick, ed., *Deviance and Mass Media*, 203–24. Beverly Hills, CA: Sage.

Sinclair, Kate. 1995. "Responding to Abuse: A Matter of Perspective." *Current Issues in Criminal Justice* 7:153–75.

Skolnick, Jerome. 1966. *Justice Without Trial*. New York: John Wiley and Sons.

Solot, Dorian. 1997. "Untangling the Animal Abuse Web." *Society and Animals* 5:257–66.

Solot, Dorian, and Arnold Arluke. 1997. "Learning the Scientist's Role: Animal Dissection in Middle School." *Journal of Contemporary Ethnography* 26:28–54.

Sorokin, Pitirim. 1950. *Altruistic Love*. Boston: Beacon.

Spector, M., and J. Kituse. 1977. *Constructing Social Problems*. Menlo Park, CA: Cummings.

Stark, M. 1993. Unpublished document prepared for The Fund for Animals, Inc., New York.

Staub, Ervin. 1989. *The Roots of Evil: The Origins of Genocide and Other Group Violence*. New York: Cambridge University Press.

Sudnow, David. 1967. *Passing On: The Social Organization of Dying*. Englewood Cliffs: NJ: Prentice Hall.

Swabe, Joanna. 1996. "Dieren als een Naturrlijke Hulpbron: Ambivalentie in de Relatie tussen Mens den Dier, binnen en buiten de Veterinaire Praktijk." (Animals as a Natural Resource: Ambivalence in the Human-Animal Relationship and Veterinary Medicine.) In B. Heerikhuizen, B. Van Kruithof,

C. Schmidt, and E. Tellegen, eds., *Milieu als Mensenwerk*, 12–37. Groningen: Wolters-Noordhof.

Tapia, Fernando. 1971. "Children Who Are Cruel to Animals." *Child Psychiatry and Human Development* 2:70–77.

Thorne, Barrie. 1993. *Gender Play: Girls and Boys in School*. New Brunswick, NJ: Rutgers University Press.

Tittle, Charles, and Raymond Paternoster. 2003. "A Typology of Deviance Based on Middle Class Norms." In Patricia Adler and Peter Adler, eds., *Constructions of Deviance: Social Power, Context, and Interaction*, 19–29. Belmont, CA: Wadsworth/Thomson.

Tyler, Stephen, ed. 1969. *Cognitive Anthropology*. New York: Holt, Rinehart and Winston.

Vermeulen, H., and J. Odendaal. 1993. "Proposed Typology of Companion Animal Abuse." *Anthrozoos* 6:248–57.

WCVB-TV. 1992. Newscenter Five Eyeopener, Channel Five, Boston. June 24.

White, D., and R. Shawhan. 1996. "Emotional Responses of Animal Shelter Workers to Euthanasia," *Journal of the American Veterinary Medical Association* 208:846–49.

Whittier, Nancy. 2001. "Emotional Strategies: The Collective Reconstruction and Display of Oppositional Emotions in the Movement Against Child Sexual Abuse." In Jeff Goodwin, James Jasper, and Francesca Polleta, eds., *Passionate Politics: Emotions and Social Movements*, 233–50. Chicago: University of Chicago Press.

Wilczynski, A., and K. Sinclair. 1999. "Moral Tales: Representations of Child Abuse in the Quality and Tabloid Media." *Australian and New Zealand Journal of Criminology* 32:262–83.

Wolfe, Alan. 1998. *One Nation, After All*. New York: Penguin.

Worth, Dooley, and Alan Beck. 1981. "Multiple Ownership of Animals in New York City." *Transactions and Studies of the College of Physicians of Philadelphia* 3:280–300.

Yaffe, Barbara. 2004. "A Prison Camp for Animals." *Vancouver Sun*, April 29.

Index

Arnold Arluke is Professor of Sociology and Anthropology at Northeastern University and Senior Scholar at Tufts University Center for Animals and Public Policy. He has published over 70 articles and eight books, including *Regarding Animals* (Temple), *Brute Force: Animal Police and the Challenge of Cruelty*, and *The Sacrifice: How Scientific Experiments Transform Animals and People*. He also edits with Clinton Sanders the *Animals, Culture, and Society* series at Temple University Press.